HERMANN SASSE:
A MAN FOR OUR TIMES?

HERMANN SASSE: A MAN FOR OUR TIMES?

Essays from the Twentieth Annual Lutheran Life Lectures
Concordia Lutheran Theological Seminary
St. Catharines, Ontario, Canada
(30 October – 1 November 1995)

An International Theological Symposium
marking the centennial of the birth of Dr. Hermann Sasse

Editor
John R. Stephenson

Technical Editor
Thomas M. Winger

Concordia Academic Press

A Division of

Concordia Publishing House

Saint Louis, Missouri

Unless otherwise stated, quotations of the Lutheran Confessions are from *The Book of Concord: The Confessions of the Evangelical Lutheran Church.* Edited by Theodore G. Tappert, © 1959, Fortress Press. Used by permission of Augsburg Fortress, Minneapolis.

Copyright © 1998 Concordia Academic Press
3558 S. Jefferson Avenue, Saint Louis, MO 63118-3968

All rights reserved. No part of this publication may be reproduced, stored in a retrieval system, or transmitted, in any form or by any means, electronic, mechanical, photocopying, recording, or otherwise, without the prior written permission of Concordia Publishing House.

Library of Congress Cataloging-in-Publication Data

    Lutheran Life Lectures (20th : 1995 : Concordia Lutheran Theological Seminary,
    St. Catherines, Ont.)
    Hermann Sasse : a man for our times? : essays from the 20th Annual Lutheran Life Lectures,
      Concordia Lutheran Theological Seminary, St. Catherines, Ontario, Canada (30 October-1
      November 1995) : an international theological symposium marking the centennial of the
      birth of Dr. Hermann Sasse / editor, John R. Stephenson : technical editor, Thomas M.
      Winger.
        p. cm.
    ISBN 0-570-04274-7
1. Sasse, Hermann, 1895- --Congresses. I. Stephenson, John R.
    (John Raymond) II. Winger, Thomas M. III. Title.
    230 '. 41-dc21   98-17203

Contents

Abbreviations	7
Editorial Foreword *John R. Stephenson*	9
Hermann Sasse: Theologian of the Church *Ronald R. Feuerhahn*	11
Hermann Sasse's Relations with His Erlangen Colleagues *Lowell C. Green*	37
Hermann Sasse and Third Reich Threats to the Church *John R. Wilch*	65
Sasse on Worship *John W. Kleinig*	106
The Confessing Church: Catholic and Apostolic *Thomas M. Winger*	123
In the Forecourts of Theology: The Epistemology of Hermann Sasse and the Relationship between Philosophy and Theology and between Natural Theology and Revelation in His Works *Tom G. A. Hardt*	155
Hermann Sasse and the Mystery of Sacred Scripture *Kurt E. Marquart*	167
Where Rhine and Tiber Met: Hermann Sasse and the Roman Catholic Church *Gottfried Martens*	194
Holy Supper, Holy Church *John R. Stephenson*	224

Consubstantiation
Norman E. Nagel 240

Hermann Sasse, a Man for Our Times
Edwin Lehman 260

List of Contributors 269

Abbreviations

Writings of Hermann Sasse:

CC *Corpus Christi: Ein Beitrag zum Problem der Abendmahlskonkordie.* Edited by Friedrich Wilhelm Hopf. Erlangen: Verlag der Ev.-Luth. Mission, 1979.

HWS *Here We Stand: Nature and Character of the Lutheran Faith.* Translated by Theodore G. Tappert. Adelaide: Lutheran Publishing House, 1979.

ISC *In Statu Confessionis: Gesammelte Aufsätze und Kleine Schriften von Hermann Sasse.* 2 vols. Edited by Friedrich Wilhelm Hopf. Berlin and Hamburg: Lutherisches Verlagshaus, 1966 and 1976.

K&H *Kirche und Herrenmahl: Ein Beitrag zum Verständnis des Altarsakraments. Bekennende Kirche*, vol. 59/60. Edited by Christian Stoll with Georg Metz and Hermann Sasse. Munich: Chr. Kaiser, 1938.

S&C *Scripture and the Church: Selected Essays of Hermann Sasse.* Edited by Jeffrey J. Kloha and Ronald R. Feuerhahn. St. Louis: Concordia Seminary, 1995.

SS *Sacra Scriptura: Studien zur Lehre von der heiligen Schrift.* Edited by Friedrich Wilhelm Hopf. Erlangen: Verlag der Ev.-Luth. Mission, 1981.

TMB *This is My Body: Luther's Contention for the Real Presence in the Sacrament of the Altar.* Minneapolis: Augsburg, 1959. [Revised edition, Adelaide: Lutheran Publishing House, 1977].

VSA *Vom Sakrament des Altars: Lutherische Beiträge zur Frage des heiligen Abendmahls.* Edited by Hermann Sasse. Leipzig: Dörffling & Franke, 1941.

WCJC	*We Confess Jesus Christ*. Translated by Norman Nagel. St. Louis: Concordia, 1984.
WCS	*We Confess the Sacraments*. Translated by Norman Nagel. St. Louis: Concordia, 1985.
WCC	*We Confess the Church*. Translated by Norman Nagel. St. Louis: Concordia, 1986.
Z	*Zeugnisse: Erlanger Predigten und Vorträge vor Gemeinden, 1933-1944*. Edited by Friedrich Wilhelm Hopf. Erlangen: Martin Luther Verlag, 1979.

Sources and Secondary Literature:

CTM	*Concordia Theological Monthly*.
EC	Feuerhahn, Ronald R. *Hermann Sasse as an Ecumenical Churchman*. Unpublished Ph.D. Dissertation. Cambridge University, 1991.
E-TFA	*Archives of the Erlangen Theological Faculty*.
E-UA	*Archives of Erlangen University*.
Huß	Huß, Siegfried. "'Was heißt lutherisch?' Zum Gedenken an Hermann Sasse. *17. Juli 1895." *Lutherische Kirche in der Welt: Jahrbuch des Martin-Luther-Bundes* 42 (1995): 83.
LB	*Lutherische Blätter*.
LTJ	*Lutheran Theological Journal*.
RTR	*Reformed Theological Review*.
ZKG	*Zeitschrift für Kirchengeschichte*.

Editorial Foreword

The Sasse Symposium, held from 30 October to 1 November 1995, was a landmark event in the life of the St. Catharines seminary, which gladly expresses gratitude to four groups whose support enabled the staging of a longer and more intensive installment than usual of the annual Lutheran Life Lectures. This conference, which involved transporting and accommodating speakers from Australia, Germany, Sweden, and the United States, was made possible by a fraternal grant received from the members of the Lutheran Life Insurance Society of Canada. President Stephen Taylor of Lutheran Life was a welcome guest for a good part of the proceedings. Moreover, we should have hesitated to proceed with this ambitious project apart from the decision of the pastors of Lutheran Church–Canada's East District to designate the lectures given at the Symposium as the agenda of their Autumn Conference. We would also voice appreciation for financial assistance from the Luther Academy of North America, whose then president, Dr. Robert Preus, participated with gusto throughout the Symposium, which ended just three days before his sudden death. Nor can we fail to rejoice in the willingness of so many pastors and laypeople to journey from all corners of Canada and the United States to take part in the centenary commemoration of Dr. Hermann Sasse's birth.

We salute Concordia Publishing House's readiness to publish the symposium essays, which can now foster the ongoing study of Hermann Sasse's fruitful legacy as they are made available to a wider public. The lectures are here printed in order of delivery, with the single exception of President Edwin Lehman's banquet speech, which fitly features as a postscript to this volume. A special words of thanks is due to Dr. Dale Griffin of Concordia Publishing House, who unflaggingly and expertly superintended the editing process with much kindness and no little humor.

The event which marked the seminary's twentieth anniversary owed much to the efforts of my fellow members of the Sasse

Symposium Committee: Dr. Jonathan Grothe, Dr. John Wilch, Mr. Glenn Stresman, and Mrs. Alison Wittig. The two last named labored beyond the call of duty on the unseen administrative preparations for the symposium, as did Mrs. Laurie Schaeffer, administrative assistant at the seminary. Thanks go also to Dean and Mrs. Roger Humann who were responsible for the liturgical and musical content of the conference worship.

Last but not least, I gladly acknowledge the unstinting assistance given by my friend and colleague, Dr. Thomas M. Winger, whose remarkable technical skills have done much to accelerate what would otherwise have been an interminable editorial process.

John R. Stephenson
St. Catharines, Ontario
Tuesday in the Week of Epiphany II, 1998

Hermann Sasse:
Theologian of the Church

Ronald R. Feuerhahn

I. Introduction

President Lehman, Dr. Grothe, and Dr. Hempelmann; Colleagues of Concordia Lutheran Theological Seminary, St. Catharines, and of Concordia Lutheran Seminary, Edmonton; *Amtsbrüder*, Candidates, and Fellow Guests: It is an honor to be numbered among your guests at this symposium. I am especially honored to be in the midst of such great witnesses, that is, speakers who knew our subject personally. I speak, of course, of Brothers Nagel and Kleinig, students of Sasse; of Marquart, his pastoral colleague; and especially of Dr. Tom Hardt, since his relation to Professor Sasse was indeed unique. From the time they started their correspondence in the mid-1950s until Sasse's death in 1976, Sasse wrote Hardt on average nearly one letter a week. This is a remarkable chronicle of Sasse's life and thought. It is, of course, a personal chronicle—at times intimate. It is also a very interesting commentary on the ecclesiastical events of modern times, their literature, persons, and events, their tragedies, witness, and confession. But one of the most beneficial features of this correspondence is its pastoral nature. One could publish many of these letters under the title "Letters of Spiritual Counsel," a title which has already been used in the *Library of Christian Classics* series for a collection of Luther's letters.

I am grateful to acknowledge also the contributions of Dr. John Stephenson who has done so much to foster this gathering and who, on a more personal note, taught me much—also about Hermann Sasse—during our two years together at Westfield House in Cambridge. I have treasured many hours in the company of Dr. Lowell Green whose breadth of knowledge about theological Germany and especially about Sasse's Erlangen I have found engrossing.

Dr. John Wilch joins us with a paper on Sasse's important confrontation with National Socialism, and Dr. Gottfried Martens, as a

German theologian dealing with a German theologian, on a subject of great importance to Sasse, the Roman Catholic Church.

We actually find ourselves in a train of generations of Sasse students. Before World War II there was Michael Reu who found substance in Sasse's writings and published many of them in the *Kirchliche Zeitschrift* (Columbus, OH). After the war there were "friends" with whom he corresponded regularly, for example, Herman Preus of Luther Seminary, St. Paul, and F. E. Mayer of Concordia Seminary, St. Louis. But it was the men of the Wisconsin Synod who generously offered space in their journal for a period of time.

In the mid-1960s a *Festschrift* was in preparation under the editorship of Professors Heino Kadai and Richard Jungkuntz.[1] In addition to essays by Sasse himself, the intention was to include six to nine essays by scholars who appreciated Sasse's contributions. The list of possible contributors included, in addition to the editors, the following: Paul Bretscher, Robert Bertram, George Forell, Martin Franzmann, Ralph Gehrke, Ralph Bohlmann, Fred Kramer, John Behnken, Herman Preus, Leiv Aalen of Norway, Friedrich Wilhelm Hopf of Germany, Henry Hamann, Jr. of Australia, and Norman Nagel of England.[2]

How encouraged we are today, as we have been so often in the past, that "Nagel of England" is here for our symposium; he as much as anyone has made Sasse available to North American readers. That proposed *Festgabe*, which according to one of its editors, "CPH refused to publish, alas,"[3] may well appear yet—in another form and in this later day. Concordia Publishing House is committed to publish a large collection of newly translated writings of Sasse under the able editorship of Matthew Harrison and Paul McCain.

We furthermore find ourselves, therefore, in the company of promising scholars who have already shown themselves ardent and astute students of Sasse; "promising" also for the benefit of the church. I risk overlooking many when I mention only a few today: Jeffrey Kloha, Thomas Winger, Scott Bruzek, and especially Matthew Harrison for his persistence as well as his scholarship in making more of Sasse's writings available for another generation.

Lest my remarks so far appear an unseemly exercise in self-indulgence, I hasten to explain that I have endeavored with these opening comments not to draw attention to my own associations with these men but rather to chronicle the abiding, even persistent, interest in Dr. Sasse and to express our common gratitude to an increasing number who, as students of Sasse, are themselves growing as teachers of the church today. I also want to whet your appetite, as many of these men will address us on the subject at this symposium or in publications elsewhere. These latter include the Reformation 1995 issue of *Logia*, due out in about three weeks, and *Lutheran Quarterly*, whose next issue will feature an article by Norman Nagel on one of Sasse's earliest works.

II. Hermann Sasse, Servant of the Church—the Man and His Life

On the occasion of remembering H. Richard Niebuhr during the centennial year of his birth, his student and colleague, James Gustafson, observed that a conference on his theology seems impoverished without a session on his personal qualities.[4] It seems that we have learned so much from Hermann Sasse without knowing much about his life and person. Nevertheless, we too would be impoverished without a session on just that.

The life of Hermann Sasse is a fascinating story. We might be excused if this assertion surprises us: we do not usually associate the description "fascinating" with the life of a theologian, especially of a historian! His was not a life dominated by cloistered academia. He was indeed a student and scholar. He had also been a soldier—a combatant in the worst battle of World War I. He was even given to a bit of intrigue, as for instance when he traveled—illegally—to a meeting with the Archbishop of York in July 1936. The authorities of the Third Reich had denied him permits for such travel from the year before. He traveled on false papers.

But it is not only these events, sometimes dramatic, which make for an interesting story. Hermann Sasse has captured our attention for other, more important reasons. First, one is drawn to his works by his mastery of history, the breadth of his knowledge, the clarity of his writing, and the forthrightness of his confession. His synthesis of disciplines and powers of analysis give his work an authority. His writing, as noted, is lucid, in contrast to much theological literature of his day.

Hermann Otto Erich Sasse was born in Sonnewalde (Niederlausitz) in Thuringia on 17 July 1895, the eldest of five children. He was named after his father, a druggist, the proprietor of a pharmacy. When his father's business partner disappeared with the cash, the family was left in very severe financial difficulty. Young Hermann was at this time a student and his scholarship had to be used to tide the family over the worst.[5] It became necessary for the young student to work for the sake of the family. His father was also a literary man who wrote on the history of pharmacies and the question of the reform of the whole trade.[6] Among Sasse's ancestors was Valentine Ernst Loescher (Timotheus Verinus).[7]

He was a good student, attending several *Gymnasia* before matriculating at the University of Berlin in the summer semester of 1913.[8] He was inscribed in two faculties simultaneously, theology and classical philology.[9] Berlin was at the height of its powers then and young Sasse relished the experience. The faculty included some of the greats of modern theology: Adolf von Harnack, Karl Holl, Reinhold Seeberg, Julius Kaftan, and, of course, Adolf Deissmann, who would later become his doctoral supervisor (*Doktorvater*). Many years later he described his work under Deissmann:

> Thus my studies, mainly centered in New Testament and patristics, were divided between two loyalties. My main work I did with Adolf Deissmann. From him I learned not only the love for the language of the New Testament and for the Greek-speaking church, but also a deep appreciation of the Septuagint as also for the mission of the synagogue which preceded the mission of the church in East and West. My main teachers in church history were Harnack and Holl.[10]
>
> Old Testament I did with Baudissin, Gressmann (who later as dean conferred my first academic degree on me) and Eissfeld. ... My great teacher in systematic theology was Heinrich Scholz who later as colleague and friend of Karl Barth in Münster taught philosophy and helped, as one of the great polyhistorians of our time, to lay the philosophical foundations of modern mathematics and physics.[11]

Sasse then recalled, perhaps whimsically, "The gaps in practical theology were later filled at the *Kriegsschule* and in the first years in the ministry."[12]

His military service came between the two important exams of his education. Again, with some wit he recalled this:

Since in the beginning of the war the army had committed the great blunder to believe that a world war could be won (or lost) without my participation, I had been able to reach just the minimum of time required.[13]

He entered the army in October 1916. He was in Infantry Regiment 51. In just over a month he saw battle.[14] He took part in what was arguably the worst battle of the First World War, the Battle of Passchendaele in Belgium. In his two years of service he reached the rank of sergeant 1st class and was awarded the Iron Cross, 2nd Class, the second-highest honor in the German military at that time.[15] Having been cut off in the Battle of Passchendaele, Sergeant Sasse brought his men back alive, the few who were left—six out of 150 who went into battle. For that he was awarded the medal.[16]

He passed his second theological exam, for the ministry, with the Consistory of Berlin. He was ordained in St. Matthew's Church, Berlin, on 13 June 1920, having "reached the canonical age of 25 years."[17] He served first as assistant pastor (*Hilfsprediger*) at churches in Berlin, first at Advent (1920) and then in Templin (1920-21). In October 1921 he was called to the fourth pastoral position at St. Nicolai in Oranienburg, about 20 kilometers north of Berlin, a working class, large double parish of 10,000 souls.[18] In the same year came his first publication, a book review.[19]

In 1924 he married Charlotte Naumann.[20] She was "Lotte" to her family and friends. The daughter of the postmaster of Oranienburg, she was an accomplished pianist. They made their first home on the same street as her parents. A year after their marriage, Hermann traveled to the United States as an exchange student at Hartford Theological Seminary to do an STM [master of sacred theology degree].[21] He traveled on ship with two other participants in the program, Wilhelm Pauck and Peter Brunner.[22] Sasse would later explain: "However, what Lutheranism is, I learned in America 1925/26."[23] He described the importance of this study exchange for his theological development.[24] Of particular impact during this time was his reading Wilhelm Löhe (1808-72)'s *Drei Bücher von der Kirche*[25] and his exposure to the liberalism and pluralism of American Christianity. During this period also he was reading Luther and the Lutheran Confessions.

Another fruit of this visit was his first book, *American Christianity*.[26] Dietrich Bonhoeffer read it in preparation for his own study at Union Theological Seminary, New York.[27]

While still *Pfarrer* in Oranienburg he had become involved in the Conference on Faith and Order. A member of the German delegation at Lausanne in 1927, he was the editor of the official German report[28] as well as the continental secretary and eventually, in 1928, a member of the Continuation Committee. His participation grew until he was forced by government travel restrictions to withdraw (1935):[29] he was elected a member of the Committee of Reference (1931)[30] and of the Study Discussion Group on "The Oecumenical Work of the Church" (1933);[31] in 1934 he was elected to the Executive Committee.

Meanwhile, during this period, Sasse was prominent in movements which challenged the increasing encroachment of the National Socialists into the affairs of the church. While not a signer of the original manifesto of the "Young Reformers" of Berlin (*Jungreformatorische Bewegung*), he was involved in the movement at an early stage.[32] He was one of the chief drafters of the Bethel Confession of 1933[33] and a leading participant in the famous Synod of Barmen of 1934.[34] Although this venture was for him confessionally burdensome,[35] he nevertheless continued for a time serving the Confessing Church.[36]

Perhaps Sasse's most significant contribution to the anti-Nazi cause was his bold critique of Article 24 of the program of the National Socialist Party (*Nationalsozialistische Deutsche Arbeiterpartei* or *NSDAP*) in 1932; it has been identified as one of the first by a German churchman and is therefore prominent in the literature on the Church and the Third Reich.[37]

The period immediately following the Second World War was in some respects equally difficult for Sasse. First, there was the physical hardship: the lack of coal and food. The family was terribly undernourished and had to scramble for wood to burn. In 1946 Sasse suffered a heart attack which prevented him attending his first post-war meeting of the Faith and Order Committee.[38] While he finally received his chair[39] and was appointed pro-rector of the university,[40] these honors were hardly enough to compensate for the conflicts to come. His appointment as *Prorektor* added to the tension with his colleagues.

Just over a month after assuming that office he wrote to President John Behnken of the Missouri Synod:

> My situation here in Erlangen is often hopeless as you can imagine. For years I have been completely isolated; recently even a boycott movement against me is under way since the military government in Frankfurt made me Prorector. Therefore to speak frankly, as I did in the memorandum which I gave you concerning the situation of Lutheranism, is impossible in public.[41]

He had been, unlike most of his colleagues, "passionately stirred by the ecclesiastical dispute in the Third Reich."[42] Now he was called upon by the occupation authorities to offer an opinion on the political stance of those colleagues in the theological faculty. "What Sasse wrote concerning his colleagues, conforms with the facts," observed a colleague, Walther von Loewenich.[43]

But while that personal burden along with the hardships of poor health and lack of heating and food in the grim post-war days was great, perhaps of even greater pain was the course of church affairs. Hoping that the crisis of the war would give opportunity for renewal, the move toward the formation of the *Evangelische Kirche in Deutschland* (*EKD*) was a great disappointment. In his view it suffered the same misconception as did Barmen. It was the triumph of Barthian ecclesiology.[44] The Erlangen professor finally withdrew, resigning his post as *ordinarius* and his membership of the Bavarian Church. He joined the *Evangelisch-lutherische (altlutherische) Kirche*[45] and then accepted the call of the United Evangelical Lutheran Church of Australia to be professor of church history at its Immanuel Seminary, North Adelaide, Australia. He was installed in this new office on 12 October 1949.[46]

In his correspondence in later years he frequently spoke of the great limitations in this new setting, chiefly of library resources. He was forced to end his research on further articles for the Kittel *Wörterbuch* for instance.[47] But it also provided new challenges, chief of which was the union of the two Lutheran churches in Australia. He related to his friend, Herman Preus, that this was one of the chief reasons he had gone to Australia. As a UELCA member of the Intersynodical Committee, he was instrumental in preparing for the merger achieved in 1966 with the Evangelical Lutheran Church of

Australia; this formed the Lutheran Church of Australia. From this outpost of the Christian world, Sasse also commenced his *Briefe an lutherische Pastoren*, a series of essays published by his disciple and friend in Germany, Friedrich Wilhelm Hopf.[48]

Professor Sasse's own words briefly summarize his estimation of the transitional period of his life. Describing in 1948 the situation for a confessionally minded pastor in the Bavarian Church, he explains his resignation and planned move to Australia:

> All the men who cannot give up the Formula of Concord which is among the official Confessions of the Church of Bavaria must either go or subscribe to the new church laws with a broken conscience. This is the reason why I accepted the first call which came to me, and that was the call from Australia. . . . You know, and your friends know it also, that I am not a fanatic. I spent more than 20 years in the Ecumenical Movement. I gave more time to it than any other theologian in this country. But since this movement has become a means to further the political plans of Geneva I cannot take part in it any longer. During the Third Reich the party and the Kirchliches Aussenamt prevented me from attending ecumenical conferences. Since 1945 Niemoeller and Barth are doing the same. Can you understand that I am longing for a country in which the Lutheran Church is still free? I shall go, if my plans can be carried out, to one of the smallest and poorest Lutheran churches. My Bavarian Government is trying to keep me here. They are prepared to pay me the highest salary a German professor can get. But if I see the distress of my students I must go, and I hope that God will show me the way. "Weg hast du allerwegen, an Mitteln fehlt dir's nicht", as we sing with Paul Gerhardt.[49]

Among the few things that brightened this traumatic period was Sasse's participation "in the first official conference between Roman Catholic and Evangelical theologians in Germany after World War II."[50] More and more his theological contacts were outside the Bavarian Church, even outside Germany, with one notable exception. That was his participation in the *Schwabacher Konvent*, a group of churchmen devoted to the preservation of confessional Lutheranism.

The contacts outside Germany were chiefly in the United States. He carried on an active correspondence with Herman Preus at Luther Seminary, St. Paul. But the most important contact, at least in terms of its sustained impact, was that with the Missouri Synod and particularly with its president, Dr. John Behnken. Their first meeting at Sasse's home in Erlangen in November 1945 was a momentous occasion for Sasse, as is indicated in the number of references in his correspondence at the time.[51] In a report on this first meeting, Behnken observed: "Dr. Sasse is probably closer to us in doctrine than any other leader in Germany."[52]

The relations with Missouri, however, were not in all respects comfortable. While Behnken's estimation of Sasse grew, others in the church were decidedly uneasy with the Erlangen professor, none more so than the faculty of Concordia Seminary, St. Louis. Sasse had the respect of Professor F. E. Mayer and their correspondence illustrates that; however, even Mayer's treatment of Sasse is not without a certain ambiguity. When in 1947, for instance, Behnken asked the seminary to invite Sasse to give some lectures, Mayer was a member of the small committee of the faculty which sought to block the invitation.[53] The reasons offered by the faculty are not merely interesting; they also may indicate something about the changing theological climate of the Missouri Synod which is very instructive for today.[54] In the end he was invited and arrived on 5 June 1948.

Once in St. Louis, discomfort with Sasse's opinions continued. His "pessimistic" view of things in the German churches, noted in the faculty concerns, stood in contrast to the optimism of the St. Louis theologians.[55] It is perhaps significant that on this visit Sasse was given more time for lectures for the Wisconsin Synod and the American Lutheran Church than for his hosts.

It was, in fact, the Wisconsin Synod, which, through its journal, then known as the *Quartalschrift*, did more to publish Sasse's writings than anyone else in North America; in it were published twelve of his essays over fourteen issues.

It was at the Springfield seminary that Sasse would be welcomed to give regular lectures. He was invited to lecture at Concordia Theological Seminary in January and February 1962.[56] He was invited back for the winter quarter in 1964-65. It was this seminary which would always hold a special place in his regard and affections, not least for the fact that it honored him with the doctor of divinity degree on Friday 20 January 1967.

In the years following, he maintained a regular correspondence with churchmen in North American Lutheranism; while most of the letters were exchanged with churchmen of the Synodical Conference, many leaders of the ALC and ULCA/LCA were included. In fact, one of the remarkable things about Sasse was the extent, both in sheer volume and in scope, of his correspondence. Many of these letters were treatises in themselves. This has caused me to include them as unpublished manuscripts in the *Bibliography*.[57] His son, Wolfgang, observed that there were at least four, if not five, typewriters in the house, each with its own project or manuscript in process.[58]

Life in Australia was difficult for the Sasses. For him it was due chiefly to the isolation, although there were also the more mundane hardships of very low salary and poor resources. The isolation was mainly intellectual but was also personal. He was very conscious of being an immigrant within a society, and even a church, which was very close knit. For that reason he had a very great affection for the immigrant community in Australia.

When Sasse spoke, as he often did, of the "lonely Lutherans" in the world to whom he addressed his letters and essays, it may have been due in part to a projection of his own circumstances, but by no means that only. It was spoken also in the context of a world Lutheranism which, in his estimation, was shrinking.

For Frau Sasse, Lotte, the adjustment to Australia was even more difficult. While they both suffered serious illnesses of various kinds, she was particularly plagued. She very much missed Europe, its climate and presumably its culture. Christmas was a time of longing for snow and winter. Many of Dr. Sasse's letters mention her poor health and the necessity for much attention on his part.

There was obvious joy and pride in their two sons, Wolfgang and Hans. Wolfgang was 20 when they arrived in Australia in 1949 and Hans was 13. A daughter, Maria, had died, after being baptized, on the day of her birth in December 1930. The elder son became a research chemist in Australia and even did post-doctoral work at Harvard. Hans, who died at Easter 1982, was a lecturer in German at the University of Newcastle in England.

A side of Sasse that we don't see then, but which one could expect, was of a man who delighted in his family. He was very excited at the birth of his first grandson, Stephen. After he learned of the birth, he could not sleep. He wrote a poem and then, in the middle of the night, brought it to his son's house and placed it on the window.[59]

His concern for people was evident to students and correspondents. One former student in Adelaide tells that it was to Sasse, more than any of their other professors, that the students would turn for advice; they always felt welcome at his home even when they knew he was very busy.[60] He kept a diptych[61] with the names of those whom he kept in his prayers.

As one imagines Sasse through reading his works or even his letters, one might be prompted to ask if he had a sense of humor. Here was a man whose life was threatened seriously on more than one occasion, who had suffered much hardship and bore the marks of tragedy, personally and ecclesiologically. Yet, if one meets his colleagues and students, or if one reads his letters, one can learn of a very pastoral concern, a warmth and even at times a sentimentality. Among these are notably stories of his sense of humor as well.

I'll leave it to Dr. John Kleinig to tell the stories about the moving desk or holding hands in church. Another student tells this story:

> Students went with Sasse to a Quaker meeting near the cathedral on a Sunday evening. On the way back there would be discussion on the meeting. On the street the group was approached by a young man holding a Bible. He addressed the question to Sasse: "My dear sir, have you found your Saviour?" Sasse paused as if in deep thought—on which occasions he would often rub the side of his nose: "I didn't know that he was lost!"[62]

Actually, the answer, even if meant to be humorous, was very theological.

Hermann Sasse died tragically on 8 August 1976 due to an accident in his home. It seems likely that he fell, knocking over a paraffin oil (American: kerosene) heater. The death was due to fumes rather than flames.[63]

III. The Churchman—His Office

As a churchman, it is important to know that Dr. Sasse came out of the old Prussian Union.[64] To one correspondent he noted:

> I came from the theology of Berlin as it was taught before World War I and from the Church of the Prussian Union in which I was a pastor. In Sweden I had for the first time seen a Lutheran Church.[65]

He was a Lutheran within that union of Reformed, Lutheran, and United churchmen, but still it was in the United States that he learned what Lutheranism was.[66] That was while on the study visit in 1925-26.

It was in America, then, that Sasse claimed the confession of the church:

> ... he learnt that the Church needs a confession and that, indeed, the Church has one which is the answer of faith to the revelation of God and now somehow the expression of a pious soul. **There he found the "Us" of the Church.** He often spoke about this.[67]

Many, then, have commented on the significance of this background to explain the man, Hermann Sasse. An interesting, even curious, comment is that of Theodore Bachmann, who observed that "Sasse was given to rigorous interpretations," both about the Union and because of it:

> He was, in a way, if you can sum it up, to me anyhow, he seemed like a Prussian Evangelical who became utterly convinced of Lutheranism and proceeded often without meaning to [hurt?] maybe because he meant to overkill.[68]

It can be asserted, however, that Sasse was not given to *ad hominem* argumentation. His letters, for instance, could be published without embarrassment. Karl Barth was his greatest nemesis, yet he could express the greatest admiration for Barth, even at the expense of his mentor and colleague, Werner Elert:

> If one compares the most outstanding work of this theology, the Dogmatics by Werner Elert (Der Christliche Glaube, 1941) with the Dogmatics by Karl Barth, the limitations of Elert's theology become obvious.[69]

In his diagnosis Sasse pointed to Elert's failure to deal adequately with the problem of Holy Scripture and especially of the Old Testament:

> Whatever there may be to criticize in Karl Barth's doctrine of the Holy Scripture—especially in regard to his teaching of Law and Gospel—on the authority of the Old Testament in the Church he stands closer to Luther than the Lutheran Elert.[70]

Sasse could be rather dismissive about Martin Niemoeller's weakness as a theologian, but maintain a very deep and open admiration for the man's courage and act of confession.[71]

Sasse fits a pattern in the life of the church: he is the type of churchman who appears at a time of renewal. There are perhaps many features of renewal which have marked the church's history. But for Lutheranism especially such renewals have shared the concerns and emphases of Sasse.

1. He has given emphasis to doctrine rather than to life. He is concerned to teach the church not so much for a renewal of ethics and morality, but rather for a renewal of its teaching and confession.

2. In the past—the 19th century for instance—there arose a renewal in response to a great emphasis on the experiential in religion; with it came a neglect of doctrine and theology, of catechesis and preaching, of sacraments and liturgy.

3. In such times there come pastors and leaders who find it necessary, and comforting, to return to a confession of the faith, especially the doctrines of Holy Word, Holy Baptism, Holy Absolution, Holy Supper, Holy Church and Holy Office. This was Sasse's service, to focus again on these dogmas for the sake of the church.

Shortly after arriving in Australia, Sasse was appointed to the Union Committee between the two Lutheran churches. In this work he identified his chief purpose for coming to Australia. The union of the two churches in 1966 was to be, humanly speaking, the culmination of all his ministry.

His interest in and knowledge of Catholicism (east, west, and "original") was very impressive.[72] His essays and correspondence reveal an extraordinary awareness of the literature of the Roman Catholic Church; he would regularly assign official documents for study by his students.

It seems ironic to some, therefore, that from 1960 he became so involved in the Inter-Varsity Fellowship movement in Australia. In 1960 he was vice-president, and in 1967 he was invited to be president. For a man of such "catholic" awareness to become so closely associated with "evangelicals" was a puzzle. For Sasse, it was not a problem. First, it was in these that he found an awareness and confession of the orthodox faith. Secondly, he was at the same time in very regular communication with Roman Catholics, with Cardinal Augustin Bea in the Vatican, for instance.[73]

He was a gifted teacher, impressive not only in his sweep of church history, but also clear in its articulation. About his lectures at the Springfield seminary it was observed:

> It was both amusing and thrilling to see these so-called "practical" students taking in hours of lectures, well-larded with foreign quotations from all ages of the church by this soft-spoken yet remarkably keen and winning man.[74]

IV. The Confessor—His Faith

Sasse felt very responsible for colleagues and especially young men whom he had influenced and by that influence had brought trouble. Tom Hardt mentions this about Hopf, as an example, and even himself:

> Sasse was of an affectionate nature, a man who felt a great responsibility towards young men whom, so he thought, he had more or less brought into problems and difficulties through his own teaching. That, for instance, is how he felt towards Hopf. He left Germany partly because he didn't want to repeat that again among his students, that they would suffer for his doctrine. If he were safely in Australia, he thought it would not happen again.[75]

Sasse gave his own explanation:

> We Lutherans in Germany were the loneliest of men. For me the only way of working for our church was to emigrate and try to work for the preservation of the Lutheran Church in the English-speaking countries.[76]

But even in Australia he found the need to confess. When, after much discussion, his own church, the United Evangelical Lutheran Church of Australia, would not leave the LWF, and, in fact became more involved, he was distressed. "Our church," he once wrote, "is completely in the wake of the LWF, the ALC, and ULCA and the hope for a union is slowly fading away."[77] A few years later, in 1958, the story was the same:

> I accepted the call to Australia to help to unite the two Lutheran bodies of the Missouri and the Löhe-tradition. The influence of the Luth. "Oekumene" smashed all our plans, frustrated the work of many years. Now our church is under the spell of Geneva.[78]

It was about this time, 1958, that he declared himself to be *in statu confessionis* toward his own church:

> [I have been] fighting in my own church for the Lutheran faith against the terrific influence of the Lutheran World Federation. Our poor little church has accepted so much assistance from Geneva that we cannot get out. I am in a *statu confessionis* again. My attempts to bring about the union have been in vain, though we have reached an amazing agreement. I am again lonely.[79]

He declared the situation even more clearly in the next year:

> It may become my duty to separate from my present Church if she continues to remain a member of the LWF. Lund-Quist [executive secretary of the LWF] is here. At the pastors' conference I shall confess; at synod I shall not be present. Since 6 years I am *in statu confessionis*. I cannot receive Holy Communion in my congregation or at the pastors' conference. The logical step would be to transfer to the ELCA. This would smash all hopes for a union of the two churches. Besides, it would kill my wife. What shall I do? I confess by word and deed, but I cannot leave my office, my honre [*sic*]. It is a tragic situation. Tell me what I should do.[80]

Thus he denied himself Communion in his church, even at Immanuel congregation in North Adelaide. For a period of time he would approach his pastor, Konrad Hartmann, to request *Hostien* for communion with his wife at home.[81] He explained this act of confession:

> We can stay for quite a while, but in statu confessionis. This means that we publicly confess and refuse obedience to any demands which violate our confessional obligation. This status confessionis, however, includes that we heed Titus 3:10. If our superiors have become heretics, we should admonish them, even seriously pray for them (see the prayer for haeretics and schismatics in the Prayers of the Faithful, preserved on Good Friday in the Western Church), but the time comes when we have to reject and avoid them (Rom 16:17).[82]

Sasse could be an uncomfortable colleague, a "Cassandra" figure, dour and pessimistic, calling to repentance. First, to those of the Enlightenment era: ". . . to the chorus of present-day Protestant theology, Sasse's voice sounds foreign and shrill."[83] For them he was too given to making assertions, shunning ambiguities. Albrecht Peters, for instance, challenged Sasse's historical judgments as well as his theological assertions.[84] Others, those who even paid attention to him, have articulated this view of Sasse as "a tragic figure in pursuit of an ideal which belonged to a bygone time."[85]

There has been a discomfiture also among the more conservative and confessional Lutherans among whom Sasse has registered theological dilettantism, un-catholic and sectarian churchmanship, un-historical perceptions. He has called us to a serious engagement in doctrine, especially the doctrines of church, office, and sacraments.

For a man of Sasse's theological gifts there were also some questionable assertions and even inconsistencies. He never really seemed to break from an ecclesiology rooted in the *Volkskirche* for which one could still make a legal appeal to the *Augustana*.[86] Does it not at least surprise us that a man with such a high view of the sacraments of the church could consistently practice private baptisms and even private communion?[87] There were also annoying features of his character. He seemed a bit self-indulgent about his poverty and his poor health, both of which, at least for periods of time, featured as a constant litany in his letters.

Yet he was not given to elevate himself. He did not encourage or attract a school. Sasse has fostered not so much a school as a following:

> Not that his friends . . . would want to promote a theological movement under his name. This itself would be completely alien to the nature of the influence he has in fact exerted. Dr. Sasse has founded no "school" of disciples. There are no Sassians—as there are Barthians, Bultmannians, Tillichians, and even Elertians in the Lutheran Church.[88]

A school implies a system. Sasse devised no system of theology. Rather, he was himself something of a follower among a train of followers, making the confession of the fathers and encouraging those who would follow next to make the confession. Sasse's gift is not to draw us to himself or to his theology, but rather to the theology of the church and especially to the church's confession. He did this so admirably because he was such a gifted student of the church's history. Sasse was a church historian. As a confessor, then, he was given to speak with the fathers, not so much a new word, certainly not a new theology. Rather, he conversed with the fathers in the language of today—and he drew his readers into that conversation.

In doing so, he restored to our conversation a whole vocabulary that had been lost to the church, or at least neglected; that was the vocabulary, for instance, of Holy Absolution, Holy Office, Body and Blood, hiddenness of the Church, the language of Creed and Confession. He taught us that theology really counts, that history is beneficial, yes, perhaps even utilitarian, that a time of confession is a gift.

Sasse was one of those men who was particularly gifted to speak to the church in a time of crisis. The crisis was the demise of confessional Lutheranism, of Lutheranism itself. Sasse became, therefore an "apostle" to "lonely Lutherans." All such "lonely Lutherans," Sasse as well as we, can rejoice in the words of one of his church fathers, Wilhelm Löhe:

> Behold the church! It is the very opposite of loneliness—blessed fellowship! There are millions of saints and believers who are blessed in it, and in the midst of their songs of praise is the Lord. No longer lonely, but filled, satisfied, yes, blessed is he who is one of these millions who completely and fully have Christ and with him have heaven and earth![89]

Conclusion

Hermann Sasse was a churchman: he taught about the Church and he taught the Church. He was that unusual, in German academic circles at least, amalgam of scholar and pastor, who could address a matter with the most critical scrutiny, but with a clarity rare among his contemporaries. In the language of our fathers he was a "teacher" or "doctor" of the church. In an early letter to Tom Hardt he addressed this office very specifically:

> You call me "father,"[90] so you will permit me to speak to you in my office as doctor which, according to the old rule and to the practice of the

Church of the Apostles, is not limited to a certain place or local church . . . .[91]

In summary, we describe the man and his work:

> he led no school; yet
> he gave encouragement to followers (see below)
>
> he was not a comfortable man to hear; yet
> he could be comforting
>
> he was a churchman
> in a scholar's vocation
>
> he was a theologian; yet
> he was also a pastor
>
> he was a man untimely born
> a "lonely Lutheran"—in a time of great "tragedies"
>
> he was a pre-Enlightenment man
> in an Enlightenment world
>
> he was a man of assertions
> in an age of ambiguity
>
> he was a confessor
> in an anti-confessional church
> -or-
> to a timid church
> he was a prophet
>
> amongst his own people
> he called to repentance

I here recall the words of John Bright about Jeremiah, the prophet. I would assign them to Sasse:

> ... for violence of passion
>   and tenderness of feeling
> for agony of spirit
>   and plain raw moral courage—
> stands out as a man of mark . . . .[92]

The following tributes to Sasse are fitting for the conclusion to my paper:

> Sasse pointed out that "orthodoxy" means more than pure teaching, though it does mean that; but it also means the right and correct praise of God. Hence there is a call not only for study and academics; but for a heart-born praise of God for His grace toward us. Orthodoxy means sound doctrine, worthy liturgical practices, a faithful ministry, adherence to the great Confessions of the church, a love for the truth as God has shown it to us in His Scripture. This is what Sasse told us. We are glad he was here.[93]

But there are Lutherans in America, as there are in Europe and Australia, who today thank God that from Hermann Sasse they have learned—in a better way than they knew before—"*was heißt Lutherisch*": what it means to be Lutheran.[94]

Notes

[1] The proposed title was *In Conspectu Dei; Lutheran Essays on The Gospel and the Church by Hermann Sasse* (Concordia Theological Seminary [hereafter CTS], Ft. Wayne, IN—Jungkuntz Collection).

[2] See H. Kadai's letter of 7 July 1965 to Roland Seboldt of Concordia Publishing House (CTS–Jungkuntz).

[3] Jungkuntz to Feuerhahn (4 Oct. 1995).

[4] James Gustafson, "Faithfulness: Remembering H. Richard Niebuhr," *Christian Century* 111.27 (5 Oct. 1994): 884.

[5] Wolfgang Sasse, Interview (2 Sep. 1994), Tape 1a.

[6] Ibid.

[7] There is a rather detailed genealogy tracing the family link in the collection of documents of Wolfgang Sasse.

[8] *The Bond* [Immanuel Seminary, Adelaide] 3 (July 1949): 9.

[9] "Reminiscences of an Elderly Student," *Tangara* [Luther Seminary, Adelaide] 9 (1976): 4-5; Biographical Note, File of Dean of Faculty, University of Erlangen (*E-TFA*).

[10] Harnack for early church history; Holl for 19th-century theology. "Said Sasse later: it is easier to live by Harnack's theology than to die by it." Heino O. Kadai, "Professor D. Hermann Sasse: Congratulations for a Septuagenerian [sic]," *The Springfielder*, 29.2 (Spring, 1965): 5

[11] "Reminiscences of an Elderly Student." Those mentioned by Sasse include Adolf Deissmann (*neutestamentliche Exegese*), Prof. Wolf, Graf v. Baudissin (*alttestamentliche Exegese*); a.o. Prof. Hugo Gressmann (*alttestamentliche Exegese*); Privat-Dozent Otto Eissfeldt (*alttestamentliche Theologie*); Heinrich Scholz, (*systematische Theologie*). For a full list of faculty see J. Schneider, ed., *Kirchliches Jahrbuch für die evangelischen Landeskirchen Deutschlands 1916*, 43. Jahrgang (Gütersloh: C. Bertelsmann, 1916), 583.

[12] Ibid. Since Sasse was not an officer, "university of life" might be an apt translation of *Kriegsschule*.

[13] Ibid.

[14] *E-TFA*. The expression "im Felde" indicates combat.

[15] Letter of Lt. Col. op de Hipt, German Military Attaché, Washington, D.C. to R. Feuerhahn (1 Aug. 1994). See Alec A. Purves, *The Medals Decorations & Orders of the Great War 1914-1918* (London: J. B. Hayward & Son, 1975), 111-115

[16] Interview, Wolfgang Sasse (2 Sep. 1994), Tape 1, Side 2. See Sasse's own description in "The Impact of Bultmannism on American Lutheranism," *Lutheran Synod Quarterly* 5.4 (June 1965): 2.

[17] "Reminiscences of an Elderly Student." Correspondence relating to his ordination by the *Konsistorium der Mark Brandenburg* is found in the Huß Collection.

[18] "Berufung des Hilfspredigers Hermann Sasse zum vierten Pfarrer bei den Evangelischen Gemeinden der Parochie Oranienburg, Diözese Oranienburg." J. T. E. Renner Collection, Adelaide. See also *E-TFA* and *The Bond* [Adelaide] 3 (July 1949): 9.

[19] "Rezension: Conrad Lakeit, Aion. Zeit und Ewigkeit in Sprache und Religion der Griechen, Teil I: Sprache (Königsberg, 1916)," in: *Neugriechische Jahrbücher* 2.3/4 (1921): 462-6.

[20] *Heiratsurkunde* dated 11 Sep. 1924 (Wolfgang Sasse Collection). This marriage certificate gives her name as Margarethe Charlotte. Even son Wolfgang admitted that he never knew she had both names until he saw her birth certificate (Interview, 2 Sep. 1994, Tape 1, Side 1).

[21] His thesis, "Der Begriff des Aion in der Bibel," is no longer available. Letter of Wm. Peters, Librarian, Hartford Seminary (14 Mar. 1989).

[22] Or so we conjecture on the basis of the interview with E. Theo. Bachmann (9 Nov. '90) and of a photograph in the Wolfgang Sasse Collection.

[23] Letter to Tom Hardt (18 June 1958).

[24] Klaas Runia, "Dr. Hermann Sasse 'In Statu Confessionis'," *RTR* 27.1 (Jan./Apr. 68): 1 [review article quoting a letter from Sasse].

[25] *Drei Bücher von der Kirche, Gesammelte Werke*, 7 vols., ed. Klaus Ganzert (Neuendettelsau, 1951-) V/1:85-179; ET by James L. Schaaf, *Three Books About the Church* (Philadelphia: Fortress Press, 1969).

[26] A series of lectures on this topic given at Frankfurt an der Oder were published as *Americanisches Kirchentum* (Berlin-Dahlem, 1927). A translation is scheduled to appear in the collection from Concordia, edited by Matthew Harrison & Paul McCain.

[27] Eberhard Bethge, *Dietrich Bonhoeffer, Man of Vision, Man of Courage* (New York, 1970; qtd from Fountain Edition, 1977), 105. By the way, the index of the original edition of the English translation did not distinguish Hermann Sasse from his close namesake Martin Sasse, Bishop of Thuringia; as the latter is described as favorable to the Nazis, the distinction is important. See index entry on 863, "Sasse, Hermann, Bishop of Thuringia," which indicates this conflation; 503-4 refer to Martin Sasse.

[28] *Die Weltkonferenz für Glauben und Kirchenverfassung. Deutscher amtlicher Bericht über die Weltkirchenkonferenz zu Lausanne 1927. Im Auftrage des Fortsetzungsausschusses* (Berlin: Furche-Verlag, 1929) [hereafter: Bericht].

[29] Klaas Runia, "Dr. Hermann Sasse . . .," 1 (quote from a letter of Sasse).

[30] *Faith & Order Papers* [Hereafter *F&O*], Series I, No. 65.

[31] *F&O*, 72.

[32] Bethge, ibid., 214 & 229.

[33] At least of the first draft. See Sasse, "Impact of Bultmannism . . . ," 10; Bethge, ibid., 229, esp. 231-33; and Guy C. Carter, *Confession at Bethel, August 1933—Enduring Witness: The Formation, Revision and Significance of the First Full Theological Confession of the Evangelical Church Struggle in Nazi Germany* (Dissertation [PhD], Marquette University, Milwaukee, 1987), 6, 61, 66, 71-3, 78, 84, 89, 92, 95, 103, 110-11, passim. See also Christine-Ruth Müller, *Bekenntnis und*

Bekennen, Dietrich Bonhoeffer in Bethel (1933), Ein lutherischer Versuch, Studienbücher zur kirchlichen Zeitgeschichte, Bd. 7 (München: Chr. Kaiser, 1989).

[34] Arthur C. Cochrane, *The Church's Confession Under Hitler* (1st ed. Philadelphia: Westminster Press, 1962; repr. Pittsburgh Reprint Series 4, Pittsburgh: Pickwick, 1976). By special request of his Bishop, Hans Meiser, Sasse was included in the committee for drafting the declaration (ibid., 54). Hannelore Braun and Carsten Nicolaisen, eds., *Verantwortung für die Kirche, Stenographische Aufzeichnungen und Mitschriften von Landesbischof Hans Meiser 1933-1955*, Band 1: *Sommer 1933 bis Sommer 1935* (Göttingen: Vandenhoeck & Ruprecht, 1985), 278, n.3.

[35] "The Impact of Bultmannism . . . ," 10.

[36] For example, he attended and contributed to the Berlin-Dahlem Synod of 1934. See Wilhelm Niemöller, ed., *Die zweite Bekenntnissynode der Deutschen Evangelischen Kirche zu Dahlem, Text–Dokumente–Berichte* Arbeiten zur Geschichte des Kirchenkampfes 3 (Göttingen: Vandenhoeck & Ruprecht, 1958), 33; cf. also 89, 95, 101f., 104, 106.

[37] See, e.g., "Saat auf Hoffnung," *Zeitschrift für die Mission der Kirche in Israel* 69 (1932): 105-7; Alfred Rosenberg, *Protestantische Rompilger* (1st ed. Munich, 1935; 4th ed., 1937), 29-31; Joachim Beckmann, ed., *Kirchliches Jahrbuch für die Evangelische Kirche in Deutschland 1933-1944*, 60. 71. Jahrgang, Gütersloh, 1948, 2-7; Klaus Scholder, *The Churches and the Third Reich*, 2 vols. (London: SCM/Philadelphia: Fortress, 1987-8), 1:125f.; Cochrane, *The Church's Confession under Hitler*, 78; Peter Matheson, ed., *The Third Reich and the Christian Churches* (Edinburgh: T. & T. Clark; Grand Rapids: Eerdmans, 1981), 1f; E. Clifford Nelson, *The Rise of World Lutheranism, an American Perspective* (Philadelphia: 1982), 314; Guy C. Carter, *Confession at Bethel*, 6.

[38] Interview with Wolfgang Sasse (2 Sep. 1994), Tape 1, Side 2.

[39] The promotion was official on 25 February 1946 (*E-UA*).

[40] The notice announcing his appointment was made on 29 September 1945; it was to take effect on 1 October (*E-UA* [062]). See also von Loewenich, *Erlebte Theologie*, 134; Letter, Herman Preus to Sasse (24 Jun. 46), available in *Archives of the American Lutheran Church*, Luther Seminary Library, St. Paul, MN; hereafter STP.

[41] Sasse to Behnken (21 Nov. 1945), Concordia Historical Institute [hereafter CHI] 200-BEH Suppl. II Box 20 [56243]; my trans.

[42] Von Loewenich, *Erlebte Theologie*, 133; my trans.

[43] Ibid., 134; my trans. This conflict was to be waged even in the United States: see the charges of his colleague Hermann Strathmann and others in *The Lutheran* [Philadelphia], 28.48 (Aug. 28, 1946): 13-14, 37; and *The Christian Century*, 63.39 (25 Sep. 1946): 1152-53; and the defense offered by Sasse, *The Lutheran*, 29.16 (15

Jan. 1947): 35 and others; ibid., 29.1 [marked as 28.53] (2 Oct. 1946): 32; *The Christian Century*, 64.7 (Feb. 12, 1947): 209; *CTM*, 18.4 (April 1947) 301-2.

⁴⁴ Henry P. Hamann, Jr., "The Adelaide Chapter," in idem, *Theologia Crucis; Studies in Honour of Hermann Sasse* (Adelaide: Lutheran Publishing House, 1975), 5.

⁴⁵ On the unique position of the *altlutherische Kirche* in Germany see "Die Evangelisch-lutherische (altlutherische) Kirche," in Manfred Roensch & Werner Klän, *Quellen zur Entstehung und Entwicklung selbständiger evangelisch-lutherischer Kirchen in Deutschland*, Europäische Hochschulschriften: Reihe 23, Theologie; Bd. 299, (Frankfurt am Main, Bern, New York: Peter Lang, 1987), 23-137; also Klän, "Die Evangelisch-lutherische (altlutherische) Kirche," in Hubert Kirchner, ed., *Freikirchen und konfessionelle Minderheitskirchen, Ein Handbuch* (Berlin: Evangelische Verlagsanstalt, 1987), 127-135.

⁴⁶ Proeve, "Hermann Otto Erich Sasse," 64-65.

⁴⁷ J. T. E. Renner, "Biography of Hermann Sasse," Appendix to *WCJC*, 102. In Kittel: "H. Sasse undertook the art. *ouranos* along with the arts. on *gay* and *kosmos*. Because of his departure for Australia he was not able to get the work ready for the press. On the basis of his extensive preparatory labours H. Traub has written the art." *TDNT* V: 497n; *ThWbNT* V: 496 has a similar note.

⁴⁸ Hopf had also left (or rather been expelled from!) the Bavarian Church to join the *Altlutherische Kirche*. He published the *Lutherische Blätter* chiefly as a vehicle for the "Letters" and reprints of earlier essays by Sasse. The *Briefe* began appearing in 1948, before Sasse left Germany.

⁴⁹ Letter to Herman Preus (27 Nov. 48) (STP).

⁵⁰ Introductory letter (Easter 1967) to "Confessional Churches in the Ecumenical Movement with Special Reference to the Lutheran World Federation," *Springfielder* 31.1 (Spring, 1967): 3; see also letter to Meiser (22 Apr. 1946) (HLA D15 V Nr.27).

⁵¹ Behnken was accompanied by Lawrence Meyer. Letters to (a) Ralph Long (18 Nov. 1945) CHI 200-BEH Suppl. II B20 F06 [56241]; (b) Behnken (21 Nov. 1945) CHI 200-BEH Suppl. II Box 20 [56243]; (c) Martin Kiunke (24 Nov. 1945) HLA [205-207] 3.

⁵² Behnken's report is dated 28 Dec. 1945. See esp. items 21 & 30. CHI 200-MEY Suppl. I Box 1 File 1.

⁵³ See, e.g., the memo of a meeting dated 29 Oct. 1947, CHI 200-SAS/BF21a.

⁵⁴ For a detailed account of this matter, see my article, "Hermann Sasse and North American Lutheranism," in *Logia* (Reformation 1995).

⁵⁵ See, e.g., Theodore Graebner, "Some Impressions of Germany," *The Cresset*, 11.10 (Sep 1948): 18-22, esp. 20f. This has been illustrated in a paper by Edward

Engelbrecht, "Lutheran Confessional Optimism after World War Two: Hanns Lilje and Theodore Graebner," (July 1992, 50pp.), to be published in *Logia*.

[56] President George Beto to Sasse (9 Oct. 1961); document not available.

[57] Ronald R. Feuerhahn, *Hermann Sasse: A Bibliography*, American Theological Library Association Bibliography Series 37 (Lanham, MD and London: The Scarecrow Press, 1995).

[58] Interview (2 Sep. 1994).

[59] Interview, Wolfgang Sasse (2 Sep. 1994), Tape 1, Side 2.

[60] Interview, Victor Pfitzner (22 Sep. 1994).

[61] A list of names for whom special prayer is made; term derived from the two-leaved folder within which the list was written. Interview, Tom Hardt.

[62] Pastor Fred Kummerow, retired Archivist of the LCA (12 Sep. 94).

[63] Interview, Wolfgang Sasse (2 Sep. 1994).

[64] An emphasis of the interviews with Tom Hardt & Martin Wittenberg.

[65] Sasse to E. Theo. Bachmann (2 May 61); CHI 200-BEH/Suppl. II/Box 2/File 13.

[66] Letter to Tom Hardt (18 June 1958).

[67] Interview, Hans-Siegfried Huß (28 Sep 1989), Tape II. 1a [p. 6], bolding added.

[68] Interview, E. Theo. Bachmann (9 Nov. 90).

[69] This quote is from "The Situation of the Lutheran Church," p. 6, a translation by G[eorge] W[olfgang] Forell (in STP) of Sasse's "Zur Lage des Luthertums nach dem Zweiten Weltkrieg." Teil III, *Lutherische Blätter* 1.3 (Oct. 1949): 15 (reprinted in *In Statu Confessionis* I:294). Note that the German original in neither *LB* nor *ISC* gives the text for Forell's translation. However, it is not only possible but even likely that Forell worked from a duplicated copy of the essay which had been altered for publication; see also the editor's footnote in *ISC* I:294 which supports Forell's translation.

[70] Ibid., 7. Original in *LB* 1.3 (1949): 16 and in *ISC* I: 295; my trans.

[71] Interview with Dr. J. T. Erich Renner (Sep. 1994).

[72] For a detailed treatment of Sasse's assessment of Catholicism, particularly the Roman Catholic Church, see my dissertation, Chapter 6.

[73] There are 48 letters in the Sasse-Bea correspondence: four letters of Sasse addressed to Bea himself; 29 to Stjepan Schmidt, S.J., Bea's secretary, and later, his biographer; he received one letter from Bea (copy not available) and 14 letters from

Schmidt. I am profoundly grateful to Fr. Schmidt for making copies available to me and for generously answering my queries.

[74] "Hermann Sasse," Editorial by J. A. O. P[reus], *The Springfielder* 26.1 (Spring 1962): 3-4.

[75] Interview, paraphrase of remarks (3 Mar. 89), Tape 1a.

[76] Letter of Sasse to H. Preus (22 Mar. 1956) STP [249-253].

[77] Letter of Sasse to Ralph Gehrke (5 Nov. 54).

[78] Letter of Sasse to Tom Hardt (18 June 1958).

[79] Letter to Tom Hardt (4 Aug. 1959), italics added. See similarly letter to Hardt of 12 Sep. 1959.

[80] Letter to Tom Hardt (17 Sep. 1959).

[81] Interview, Pastor Hartmann, Canberra (25 Sep. 1994). I have found no explanation given by Sasse for this action.

[82] Letter to Tom Hardt (18 Dec. 1958), underlining original.

[83] Albrecht Peters (prof. at Heidelberg), Review of *In Statu Confessionis* I, *Theologische Literaturzeitung* 92 (1967): 700; trans. from Gordon J. Gerhardy, "Hermann Sasse on Confession and Culture for a Younger Church," Thesis [MTh] (Luther-Northwestern Seminary, St. Paul, 1981), 39, 63.

[84] Ibid.

[85] Walther von Loewenich, *Erlebte Theologie*, 136.

[86] For example, at Barmen or at Wittenberg in September 1933. This can be called a *kirchenrechtliche* (canon law-style) view.

[87] He baptized all four of his Australian grandchildren in private services. It was likely a remnant of his German churchmanship. See, e.g., even Peter Brunner, *Worship in the Name of Jesus* (St. Louis: Concordia Publishing House, 1968), 336, n. 230: "However, we must oppose the demand that Baptism must be administered in the main service." On private communion, see supra.

[88] Richard Jungkuntz, "Dedication" for the never-to-be-published *Festschrift*, *In Conspectu Dei* (CTS - Jungkuntz).

[89] Three Books About the Church, 51

[90] In each letter Hardt used the salutation, "Dear father in Christ."

[91] Letter to Hardt (21 May 1958). In a letter to J. A. O. Preus (31 Oct. 1968) he spoke of "my privilege as a public teacher of theology in the Lutheran Church . . ." (CTS [418-428]; CTS-CTCR; CTS-Otten). He commented on the "old rule and

practice of the Church," mentioned in the Hardt letter, in a letter to Hans Rottmann [Porto Alegre] (21 Jan 1960); CHI 200-BEH Suppl. II B2 F13 [52320].

[92] John Bright, *The Kingdom of God* (New York & Nashville: Abingdon, 1953), 98f.

[93] "Hermann Sasse," Editorial by J. A. O. P[reus], *The Springfielder* 26.1 (Spring 1962): 3-4.

[94] Richard Jungkuntz, "Dedication."

Hermann Sasse's Relations with His Erlangen Colleagues

Lowell C. Green

Back in the 1940s, when I was a student at Wartburg Theological Seminary, we students were told that every one of us must read these three books: C. F. W. Walther's *The Proper Distinction Between Law and Gospel*, Adolf Köberle's *The Quest for Holiness*, and Hermann Sasse's *Here We Stand*. Johann Michael Reu had had a high opinion of Sasse, who thus became somewhat of an icon for us students. The centennial of the birth of Hermann Sasse gives us the occasion to remember the words and deeds of this great Lutheran scholar and confessor, and my topic shall be "Hermann Sasse's Relations with His Erlangen Colleagues." This is a difficult topic because those relationships were complicated and often neuralgic. We can learn much about Hermann Sasse as we turn our attention to his career at Erlangen, the place where he spent sixteen of the most important years of his life.

I. Erlangen, the Scene of Sasse's Work

During the 19th century the Theological Faculty at Erlangen was a stronghold of Lutheran theology, building upon a conservative interpretation of the Scriptures, commitment to the Lutheran Confessions, and emphasis upon personal piety and faith as the source of religious certainty. The renowned theologians included Adolf Harless, Johann Christian Konrad von Hofmann, Gottfried Thomasius, Theodosius Harnack, Franz Delitzsch, Franz Hermann Reinhold Frank, and Heinrich Schmid. Many of their works have been translated into English, including the Old Testament commentaries of Delitzsch and the dogmatics of Schmid.

As superintendent of the Protestant State Church of Bavaria, Harless worked together with Pastor Wilhelm Löhe to form a separate confessional Lutheran group, which became the Lutheran Territorial ["*Land*"] Church of Bavaria, a stronghold for Lutheran doctrine and practice. Löhe is regarded as one of the founding fathers of both the

Missouri and the Iowa Synods.

After the death of Frank in 1894, Erlangen theology declined, only to return to life with the arrival of Werner Elert at Erlangen in 1923, of Otto Procksch as professor for Old Testament in 1925, and later that same year of Paul Althaus as professor of systematic theology. Under these men, the "Big Three," Erlangen entered its second period of celebrity. Each man was noted for scholarly brilliance coupled with a strong fidelity to Luther and the Lutheran Church. Nowhere else in Germany was there a faculty which presented such a united confessional front. Enrollment rose from 181 in 1923 to 661 in 1933. Wolfgang Trillhaas has characterized this triumvirate as follows: the unteachable Lutheran, Procksch; the man of humane and pastoral nobility, Althaus; and the man of uncontrollable love for research, Elert.[1] Let us look briefly at the position which Sasse assumed. In a German university, a full professorship was known as an *ordinarius* or ordinary position; this meant "according to the order," a full track position within the university statutes. An assistant professorship was known as an *extraordinarius* or a position "outside the order." Just why the Bavarian Minister of Education and Culture, Dr. Hans Schemm, had insisted that Elert's successor not have the full rank of an *ordinarius*, is unclear. Because of the lowered rank, several other candidates had declined to come.[2] Nevertheless, Sasse was willing to accept the position of an *extraordinarius* when he came to Erlangen in 1933. He was formally received into the theological faculty of the Friedrich & Alexander University of Erlangen on 19 May 1933.[3] Sasse was to have a very successful teaching career. He was an excellent teacher and took a warm interest in people, so that he was very popular with his students.

A good friend of mine, Theodore Baudler, first went to Erlangen on 10 September 1933. Baudler has shared with me his impressions of the "Big Three." He was offended by Elert's public posture of supporting Nazism, and he disliked Althaus' doctrinal ambivalence, but he was strongly drawn to Otto Procksch[4] and to Sasse. He was attracted to Sasse because of the professor's great knowledge and clarity as a teacher, and because of his warm and kindly personality. He said, "Sasse regularly invited English and American students to his home."

II. Developments in Germany, 1933-1949

A. A Time of Uncertainty.

When Sasse formally joined the Theological Faculty of Erlangen University on 19 May 1933, Germany was in the throes of being taken over by the National Socialist party.[5] The Weimar Republic had abolished all the German state churches when it declared in Article 137 of its constitution that, "The state churches no longer exist" (*Es besteht keine Staatskirche*);[6] this government was often hostile to religion and the churches. But the Nazis had declared in 1920 that, "We demand freedom for all religious confessions in the State, insofar as they do not endanger its existence or offend against the ethical and moral sensitivities of the German race."[7] Sasse made the keen observation in 1932 that this statement could not protect the church, because the Christian doctrine of inherited lust and original sin militates against the Nazi ideology about Aryan perfectibility.[8]

Both Althaus and Elert supported the transformation of the old "Federation of Evangelical Churches" from 1923 into a new "German Evangelical Church" (*Deutsche Evangelische Kirche*) or *DEK*. Because perhaps 85% of German Protestants were Lutherans, they hoped that the new *DEK* would be based upon the Lutheran Confessions and put their church in the position of prominence which it deserved. It seemed as though there were only two professors at Erlangen who firmly opposed this development, and that on the grounds of "unionism": these were Sasse and Friedrich Ulmer, professor of practical theology. Elert rejected democratic notions about the church and emphasized its Christocentric nature; he wanted the position of church presidents to be replaced with bishops, and borrowed the concept of the political *Führer* to express this.[9] But Sasse devastatingly criticized the *Führer* concept: "It is the weakest place in Hitler's world view, a teaching that is unacceptable to any Christian church, when it says there: 'The first fundamental for building authority consists in popularity .... In power ..., in force, we see the second fundamental of that authority' ...." And he noted how Hitler at one point ascribed "almost religious value to the 'folk' while he disparaged the 'masses,' who are actually in both cases the same people."[10]

On 11 July 1933 the new constitution for the "German Evangelical

Church" (*DEK*) was signed by the "territorial" bishops and other leaders,[11] and on 14 July a Reich law confirmed the constitution and set 23 July for new elections. At the summit stood the "Reich Bishop" (*Reichsbischof*), who was required to be a Lutheran; in cases involving Reformed churches, the Reich Bishop was to appoint someone of that confession to represent him. Besides him there was the "Clerical Ministerium" (*Geistliches Ministerium*), which helped to set policies, and the "National Synod," consisting of 60 representatives from the provincial churches.[12]

The suspicions of men such as Sasse and Ulmer against the *DEK* were soon confirmed as, step by step, the German Christians used the *DEK* as a sort of Trojan Horse to take over the control of Protestant territorial ["*Land*"] churches and incorporate them into the new Reich Church, which was patterned after the Union Church. Already on 24 June 1933 the German Christians seized control of the largest territorial church in Germany, the Church of the Prussian Union.[13] Elert denounced this action of the "German Christians" and compared it to the famous *Latrocinium Ephesinum* of A. D. 449 as the "Robber Synod of Berlin."[14]

There was an uneasy feeling among churchmen that they were confronted with an enemy. But who was the real foe? Most churchmen at first did not see Hitler or the Nazi party as the enemy, but rather the German Christian Movement. They thought: "If only Hitler knew what these people were doing, he'd put a stop to it." A number of affirmations of loyalty to Hitler were proclaimed during the first year he was in power by those who otherwise opposed the German Christians. In a "Summons of the Young Reformation Movement" (*Der Aufruf der Jungreformatorischen Bewegung*) of May 1933, Walter Künneth, Martin Niemoeller, and Hanns Lilje, all men noted for their later resistance to Hitler, had signed a similar pledge:

> §11: We demand that the Evangelical Church, in a joyful affirmation of the new German State, fulfill its God-given task in full freedom from all political influence, and simultaneously bind itself to an indissoluble commitment of service to the German folk.[15]

And on 15 October 1933, the day after Germany declared its withdrawal from the League of Nations, Martin Niemoeller expressed this public pledge of loyalty in a telegram to Hitler:

In this hour which is so decisive for folk and fatherland, we greet you as our *Führer*. We thank you for the manly deed and the clear word which guards German honor. In the name of more than 2500 evangelical pastors who do not belong to the German Christian movement, we pledge you our loyal following and our prayerful thoughts.[16]

A similar statement was the "Ansbach Counsel" of Elert and Althaus, written in June 1934 as a statement of support for Hitler and the National Socialist government and as a repudiation of the German Christians.[17] So late as 28 April 1934, a month before the Synod of Barmen and six weeks before the "Ansbach Counsel," Bonhoeffer had complained in a letter to a Swiss friend that Niemoeller still thought he could further the objectives of the church by working together with the National Socialists.[18] The evil character of Hitler's new regime was seen only slowly and gradually, and by the time churchmen were aware of its demonic nature, it was too late to oppose him.

The seizure of the Old Prussian Union by the German Christians was the real beginning of the *Kirchenkampf* or Church Struggle. The Nazis were able to take control of all the Union Churches as well as many Lutheran Churches. These were called "destroyed" churches, whereas the churches which successfully avoided seizure were known as "intact" churches. The only intact churches were the large Lutheran territorial churches of Bavaria, Württemberg, and Hanover. In the "destroyed churches," those who resisted the German Christian Movement formed small conventicles which called themselves the "Confessing Church." This term must be distinguished from "Confessional Church," i.e., the church which follows the Lutheran Confessions. The participial construction in the word "confessing" denotes that, in their understanding, confession was the act of confessing something or other, and the content of such confessing could be very general and not at all related to the Lutheran Confessions. The Confessing Church became doctrinaire in a new sense. It replaced the totalitarianism of the Nazi government with a sort of church totalitarianism which dealt ruthlessly with the scruples of Confessional Lutherans. In spite of his relentless rejection of Nazi ideology, a man such as Sasse was bitterly attacked by members of the Confessing Church. Bonhoeffer even said that it was doubtful that anybody could be saved who did not take part in this unionistic movement.

A group of theologians from the Reformed, Union, and Lutheran churches gathered in the city of Barmen 29-31 May 1934 to discuss action against the German Christians. Hermann Sasse was among the representatives from the Lutheran territorial church of Bavaria. The meeting was dominated by the personality of Karl Barth, a Reformed theologian with whom all the professors at Erlangen disagreed. Barth succeeded in pushing through a statement which had two serious weaknesses: it assumed that the federation known as the "German Evangelical Church," or *DEK,* was a church which could pass binding doctrinal statements, and it contained statements which militated against the Lutheran distinction of Law and Gospel and the Two Kingdoms. Sasse rejected the Barmen Declaration for the first reason, its unionism, and left Barmen before the conference had ended to avoid the unionism of signing it; Elert and Althaus attacked the Barmen Declaration for the second reason, its doctrine; Sasse later joined them in assailing its confounding of Law and Gospel.

In 1934, the German Christians made several attempts to seize control of the "intact" Lutheran territorial churches of Württemberg and Bavaria. On 14 September 1934, Bishop Theophilus Wurm of neighboring Württemberg was deposed and placed under house arrest. Their attention was now directed to overthrowing Bishop Hans Meiser and seizing control of the Lutheran Church of Bavaria. Advertisements appeared in the Nuremberg papers denouncing Bishop Hans Meiser as a traitor to the church. The German Christians attempted to divide the territorial church of Bavaria into two parts, with one bishop replacing Meiser in Munich, and a new bishop seated in Nuremberg.

On Saturday, 12 September 1934, large placards were placed in the streets of the city with this message: "Away with Meiser—The man is un-Christian—He has no character—He has behaved like Judas Iscariot," etc. But the Nazis had not reckoned with the loyalty of Nuremberg Lutherans. That week there were a number of mass demonstrations, with huge crowds filling the large city churches.[19] The Theological Faculty of Erlangen issued a strong protest against these Nazi tactics on 13 October, stating that the Reich Church government had gone against the law, against the spirit of true churchliness, against Christian love for the brethren, and against the commandments of God, and had violated the divinity of the call.[20] Already on 11 October, a commission appointed by the German Christians had seized the leadership of the Bavarian church at Munich while Meiser was out of town.[21] The stalwart bishop was arrested upon his return the following day and confined to his home.[22] However, massive demonstrations continued in Munich, Nuremberg, and other cities of Bavaria. Similar demonstrations were going on in Württemberg, until at last the Nazis were unnerved and Hitler intervened. Meiser and Wurm were set free, the territorial churches were returned to their legitimate control, and both bishops, together with Bishop August Marahrens of Hanover, were invited to come to Berlin for a private meeting with Hitler. The Lutheran territorial churches of Bavaria, Württemberg, and Hanover were to remain "intact" until the fall of the National Socialist regime in 1945.

B. Elert as Dean of the Theological Faculty at Erlangen.

The career of Sasse at Erlangen was intricately interwoven with his relations with his colleagues, and, above all, with Werner Elert, with whom he had a very strong doctrinal affinity and who was also his administrative superior during most of the time Sasse was at Erlangen. In 1935, Elert had become dean of the theological faculty. Normally, this position rotated among the faculty on a yearly basis. But had Elert given up his post at the end of the first year, Hans Albert Molitaris, the so-called "Faculty Leader" set up by the Nazis, would likely have appointed a Nazi as dean. Therefore, Elert remained in that position until he was ousted in 1943 for refusing to join the Nazi party.

Elert was under intense pressure in his policy of appearing to be friendly to Hitler's government while at the same time secretly undercutting its evil activities. He carried out his policy in at least three ways: Elert steadfastly avoided the urgings to join the Nazi party or at least its German Christian movement; he successfully prevented all attempts to add Nazi professors in the theological faculty; and he shielded professors and students when they got into trouble with the government.[23]

Sasse was a marked man and the whole theological faculty was under the watchful eye of the Nazis. The Nazi rector, Fritz Specht, asked Elert why there were more theological students at Erlangen than elsewhere (over 200 in 1939), the highest in Germany,[24] and suggested suspiciously that these students had come to Erlangen because Sasse was known for his opposition to National Socialism. Following the dismissal of Prof. Friedrich Ulmer during the summer of 1937 by the

Nazis, Alfred Rosenberg had criticized the university on account of Sasse, and Rector Specht told Elert that the whole university had been brought into disgrace by Sasse. Elert defended Sasse before Specht, reminding him that the declarations submitted by Sasse on the occasion of his being called were of the nature that he could be called as a professor in a university in the National Socialist state.[25] Nevertheless, both Specht and Molitoris, the "Faculty Leader," continued to harass Elert to get rid of Sasse.

In spite of the strikes against him, Sasse asked Elert to secure him a promotion with a raise in salary. Elert comments: "Everyone who had had any dealings with the party leadership knew that the application of Dr. Sasse for promotion to the position of *ordinarius* had no chances."[26] But Sasse insisted. Elert continues: "When I, in spite of all this, approached Molitoris, the 'Faculty Leader,' with the hope of winning him for an unusual step in favor of Dr. Sasse, he urgently advised me not to present an application. First, because it was absolutely hopeless—one would have to get the approval of the Reich Minister of Finance—and second, because the question of the acceptability of Dr. Sasse from the viewpoint of the Party would be again opened to discussion; in his opinion, this could only end in misfortune for Dr. Sasse."[27]

III. Stormy Relationships of Sasse with His Colleagues.

The career of Sasse was marked by many conflicts with his colleagues, including Althaus, Strathmann, and the university music director, Georg Kempff.[28] The fiercest of these were his disputes with Hermann Strathmann, which we must now scrutinize. It appears that the first of these skirmishes broke out in 1935. Strathmann had presented an essay to a group of Erlangen students at the retreat center of Rummelsberg during the Pentecost vacation of 1935; a little later he published a version of this material as an article in *Theologische Blätter*, of which he was editor.[29] In this article, Strathmann supported the Barmen movement, and he also defended the doctrinal ambiguity of the Union Churches by means of a radical application of the *sola scriptura* principle. Strathmann wrote that we accept the Lutheran Confessions "insofar as" they agree with the Scriptures, and that since the Confessions claim validity only as interpretations of the Scriptures, Lutherans should not refuse fellowship with other Protestants who accept the Scriptures. Strathmann added that fellowship should be extended to the Union and Reformed Churches. This position was, of course, unacceptable to Sasse. But Strathmann had also made a disparaging reference to Sasse as one who had walked out on the meeting at Barmen; he said that Sasse had first approved the six theses of the *Barmen Declaration*, but had refused to sign the declaration because, as a Lutheran, he felt he could not proclaim confessional solidarity with the Reformed. Moreover, Strathmann inveighed against those who placed the Lutheran Confessions above unity with the Union Church.

Sasse wrote a letter to Strathmann in which he said that it was impossible for the two men to discuss theology or the church any longer, since their views were hopelessly divergent, and he added: "I can only ask you hereafter to abstain from any reports whatsoever about me in *Theologische Blätter*. I do not wish to be mentioned there either by name or anonymously." Sasse ended by expressing the hope that they could remain on amiable personal terms.[30]

IV. Post-War Developments and Their Impact upon the Relationship of Sasse with His Erlangen Colleagues

A. Erlangen after the War

In his published memoirs, Walther von Loewenich gives a colorful picture of the day on which Erlangen peacefully surrendered to the American army. It was 16 April 1945. He writes: "the Americans were there. They occupied the Burgberg [the highest hill above Erlangen]. For us at least, the Third Reich had ended. I shall never forget that moment. Thankfulness that we had safely come so far simply overwhelmed me. Like so many others, I experienced the Americans as our deliverers."[31]

The sermons of Althaus from that period reflect the suffering of the people who had lost husbands, fathers, and sons in the war, the refugees who were homeless and needy, and the lack of food, clothing, and heating fuel which affected everyone.[32] Most of the theological professors had lost sons in the war. In his letters to Prof. Mayer of St. Louis, Sasse described how difficult it was to spend the winter in an unheated house, and thanked him for the care packages from the Missouri Synod, which had kept him and his family alive.

B. Sasse's Confidential Memorandum

The American army occupied the city of Erlangen for several years after the war. The Americans favored the reopening of the university and the return to normal conditions as soon as possible. In order to ascertain that the remaining faculty were free of Nazi ideology, the military government chose a person from each of the colleges to give a report on whether its faculty were free of Nazi supporters. Hermann Sasse, who was known to the Americans as a dependable man who had opposed National Socialism and who spoke excellent English, was asked to prepare a memorandum on the theological professors. In compliance, Sasse wrote his *Confidential Memorandum*, dated 28 April 1945, and presented it to the military. His report had the desirable effect of clearing the theologians of all suspicion of wrongdoing, and it secured the reopening of the Theological Faculty at Erlangen, the first department of this university and the first theological faculty in Germany to begin classes in the fall of 1945.[33]

Let us look more closely at Sasse's *Confidential Memorandum*. It began with a very laudatory description of the Theological Faculty, characterizing it as very churchly in nature, devoted to the Lutheran Confessions, and dedicated to educating pastors for the church. Sasse pictured the serious problems the theological faculty had experienced and successfully overcome during the Third Reich without sacrificing their integrity to the Nazis. Sasse concluded: "The Theological Faculty of the University of Erlangen had absolutely no connections with the National Socialist Party. There can hardly have been any other Evangelical theological faculty in all Germany that remained intact like this as did ours. In this respect, the department is like the territorial church with which it is tied very closely."

If Sasse had only stopped at that point, he would have won the gratitude of his fellow professors. Why he continued to write, giving unflattering characterizations of his colleagues, is unclear. According to his letter to his friend, Friedrich Wilhelm Hopf, on 23 October 1945, at the meeting of the commission in which Sasse presented his report, he was asked to provide more elaborate descriptions of his colleagues.

Here are some of his elaborations: In the first years of Nazi supremacy, Hans Preuß had repeatedly made public statements in which he supported the Nazi movement. Hermann Strathmann was described as a man whose interest in politics had sacrificed a brilliant career as a New Testament scholar. Althaus was a Melanchthonian, a mediator, the master of a theology which says both yes and no to everything. Sasse criticized Althaus for seeking a reconciliation of Christianity within the concept of the German folk, whereby he became the theologian of the German national citizenry of the 1920s.[34]

Sasse wrote regarding Elert: "As a strongly profiled representative of Confessional Lutheranism, called to Erlangen in 1923, he could have become the theological leader of the Lutheran Church of Germany, had he not weakly failed at every decisive hour, especially during the National Socialist Revolution of 1933 and in the following Church Struggle. In the role of professor and dean he presented himself in public as a Nazi, but he was neither inwardly nor outwardly a Nazi, and more sharply than others he recognized the demonic trends of the party and he condemned them in private . . . ."

Sasse concluded: "The undersigned accepted the difficult and thankless task of writing such a report so that it would not be committed to less knowledgeable hands. He has labored to be as objective as possible, but also to speak with full openness, so that this openness will be rightly understood at the place to which this report is directed."[35]

C. *The Response of His Colleagues to the* Confidential Memorandum

In writing his report, Sasse should have been mindful that his report might reach the eyes of his colleagues. Some unknown person violated its confidentiality; within a few weeks the other professors had read his remarks about them, and Sasse faced a new storm. There is a large amount of available documentary material; because of time limitations, I must restrict myself to only a few of the angry replies addressed to Sasse.

An *Anonymous Memorandum on Sasse* appeared with the following introduction: "Among the members of the faculty who were characterized for the occupational authorities in Dr. Sasse's *Secret Memorandum*, Dr. Sasse himself is absent. By means of my observations I will attempt to fill the gap." Who was the unknown writer? Because of the information it presents, and the satirical manner and playful humor in which it was written, it points to Elert.

The writer proceeds: "Dr. Sasse had the great merit to have warned about National Socialism already before 1933. However, this did not hinder him from allowing himself [as a professor in a state university] to be made an official of the National Socialist state after the seizure of power by the party, prior to which he gave calming assurances to the Minister of Culture, [Hans] Schemm, a Führer of the Party, and then gave an oath of loyalty to the political leadership of Hitler. . . .

"Also later on, when the catastrophic development of the party had become obvious, he did not take advantage of the possibility to leave the service of the state, although a very respectable professorship was offered him in the service of the church as Director of the Seminary of the Lutheran Free Church in Breslau . . . ."

The writer further described an essay on "The American Churches" in which Sasse wrote so disparagingly of the Americans as to have seriously endangered German-American relations.[36]

Sasse's closing remarks in the *Confidential Memorandum* were subjected to a comical imitation at the close: "Sasse's tendency to remain an outsider, to put it gently, has also been noticed in the other departments. He is a man without tact, a deficiency which is excused least of all in Germany. Any group over which Dr. Sasse has any important influence will be robbed of all credit. He was forced to resign from the leadership of the *Martin Luther Bund*. But still, it is self-understood that what has been said here does not make Dr. Sasse politically unacceptable for the university."[37]

Several letters from Elert to Althaus show that he had felt betrayed as a benefactor, friend, colleague, and fellow Lutheran. But matters got worse. In a letter to Althaus dated 27 July 1945, Elert reported that Sasse, in filling out a questionnaire for the American Military Government, had added this statement on a separate sheet of paper: "In the summer of 1939, the man who was Dean at that time, after repeatedly asking me to make my literary confession to the National Socialist State, said that I was not acceptable to the state on a permanent basis . . . ." Elert now comments about this statement: "This presentation, which, inasmuch as it applies to the man who was Dean at that time, becomes a denunciation [of me] under present circumstances . . . ."[38] Elert explains that the only reason he suggested that Sasse make himself more acceptable to the Nazis lay in Sasse's repeated requests for a promotion and raise in salary. Elert finally told him that if he really wanted to obtain a promotion from the Nazis, he would have to win their confidence by doing some political writing that would win their approval. Elert, of course, meant that this was an impossibility. But Sasse evidently hadn't gotten the point.

Elert now felt under attack for his work as Dean. In a follow-up letter of 7 August, he expressed his deep disillusionment with Sasse. He announced that he would prepare a longer statement to describe his twelve years as Dean. This statement, his *Report on the Deanship of the Theological Faculty 1933-45*, contains some exceedingly valuable first-hand information about the years 1935-1943 when Elert was Dean, and it shows that he acted very courageously in difficult times. Had it been made public earlier, much of the sentiment against Elert and Erlangen would have been made impossible. For some unknown reason, the report was suppressed for many decades, and was first published by Karlmann Beyschlag in 1993.[39]

The strongest attack on Sasse came from Hermann Strathmann, in what Prof. Gerhard Schmidt amusingly dubbed the *Hermannschlacht*, the battle of the two Hermanns, an analogy to German mythology. Strathmann had been deeply angered by the *Confidential Memorandum* and had carried on an almost scandalous attack on Sasse. Nevertheless, on 26 October 1945, a meeting of the *Concilium decanale* was called by Rector Suess in which both Hermanns appeared and the matter was talked through. Strathmann conceded that the *Confidential Memorandum* had not been written out of any dishonorable intention, and both men agreed to avoid all conduct which could disturb their new agreement.

It is ironical that both Hermanns, who had come out of the Prussian Union, tended to politicize their theology. Sasse's cooperation with the American Occupational Force was seen by his colleagues as an act of betrayal, and his *Confidential Memorandum* as a political maneuver. We shall see later how Sasse politicized Elert's hermeneutics of the Old Testament and claimed that Elert thereby supported the rejection of the Old Testament by the German Christians.

Strathmann had been a member of a small Christian party which was strongly opposed to Hitler, the "Christian People's Party" (*Christlichen Volksdienst*).[40] But during the early war years, Hitler's military victories reawakened the patriotism of Strathmann, who, as editor of the journal *Theologische Blätter*, wrote glowing reports favoring Hitler's foreign policies.[41] In his "*Confidential Memorandum*, Sasse had referred to these acts of indiscretion. This was perhaps what led the Americans to find these nationalistic statements of Strathmann and, because of them, to place a ban on Strathmann's teaching. This happened late in November 1945. Strathmann at once blamed Sasse for his new misfortune.[42]

And Strathmann spread the conflict to America when he attacked Sasse in an article that appeared in *The Lutheran* on 28 August 1946: "More painful for me was that my colleague, Sasse, considered it proper in April 1945, without any compulsion, to besmear Elert, Althaus, and myself in a secret letter to the Americans. I did not learn of it until August and as a German and a theologian can only be deeply ashamed of his conduct. By perverting the truth, I was described in his letter as a 'Nationalist.' I was not dismissed, but was compelled—temporarily—to request a 'leave,' and since December 1, 1945, I cannot lecture any more . . . ."[43]

Sasse valued his relations with Lutherans in America and as soon as he learned of Strathmann's letter, he responded directly to *The Lutheran* in a letter to the editor that was published on 15 January 1947, and in which he insisted that he had had nothing to do with Strathmann's dismissal.[44] It does appear, however, that Strathmann's defamation was at least part of the reason why Sasse was not given a position at Concordia Seminary, St. Louis.

D. New Trouble from Sasse's Resignation as Pro-rector and the De-Nazification at Erlangen.

On 31 May 1946, Sasse sent a letter of resignation to Dr. Fendt, State Minister for Education and Culture in Munich. In this letter he said that he was resigning because he did not think that the composition of the Council of Deans was legitimate and that he considered its decisions invalid, that he could no longer allow his name to be associated with the false course in which the university was headed, that he could not continue selecting students as eligible for admission on the basis of their not having been Nazis when no such standards were applied to the professors, and that many in the university who had been standard-bearers for the Nazis still remained in leadership. Sasse called for a de-Nazification purge of the university which would be "righteous" and "humane."[45]

After this, Sasse had written a second, more damaging letter to a higher authority than the Minister of Education. In this letter to the Military Government and the Bavarian Minister of Education, he appealed personally to the President of Bavarian Ministers, Dr. Hoegner, going over the heads of the university administration and Dr. Fendt in Munich. Sasse explained that his resignation had been on the grounds that the University of Erlangen was a center of [Nazi] reaction. As an example of this, he referred to some publications of Althaus from the 1930s. On 14 July 1946, Werner Elert wrote an urgent letter to Bishop Hans Meiser, informing him of the new emergency awaiting the University of Erlangen.[46] He expressed the fear that if the university were closed only temporarily, the public media would doubtless take hold of Sasse's word "reaction" and connect it with the notorious "Niemoeller Affair," and with reference to the Theological Faculty, point to the Protestant character of the university. Closing the university even temporarily could have a devastating effect upon its future survival.[47] The reference to the "Niemoeller Affair" was to the cold reception Martin Niemoeller got on the occasion of a lecture he delivered in Erlangen, which afterwards was described by the press as a near-riot in the church and as a sign that Erlangen was still a stronghold of Nazi sympathy.[48]

Sasse's suggestion was followed, but the de-Nazification proved to be neither "righteous" nor "humane." The notorious de-Nazification of Erlangen began on 7 January 1947, when all professors at Erlangen were dismissed. All were placed upon one of three lists: from among the theologians, only Sasse and Friedrich Baumgärtel were on the white list, who were immediately reinstated; on the black list were Althaus, Strathmann, and Preuß, who were not allowed to teach for a year, and Friedrich Hauck, who was not allowed to teach for 21 months; on the gray list, those who were conditionally reinstated, stood the names of all others, such as Elert and Gerhard Schmidt. The only thing they had against Hauck was that he had written a school prayer which included the petition, "God bless the Führer." It was said that Strathmann was deposed because somebody had said he was a "party member"; but Strathmann had not belonged to the Nazi Party, but to the "People's Christian Party" which had opposed the Nazi Party!

The clumsiness and even dishonesty of the American military interrogators caused the investigation to be a great misfortune for many people. It was said that if one were Roman Catholic, one could go to the confessional, be absolved of the sins of Nazism by the priest, and then be acceptable to the American authorities; but Protestants were not handled so gently. Some innocent professors were hurt, and a storm of anger broke out also against Sasse on account of the De-Nazification.

E. Sasse's Attacks upon the Theology of Elert.

I have some strong reservations about the criticisms which Sasse leveled against the dogmatics of Elert. Most inappropriate was his attack upon Elert's doctrine of the Old Testament in an essay written in 1945.[49] Sasse faulted Elert for distinguishing between the Old Testament people of God and the New Testament church of Jesus Christ. Elert had written:

> For the whole New Testament, the God, who is the Father of Jesus Christ and thereby also our Father, is none other than He who spoke to the people through the prophets. Already for this reason every Christian will read the Old Testament with reverence, also in places where he himself is not addressed. But the Old Testament becomes an absolute authority for him at the point where it reaches over the boundaries of the old theocracy and turns to all people. And this is always the case where the New Testament examines the promises which have been fulfilled in Christ.[50]

Sasse uttered a lashing criticism of this position, in which he seems to have opted for the Reformed position that all of the Scriptures stand on the same level. He writes:

> This distinction of passages of the Old Testament, which are not meant for us, with others, which are valid for all peoples and therefore also for us, so that the first group are read only with reverence, but the second group are read as having unconditional authority, cannot be sustained theologically . . . . This distinction is strange to classical theology of all times, and also that of the Reformation . . . .[51]

Sasse then remarks that he prefers Barth's doctrine of the Scriptures to that of Elert before going on to make his political kill:

> And one can understand why the question has been raised again and again, whether the view that "the Gospel can also be understood without the Old Testament" is the door through which—completely against the will of contemporary Lutheran theologians who represented this position—the modern Marcionism of the Anti-Semites, National

Socialists, and "German Christians" found their way into the Lutheran Church.[52]

F. Criticism of Sasse

Space and time prevent us from a thorough discussion of the theological problems involved, but we must say that we find Sasse in the wrong. When he ascribed this position of Elert to "the theology of Neo-Protestantism," he seems to have forgotten that not only Melanchthon and Luther but also the Lutheran Confessions insisted that the civil and ceremonial parts of the Old Testament law do not apply to the Christian Church.[53] And he seems to be totally unfamiliar with the Lutheran distinction of the two testaments. This distinction was based on Gal. 4:24. English Bibles have translated διαθήκη as "covenant," which gives this misleading sentence: "For these are the two **covenants**; the one from Mount Sinai, which gendereth to bondage, which is Hagar . . . ." Luther instead translated διαθήκη as testament, yielding this meaning: "There are two **testaments**, one from Mount Sinai, which belongs to bondage, which is Hagar . . . . But Jerusalem which is above is free, which is the mother of us all." The Lutheran reformers taught that one must distinguish between the old and new testaments in studying the Sacred Scriptures. We find this in the writings of Luther, Melanchthon,[54] and Chemnitz.[55]

Luther definitely taught that not all parts of the Bible applied to everyone equally. He asserted in his sermons on Exodus:

> God commanded it to Moses and had spoken thus with the people. But we are not that people. My friend, God also spoke with Adam, but I am not on that account Adam. He commanded Abraham that he should kill his son; but I am not therefore Abraham, that I should kill my son. Thus he spoke also with David. It is all God's Word. God's Word here, God's Word there. I must always know and consider to whom the Word of God is spoken.[56]

We think that Sasse's attack upon the Old Testament hermeneutics of Elert, as well as his preference for the dogmatics of Barth rather than of Elert, represents a weak spot in the otherwise distinguished publications of Hermann Sasse.

G. Final Disillusionment of Sasse with the German Church.

Sasse belonged to a group of faithful Lutherans in the Bavarian territorial church called "The Schwabach Conventicle." When the leaders of Confessional Lutheranism in Bavaria, Christian Stoll and Wilhelm Bogner, were killed in an automobile accident, Sasse's most important fellow workers against unionism were removed. Gottfried Krodel of Valparaiso has told me how his father, a member of the Schwabach Conventicle, pleaded with Sasse not to leave Germany but to stay and lead the fight, but Sasse could not be dissuaded.

Sasse's melancholy predictions about the German churches proved correct in the long run. It seems strange that the "German Evangelical Church," the *DEK*, survived World War II after its miserable capitulation to the German Christians. Largely through efforts of the Barmen group, it managed to erase its soiled history under the Nazis and to reorganize itself as the "Evangelical Church in Germany" (*Evangelische Kirche in Deutschland*). The *DEK* was thus reincarnated as the *EKD*! At its inception, the *EKD* was only a federation and not a church. The Lutheran members of *EKD* had rejected intercommunion and had restricted the sacrament to only fellow Lutherans (closed communion); they formed a conventicle within *EKD*, the "United Lutheran Church of Germany" (*Vereinigte Evangelisch-Lutherische Kirche in Deutschland*) or *VELKD*. Sasse correctly foresaw that this was the fatal error. From the very beginning, pressure was put upon *VELKD* to change its position and to establish intercommunion with the Union and Reformed Churches.

Some years later forces within the *EKD* published, first, the *Arnoldshain Theses on the Lord's Supper*, and later the *Leuenberg Concord*, both of which advocated open communion. They used every possible form of propaganda in the news media to make the Lutherans look bad and manipulate them into communing with them. Finally, the older generation of Lutherans passed away, younger people began to clamor for pulpit and altar fellowship, and most of the Lutheran territorial churches gave in and accepted the *Leuenberg Concord*. Since the 1960s, Confessional Lutheranism has widely disappeared among the *Land* Churches of Germany. Only the Independent Lutheran Church (*Selbständige Evangelisch-Lutherische Kirche*), called *SELK*, and a few groups within the large territorial churches, such as Bishop Joachim Heubach and the territorial church of Lauenburg, have managed to maintain their Confessional Lutheran identity.

Conclusion

When I asked Theodore Baudler to characterize Sasse at Erlangen, he replied: "He was a very lonely man." Sasse's natural skepticism enabled him to see through the false claims of National Socialism at a very early period, but it also isolated him from others. He must have felt frustrated in the early years at Erlangen when his colleagues at first could not see the evils of Hitler. And his sense of justice led him to bring about the de-Nazification of the Erlangen University, which turned out very badly and must have sickened him. Furthermore, it drew down the wrath of his colleagues upon him. When Sasse emigrated to Australia, he was totally disillusioned with the Lutheran churches of Germany and completely alienated from his fellow professors. He had tried to act in full integrity, but he had also made mistakes. Sasse reminds us of Luther's profound insight that the Christian believer is *simul justus et peccator*, a sinner and a righteous man together.

Notes

[1] Karlmann Beyschlag, *Die Erlanger Theologie, Einzelarbeiten aus der Kirchengeschichte Bayerns*, Nr. 67 (Erlangen: Martin Luther Verlag, 1993), 146.

[2] Attempts to fill the position had been going on for over a year before Sasse was called. The call had been rejected by Ernst Wolf and Simon Schöffel; the attempt to call Johannes von Walter of Rostock had been rejected by the Bavarian Ministry of Education and Culture because of his advancing age, noting besides that both he and Hans Leube were ordinary professors and would hardly accept an extra-ordinary position where there was no chance of being advanced to the ordinary status. *E-UA*, 7a.

[3] *E-TFA*, 5.

[4] Many anecdotes indicative of the spunk of Procksch are related; some of the following were shared with me by Theodore Baudler in an interview at his home in Neustadt am Aisch on 28 July 1994. When Alfred Rosenberg, Hitler's intellectual guru, spoke in Erlangen, Procksch had to skip one of his lectures on the Minor Prophets of the Old Testament. At the preceding class meeting he announced to his students: "Tuesday I must skip my lecture because my colleague Rosenberg wants to speak to you. As a matter of fact, I didn't invite him." Walther von Loewenich, *Erlebte Theologie. Begegnungen, Erfahrungen, Erwägungen* (Munich: Claudius Verlag, 1979), 123. On the following Thursday, Procksch appeared at his rostrum and

remarked: "Ladies and Gentlemen, on Tuesday a substitute took my place whom I did not choose. But when the Major Prophets speak, the Minor Prophets must keep silent [Wenn die Großen Propheten reden, die Kleinen Propheten müssen schweigen]." Laughter and applause filled the room so that Procksch could not speak for thirty minutes (interview with Theodore Baudler, July 28, 1994). ... On Hitler's birthday, his classroom was always full because the students knew that something noteworthy would happen. One year it went something like this: "Heil Hitler! Today is the Fuehrer's birthday. May the blessing of Yahveh rest upon him!" *Erlebte Theologie*, 123. ... In a sermon which Procksch preached in the Neustädter-Kirche, he talked about lying. He remarked: "Die Lüge hinkt durchs Land [Lies are limping through the land]." He was summoned before the Gestapo, who asked him if he meant Goebbels. Procksch asked: "Lügt der Herr Goebbels etwas? [Does Dr. Goebbels lie somewhat?]" ... In May 1933, Pastor Kessel, later the German Christian bishop of East Prussia, spoke in the *Redoutensaal* on his goals as a German Christian. He called for the dismissal of all Jews from the pastoral ministry, and said that instead of spending their time on the Old Testament, it would be better if the students studied Eugenics. In the discussion, Procksch limped up to the podium and gave his comment. Let me give it first in his inimitable German: "Ich werde in Zukunft nicht mehr über die jüdischen Könige prüfen. Den Apostel Paulus könnte man vielleicht wenigstens als Vikar von Erlangen-Neustadt anstellen. Und was die Tante Eugenie anlangt ... "—Procksch was unable to go on because of the laughter. The same in English: "Hereafter I will no longer examine my students on the Jewish kings. Perhaps the Apostle Paul could at least become a vicar at the New Town Church. And so far as Aunt Eugenia is concerned . . . ." *Erlebte Theologie*, 124-25. These stories show how there were people during the Third Reich who showed great courage, even when others were afraid to speak out.

[5] The seizure of power by the cohorts of Hitler was a gradual process extending from 1922-1933. This began with the founding of local Nazi party groups in hundreds of communities; these later combined in the national takeover, according to my colleague in the History Department of the New York State University at Buffalo, William S. Allen. Allen has described the gradual assumption of power by the Nazis 1922-1933 in Northeim, a small town in Lower Saxony; he then continues the story until the collapse of Germany in 1945. William Sheridan Allen, *The Nazi Seizure of Power. The Experience of a Single German Town 1922-1945*, 2nd ed. (New York: Franklin Watts, 1984).

[6] The religious statutes of the Weimar Constitution of 11 August 1919, are given in Hans Liermann ed., *Kirchen und Staat* V, part 1 of Veröffentlichungen des Instituts für Staatslehre und Politik e.V. Mainz (Munich: Isar Verlag, 1954), 11-14.

[7] "Wir fordern die Freiheit aller religiösen Bekenntnisse im Staat, soweit sie nicht dessen Bestand gefährden oder gegen das Sittlichkeits- und Moralgefühl der germanischen Rasse verstoßen. Die Partei als solche vertritt den Standpunkt eines positiven Christentums, ohne sich konfessionell an ein bestimmtes Bekenntnis zu binden." From *Programm der Nationalsozialistischen Deutschen Arbeiterpartei* of 1920. Liermann, *Kirchen und Staat*, 15.

⁸ Sasse wrote: "[Die evangelische Theologie] müßte als Bedingung einer Aussprache die vorbehaltlose Zurücknahme dieses Artikels fordern. Denn die evangelische Kirche müßte ein Gespräch darüber mit dem offenen Geständnis beginnen, daß ihre Lehre eine vorsätzliche und permanente Beleidigung des 'Sittlichkeits- und Moralgefühls der germanischen Rasse' ist und daß sie demgemäß keinen Anspruch auf Duldung im Dritten Reich hat." This first appeared in Hermann Sasse, "Die Kirche und die politischen Mächte der Zeit," *Kirchliches Jahrbuch für die deutschen evangelischen Landeskirchen 1932*; repr. *ISC* I:262.

⁹ See Werner Elert, "Politisches und kirchliches Führertum," *Luthertum* (1934): 102-17.

¹⁰ "Die Kirche und die politischen Mächte der Zeit," *ISC* I:252-53, n.1.

¹¹ The forerunner of the new constitution was the "Loccum Manifesto" of May 1933. Nearly all the organizational factors of the constitution were worked out at a meeting at Loccum attended by Chaplain Ludwig Müller, Bishop Marahrens, and Dr. Hesse, professor at the Reformed seminary. In addition to matters of organization, the "Manifesto" ended with a confession of faith in the Triune God which was not included in the constitution. Kurt Dietrich Schmidt, ed., *Die Bekenntnisse und grundsätzlichen Äußerungen zur Kirchenfrage des Jahres 1933* (Göttingen: Vandenhoeck & Ruprecht, 1934), 153-54.

¹² The *DEK* constitution is printed in full by Liermann, *Kirchen und Staat* I:17-20, and by Johann Michael Reu in *Kirchliche Zeitschrift* 57 (1933): 572-76. The bill in which the constitution was approved by the civil government is in Liermann, ibid., 16. The constitution is also given, together with a number of preliminary forms, in Horst Kater, *Die Deutsche Evangelische Kirche in den Jahren 1933 und 1935*, vol. 24, in Arbeiten zur Geschichte des Kirchenkampfes (Göttingen: Vandenhoeck & Ruprecht, 1970), 195-213.

¹³ The takeover of the Old Prussian Union happened after Dr. Hermann Kapler retired as president of the Supreme Church Council (*Oberkirchenrat*) of the Old Prussian Union and thereby also as president of the German Evangelical Church Federation. To avoid a Lutheran candidate, a Union-minded faction engineered the appointment of a temporary president to serve until the new Constitution of *DEK* should go into effect; they chose Stoltenhoff, a man of the Union who insisted that the *DEK* must implement full communion fellowship among Lutheran, Union, and Reformed churches. Since the Constitution of the Prussian Union required ratification by the civil authorities, the German Christians were able to declare this action illegal and to install August Jäger, one of their number.

¹⁴ Werner Elert, "Die Verfassung der Deutschen Evangelischen Kirche," *Ecclesia Militans. Drei Kapitel von der Kirche und ihrer Verfassung* (Leipzig: Dörffling & Francke, 1933), 40. Elert was unsparing of the German Christians, here and elsewhere; but in 1933, he failed to see the close connection between Hitler, the *DEK*, the Reich Church, and the German Christians.

¹⁵ Schmidt, *Die Bekenntnisse des Jahres 1933*, 146; my trans. of: "Wir fordern, daß die evangelische Kirche in freudigem Ja zum neuen deutschen Staat den ihr von

Gott gegebenen Auftrag in voller Freiheit von aller politischen Beeinflussung erfüllt und sich zugleich in unlöslichem Dienst an das deutsche Volk bindet." This document and its origin are described by one of its authors, Walter Künneth, *Lebensführungen: Der Wahrheit verpflichtet* (Wuppertal: R. Brockhaus Verlag, 1979), 106ff. and especially 111.

[16] "In dieser für Volk und Vaterland entscheidenden Stunde grüßen wir unseren Führer. Wir danken für die mannhafte Tat und das klare Wort, die Deutschlands Ehre wahren. Im Namen von mehr als 2500 evangelischen Pfarrern, die der Glaubensbewegung Deutscher Christen nicht angehören, geloben wir treue Gefolgschaft und fürbittenden Gedenken. Harnisch, Berlin; Messow, Steglitz; Müller, Dahlem; Niemoeller, Dahlem; Röhricht, Dahlem." *Junge Kirche* 1 (1933): 252; my trans.

[17] The text of the "Ansbach Counsel" is provided by Kurt Dietrich Schmidt, *Die Bekenntnisse und grundsätzlichen Äußerungen zur Kirchenfrage*, Band II, *Das Jahr 1934* (Göttingen: Vandenhoeck & Ruprecht, 1935): 102-4, and in the *Kirchliche Zeitschrift* 58 (1934): 506-8. The withdrawal of Elert and Althaus from the Ansbach Circle in September 1934, when they realized that this group contained German Christians, is discussed by Hans Rößler, "Das Ende einer Freundschaft - Rektor D. Hans Lauerer und Pfarrer Hans Sommerer im bayerischen Kirchenkampf (1934)," *Zeitschrift für bayerische Kirchengeschichte* 57 (1988): 73-85; 79. Gerhard Niemoeller, *Die erste Bekenntnissynode der Deutschen Evangelischen Kirche zu Barmen*, vol. I, Geschichte, Kritik, und Bedeutung der Synode und ihrer Theologischen Erklärung, Arbeiten zu Geschichte des Kirchenkampfes Nr. 5 (Göttingen: Vandenhoeck & Ruprecht, 1959), lists the "Ansbach Circle" as including, besides Elert and Althaus, Pastors Fuchs, Grießbach, Seiler, Werlin, and Student Counsellor Fikenscher (142). Niemoeller tells of the withdrawal of Elert and Althaus on 17 Sept. 1934 (143, n. 29, and 149).

[18] Letter of 28 April 1934, from Dietrich Bonhoeffer to his Swiss friend, Erwin Sutz; in Eberhard Bethge ed., *Dietrich Bonhoeffer, Gesammelte Schriften* (Munich: Kaiser Verlag, 1958), I:39-40; qtd in Friedrich Baumgärtel, *Wider die Kirchenkampf-Legenden* (Neuendettelsau: Freimund Verlag, 1959), 39.

[19] Julius Schieder, director of the Lutheran Preaching Seminary in Nuremberg, and later pastor in St. Lorenz Church, describes the Nuremberg demonstrations on Saturday, Sunday, and Monday, 12-14 Sept. 1934. On Monday, while the Nazi Party held a big rally at the Market Place, a crowd entered St. Lorenz Church, which was soon filled with 6,000 people; the overflow was sent to Holy Ghost Church, and after it was filled, to St. Aegidius Church. Bishop Meiser had come up from Munich, and he preached successively in all three churches. After the last service, there was a stormy rally for the bishop in the St. Aegidius Square, and the crowd sang Lutheran chorales again for almost an hour. Schieder, "Wir hatten alle verzagten Stunden," in Helmut Winter ed., *Zwischen Kanzel und Kerker. Augenzeugenberichten vom Kirchenkampf im Dritten Reich* (Munich: Claudius Verlag, 1982), 73-74.

[20] See "Stellungnahme der Theologischen Fakultät Erlangen," *Junge Kirche* 2

(1934): 871-72; reprinted in Schmidt, *Die Bekenntnisse und grundsätzlichen Äußerungen zur Kirchenfrage*, Band 2, *Das Jahr 1934*, 154-55.

[21] Eduard Putz, a young assistant to Meiser who was later our pastor at Erlangen, relates how he intercepted the bishop while he was out of town and prevented his immediate arrest. Putz got word to Meiser that on returning to Munich he should get off at an earlier stop at Augsburg. The bishop was met at the Augsburg depot and whisked into a limousine, where the two clergymen sat in the back seat with a bridal pair in the front to serve as camouflage. Thereby they evaded the police and brought Bishop Meiser to the St. Matthaeus Church in Munich, which was filled to capacity and surrounded by thousands of supporters on the outside who chanted "Heil, Meiser!" The bishop preached to the crowded church on Heb. 10:38-39: "If any one shall yield, my soul shall have no pleasure in him. But we are not of those who yield and are damned, but of those who believe to the saving of the soul." After the service, thousands of people accompanied the bishop through the streets of Munich to his residence on the Arcis Street. Here, the stalwart bishop was arrested the next day and confined to his home. Eduard Putz and Max Tratz, "Bauern kämpften für ihren Bischof," *Zwischen Kanzel und Kerker*, 10-17.

[22] *Zwischen Kanzel und Kerker*, 18.

[23] Much of the following material is derived from Werner Elert, "Bericht über das Dekanat der Theologischen Fakultät 1935-43," in Beyschlag, *Die Erlanger Theologie*, 266-86, referred to in this paper as "Bericht" with the pagination of Beyschlag. This report will be discussed further under the events of 1945, below.

[24] "Bericht," *Erlanger Theologie*, 273.

[25] "Bericht," *Erlanger Theologie*, 284.

[26] "Bericht," *Erlanger Theologie*, 284; my trans.

[27] "Bericht," *Erlanger Theologie*, 284f.; my trans.

[28] Regarding the clash with the famous, incredibly talented, and difficult Kempff, Sasse discusses this in a letter to Meiser, dated 10 Oct. 1946, where he says little about his own embarrassment but refers to this experience of Walter Künneth, first pastor of the Neustädter-Church and Dean of the Erlangen circuit. In that celebrated case, the church was filled to its capacity of 1,300 people for the performance of Bach's "B-Minor Mass." Some prominent people, Künneth among them, had purchased the expensive seats located in the chancel; the performance was in the rear gallery. Between them and the gallery hung a huge chandelier, the *Kronleuchter*; once boasting dozens of candles, it had been electrified in recent times. This chandelier blinded the folks sitting in the chancel, and, at their request, Künneth got up and turned it off. Kempff, who was conducting the choir and orchestra, stopped the performance and bellowed out, "Who turned off the *Kronleuchter*?" Künneth, much embarrassed at the scene, said he had done it. Kempff demanded that he turn it back on. Künneth said that this light hurt the eyes of those seated in the chancel. Kempff replied: "This chandelier is the symbol of the Holy Trinity, to whom the 'B-Minor Mass' was dedicated, and the performance will not be resumed until the *Kronleuchter* is turned back on." So Künneth, like a little boy, had to get up and turn the light back on again.

[29] Hermann Strathmann, "Schrift und Bekentnnis," *Theologische Blätter* 7/8 (1935): 187-95. On Strathmann's tenure as editor of this periodical, see Friedrich Wilhelm Kantzenbach, "'Theologische Blätter': Kampf, Krisis und Ende einer theologischen Zeitschrift im Dritten Reich," in *Zur Geschichte des Kirchenkampfes. Gesammelte Aufsätze*, Band II, Arbeiten zur Geschichte des Kirchenkampfes Nr. 26 (Göttingen: Vandenhoeck & Ruprecht, 1971): 79-104; ironically, the article by Kantzenbach ends with a letter written by Strathmann to the Nazi government, seeking to reverse their abolition of his journal, and closes with the words "Heil Hitler!"

[30] Sasse to Strathmann, letter of 23 September 1935, pp. 3-4; my trans. That this controversy attracted the attention of the territorial church is shown by the fact that Sasse on 21 Nov. 1935, wrote a reply to Oberkirchenrat Semmetreuther in Munich explaining his side of the dispute.

[31] Von Loewenich, *Erlebte Theologie*, 185; my trans.

[32] See the book of sermons from 1945 by Paul Althaus, *Der Trost Gottes: Predigten in schwerer Zeit* (Gütersloh: C. Bertelsmann, 1946), especially "Die gewaltige Hand Gottes," for Jubilate (22 April) and "Die große Barherzigkeit," for the First Sunday in Advent (2 Dec.).

[33] See von Loewenich, *Erlebte Theologie*, 134-36.

[34] Sasse added this rather devastating comment on Althaus: "The tragedy of the life's work of Althaus is that, without knowing it or desiring it, he became the forerunner of the German Christians, who in a clumsy way did what Althaus had done in a fine and careful manner, when he filled Christian teaching with a secular ideology. He was never a National Socialist because every kind of radicalism lay far from his nature. More and more his eyes were opened to the demonism of modern nationalism."

[35] "Vertrauliches Memorandum von Prof. D. Hermann Sasse über die Theologische Fakultät der Universität Erlangen für die Amerikanische Militärregierung vom 28. 4. 1945," *E-TFA*, 110-14; my trans.

[36] The writer might have been referring to a shocking description of American Protestantism given in a paper delivered at a pastoral conference and later published. See Hermann Sasse, "Die Konfessionen und die Einheit der Kirche," *Korrespondenzblatt für die evangelisch-lutherischen Geistlichen in Bayern* 62.27 (6 July 1937): 237-38. This article has been translated by me and will appear in a collection of essays pending publication by Concordia Publishing House, St. Louis.

[37] *E-TFA*, no. 129-30; my trans.

[38] *E-TFA*, 37; my trans.

[39] See Beyschlag, *Die Erlanger Theologie*, Beilage 8, 266-86.

[40] The politician, Strathmann, had left the German Nationalist People's Party (*Deutschnationale Volkspartei*), for which the "Steel Helmets" (*Stahlhelm*) had become an increasingly radical support group, and whose leader, Alfred Hugenberg, eventually joined forces with Hitler, and he had become a member of the "Christian People's Party" (*Christlichen Volksdienst*). On the DVP and the "Steel Helmets," see William S. Allen, *The Nazi Seizure of Power*, 18, 38-39, *et passim*, and on

Hugenberg's alliance with Hitler, see Klaus Scholder, *Die Kirchen und das Dritte Reich* (Frankfurt: Propyläen Verlag, 1977), 1:278-79.

⁴¹ In one case, Strathmann had denounced the Poles for the atrocities which they had committed against Germans and particularly Protestants. *Theologische Blätter* 5 (1939): 317. In a later issue, Strathmann had enthusiastically praised the occupation of Norway, The Netherlands, and Belgium in a piece which bore the title, "Welch eine Wendung durch Gottes Führung!" He continued: "In the week ending May 30 [1940] the Old Europe has gone under. This is a happening of purely mythological greatness which has taken place. We Germans can do no other than to see God's finger. . . . And we see in the Fuehrer the man that God has given us to complete this work." *Theologische Blätter* 6 (1940): 171-72; qtd in Friedrich Wilhelm Kantzenbach, "'Theologische Blätter.' Kampf, Krisis und Ende einer theologischen Zeitschrift im Dritten Reich." Heinz Brunotte, ed., *Zur Geschichte des Kirchenkampfes. Gesammelte Aufsätze*, no. 26 in Arbeiten zur Geschichte des Kirchenkampfes (Göttingen: Vandenhoeck & Ruprecht, 1971), 98-100.

⁴² Although Strathmann was a very pleasant person to know, he was all too willing to spread unfavorable rumors about his colleagues, and particularly Elert. In a letter to a colleague at Göttingen he wrote on 14 Dec. 1935: "It was Elert who prevented our faculty from taking a clear stand in the church disputes of the past years. Out of church political calculations . . . I've heard that he owns a membership card in the 'Confessing Church' here in Bavaria. But he is a clear opponent of the decisions of the confessing synods so far as they do not fit in with his Lutheran church political goals . . . . But he can only play successfully where he has at his side a row of sworn Confessional Lutherans (Procksch, Ulmer, Sasse, Preuß)." Letter in Kantzenbach, ibid., 83.

⁴³ Hermann Strathmann, "German Theologian Describes Postwar Situation," *The Lutheran* 28.48 (28 Aug. 1946): 13-14.

⁴⁴ Sasse wrote: "The retirement of Dr. Strathmann, now in the 65th year of his life, was not caused directly or indirectly by a colleague of his faculty. It was based upon a decision of the military government on which none of us had any influence. The military governor at that time, Mr. Elden H. Dye, as well as the university officer at the time, Mr. Ben Kimpel, can confirm that fact at any time. I would regret very much if the arguments of Dr. Strathmann, who has been embittered by much suffering, would arouse the false impression that one of us were guilty for his retirement." *The Lutheran* 29.16:35.

⁴⁵ Sasse gave a copy of this letter to Prof. Hans Liermann, acting Rector, who evidently showed it to his friend, Elert.

⁴⁶ Elert wrote to Bishop Meiser: "Dr. Sasse, after he had already a few weeks ago submitted a memorandum to the Military Government and the Bavarian Minister of Education, in which he had given as reason for his resignation as Pro-Rector the membership of the Council of Deans, now (about fourteen days ago), and going over the heads of all the intervening authorities, has appealed personally to the President of Bavarian Ministers, Dr. Hoegner, submitting him a written complaint in which he

explained his resignation on the grounds that the University of Erlangen is a center of [Nazi] reaction. As evidence for this he mentioned among others also members of the Theological Faculty, for example Dr. Althaus, in that he quoted statements out of the writings of Dr. Althaus from the time of a decade ago. The Ministerial Council (*Ministerrat*) looked into the matter and has taken into consideration both the closing of the university and the sending of a Commissioner of the State. The President of the Ministers explained that when the Pro-Rector of the university has pictured the official condition of the university in such a way, he can choose no other procedure. The Minister of Education was not present at that meeting. Upon Fendt's intervention, the closing [of the university] has been forestalled for the present, but further steps are being announced."

[47] Elert gave this opinion in his letter to Meiser: "I fear that Dr. Sasse, without knowing it, has become the tool of other political forces who intended to pursue very definite church-political purposes with a scandal about Erlangen." A little later, a determined effort was actually made by Roman Catholics to close the only Protestant university in Bavaria; it was only the adroit statesmanship of Baumgärtel, who was Rector at that time, which saved Erlangen from being closed.

[48] Someone had invited Niemoeller to deliver a guest lecture at the university, but so many students turned out that it was moved to the *Neustädter-Kirche*, the University Church, which has a seating capacity of 1,300. There were several things in his lecture which offended the audience. Niemoeller claimed that all German veterans were "war criminals" (*Verbrecher*), and demanded that they acknowledge their transgressions somewhat in the sense of the "Stuttgart Declaration of Guilt," a statement advanced by the "Confessing Church." The church was packed with veterans who had been drafted into the army by Hitler and who had managed to survive the war and return home. They regarded Niemoeller as hypocritical, because at the outbreak of World War II he had volunteered to serve in the German armed forces in exchange for his release from the concentration camp; however, the Nazis had spurned his offer. After the war he had become a "hero" and had gone about Germany, denouncing the German soldiers who had served in the lost cause. Another point which turned the audience against Niemoeller was that he urged the Lutheran territorial churches to form a new union with the Union and Reformed territorial churches. Niemoeller claimed that the memories of their working together in the Confessing Church during the Third Reich were too precious that they should give up this fellowship for the sake of confessionalism. The result was that a number of students walked out in protest; their departure was accentuated by the noisy wooden floors of the dilapidated old church, but this was in no sense a "riot," as it was later described by the press. After Niemoeller's lecture, there was a discussion period in which men such as Gerhard Krodel, now living in Gettysburg, Pennsylvania, took part. Krodel recently wrote to me: "Yes, I was there when Niemöller tried to sell us the Stuttgarter Schuldbekenntnis. And I denounced him in no uncertain terms when he arrogantly rejected the distinction between 'Scham' and 'Schuld' [shame and guilt]. For example, if my father had been a murderer, I would be ashamed of him and would have to bear that burden. But surely I would not be guilty of murder. Niemöller rejected this.... For all of us his

presentation and his answers were one great disappointment. Today I evaluate Niemöller's speech as an exercise in Reformed/Barthian hypocrisy." Gerhard Krodel to Lowell C. Green, letter of 19 June 1995.

[49] Sasse, "Zur Lage des Luthertums nach dem Zweiten Weltkrieg." At first, Sasse circulated his essay privately in typewritten form, but then it was published in *LB* in 1949, and reprinted in *ISC* I:287-302. For his criticism of Elert, see *ISC* I:294-95.

[50] Werner Elert, *Der christliche Glaube. Grundlinien der lutherischen Dogmatik*, 3rd ed. (Hamburg: Furche Verlag, 1956), 188; my trans.

[51] "Zur Lage des Luthertums nach dem Zweiten Weltkrieg" (1945), *ISC* I:295; my trans.

[52] Ibid.; my trans.

[53] In citing the Confessions, we follow the Göttingen edition: *Die Bekenntnisschriften der evangelisch-lutherischen Kirche* Herausgegeben im Gedenkjahr der Augsburgischen Konfession 1930, 2nd ed. (Göttingen: Vandenheock & Ruprecht, 1952 et sqq.), abbreviated *BS*. For statements in *BS* that the civil and ceremonial laws of the OT do not apply to Christians, see the following: AC 28:39-41 (*BS* 126-27); AC 28:58-59 (*BS* 130); Ap 15:32-33 (*BS* 303); Ap 23:41 (*BS* 341); Ap 27:58 (*BS* 393-94); Ap 24:30 (*BS* 358).

[54] In teaching the distinction of the OT and the NT, Melanchthon commented thus on Gal. 4:24: "'These are two testaments, the one of which is from Mount Sinai gendering unto servitude,' i.e., obligating to this political arrangement, which, although it were a great blessing . . . yet it was in servitude, i.e., the highest good was not yet there, that new and eternal life, which would be the true liberty given in the new testament; but [in the old testament] there was a ministry of the law, preaching wrath against sin and forcing discipline, and teaching the people by certain shadows concerning the things to come." *Melanchthons Werke*, ed. Robert Stupperich (Gütersloh: C. Bertelsmann, 1953), II:445.8-17. Melanchthon now turned to Jeremiah (chap. 31), who calls the OT a "covenant" which had been made when God led the people out of Egypt, and "in a very erudite manner," Jeremiah taught the distinction between the Old and New Testaments. "The Old Testament was the promulgation of an external law and the declaration of judgment against sin, and the establishment of a legal structure, that it might be a definite seat of the word and testimonies of God. But the New Testament was not to be an outward promulgation of the law, but a new and everlasting life, light, and righteousness, with the law glowing within their hearts, and death and sin done away." *Melanchthons Werke* II:445.28-36. Melanchthon summarized: "Thus there is a clear distinction between the New and Old Testaments, since the New Testament is the new heavenly nature, freed from all evils, conferred upon the old nature, which had been subjected to the law and to death." *Melanchthons Werke* II:446.3-7. In Jacob A. O. Preus, trans., *Loci Communes 1543 Philip Melanchthon* (St. Louis: Concordia Publishing House, 1992), 119,A.

[55] Chemnitz wrote a commentary on the *Loci theologici* of Melanchthon in which he carried his teacher's position on the distinction of OT and NT even further. Calvin and his followers had advanced this maxim: *re ipsa unum testamentum esse* ("in fact,

there is only one testament"). Chemnitz sturdily resisted this maxim, which placed any teaching of the Bible, however minor, on the same level with a major doctrine, and which therefore leveled off the distinction of Law and Gospel. *Loci theologici D[omi]n[i] Martini Chemnitii, Theologi longe celeberrimi, atque Ecclesiae Brunsvicensis quondam Superintendentis Fidelissimi: Quibus et Loci Communes D. Philippi Melanchthonis perspicue explicantur* ... (Frankfurt: Tobias Mevius, 1683), III:89,B. In his criticisms of the Roman doctrine of the Sacred Scriptures in his *Examination of the Council of Trent*, he also made a clear distinction between the OT and the NT. Cf. the following, in his debate with Andradius: "Vide jam Andradi, quomodo constet, quod contendis aequum fuisse, ut populus Dei sub veteri Testamento, doctrinam coelestem literis haberet comprehensam: Novi vero Testamenti plane diversam esse rationem. Quod si vetus Testamentum intelligant de doctrina legis quae in monte Sina promulgata fuit: certe praecepta Decalogi, et ante et post diluvium, voce divina proposita, et a Patriarchis tradita leguntur in Genesi. Et Paulus Romanorum 2 affirmat opus legis natura scriptum esse in omnium hominum cordibus etiam illorum qui legem scriptam non habent. Etiam consideretur, quae insania sit, Jeremiae tribuere illam sententiam, quasi discrimen Veteris et Novi Testamenti in eo potissimum constat, quod doctrinam legis, scriptis comprehendi aequuum fuit, doctrinam vero Evangelii, per traditiones sine scripto cordibus commendandam esse." *Examen Concilii Tridentini*, ed. Eduard Preuss (Berlin: Gustav Schlawitz, 1861), 17.

[56] *WA* 16:384; my trans.

Hermann Sasse and Third Reich Threats to the Church

John R. Wilch

Introduction

Most church people in Germany in the early 1930s could not have been expected to see what was coming with the National-Socialists. Most of them were very strongly influenced by many factors: on the one hand, by loyalty to the state, by nationalism, by the glorification of the *Volk* (people), and by the concept of *Führer*; and, on the other hand, by the economic and political chaos (largely blamed on the grossly unfair Versailles Treaty), by ethnical and socio-economical anti-Semitism, by a fear of communism and of democratic parliamentarianism, as well as by liberalism, rationalism, and church unionism. Thus, many Christians simply could not imagine that the *Führer* and the state could become the enemy of the church, and that folk ideology, unionism, and anti-Semitism could go too far, e.g., that what was happening to the Jews was blasphemy against God. That is, they could not have been expected to realize any of this until it was too late to take any positive action, when clear opposition meant endangering oneself and the ability of the church to function.

How did Hermann Sasse respond to the threats to the church presented by the Third Reich? First, Sasse was "the first important German theologian to raise his voice against Nazism,"[1] for he attacked six threats to the church by the Nazis' church program, even before they came to power. These were the threats: first, of the idolatry of the old Germanic heathen religion; secondly, of glorifying the *Volk*; thirdly, of glorifying the concept of the divinely-given leader; fourthly, of rejecting the Old Testament as Jewish propaganda; fifthly, of unionistically establishing one national Protestant church; and especially, sixthly, of controlling the administration, ethics, and theology of the church by the state. Secondly, Sasse's consistent Lutheran confessionalism appeared to divide the forces of the *Bekennende Kirche* (Confessing Church) in its opposition and stand against the Nazis' threats and proceedings against the churches. However, in contradiction to most historians of the German Church Struggle (*Kirchenkampf*) that is not where the principal fault lies. Instead, it lies with those theologians and church leaders who took advantage of the Church Struggle to press for the realization of their dream of one united Protestant church in Germany. Sasse clearly saw that such a union, without first arriving at doctrinal unity, would nullify the Lutheran Confessions for the Lutheran territorial churches (*Landeskirchen*). So he pleaded for cooperation among the different confessional churches in all ways except in matters of doctrine and confession. If his proposed procedure would have been followed, the churches could have presented an opposition united in purpose and goal. Unfortunately, this was not done, and his prophecy was ultimately fulfilled, namely, that the Lutheran territorial churches have since lost their confessional Lutheranism. Perhaps Sasse should have realized that already in his own day unionism was more important for most Lutherans than the Confessions.

Thirdly, however, Sasse failed to realize that anti-Semitism was also a major hindrance to effective opposition to the Nazis: the Nazis attacked Jewish-Christians, Christian mission among Jews, and anything in Christianity perceived as Jewish, as well as Jews in general. This alone was cause enough for *status confessionis*, that the church should take a stand whereby it would rather risk martyrdom than retreat.[2]

A. Sasse and the Threats of the Third Reich to the Church

1. Sasse as an Ecumenical Critic of World Events

"Loyalty to the Confessions and true ecumenicity belong together,"[3] Sasse could say, for Jesus Christ is the Lord of His worldwide church. This confessionalist "was a passionate ecumenist with world-wide vision."[4] As an example of his ecumenicity, he received letters during World War II from both Japan and China.[5] Sasse declared at a meeting of the Continuation Committee of the World Conference on Faith and Order in 1934: "If we could agree over what the church and the Word of God are and in which relationship they stand to each other, then nothing more would stand in the way for the union of the churches."[6] He pleaded: "Let us again become confessional Lutherans for the sake of the unity of the church." One "acts in an ecumenical fashion who . . . , like Luther, searches for the one truth of the one gospel for the one church."[7]

2. Sasse and the Background of the Church Struggle

A crystal-clear, "exact cartographer of church doctrine,"[8] Sasse rightly interpreted the wider nationalistic movement in the Germany of 1930 as a reaction against internationalism, a late awakening of the Germans to the self-consciousness of a united people, and the only hope for the younger generation after the humiliation of the capitulation at Versailles.[9] Protestant pastors in general were proud of their loyalty to the fatherland, state, and emperor. After the fall of the throne, the altar joined up with nationalism, and the concept of the folk church arose.[10] Pacifism was ridiculed, and nationalism was exploited by the Nazis for racism and anti-Semitism with agitation against the Old Testament.[11] The economic and political confusion in the 1920s led to the yearning for a new ideology to ensure security.[12] But the church experienced renewal from dialectical and Biblical theology, from a Luther renaissance, and from fundamentalistic piety.[13]

3. Early Exposure of Major Threats to the Church by the Third Reich

Hermann Sasse proclaimed in a sermon during the Nazi era that, "False, crazy prophets have broken into our church and are destroying it!"[14] Bishop Hermann Dietzfelbinger of Bavaria later said of him that, "He accepted the authority to expose the idols of his time."[15] He saw that people were being swept up into the enthusiastic proclamation of conflicting world-views, of communists and nationalists, of socialists and democrats; so he warned against their godless enthusiasm.[16] He recognized early that the ideology of the Nazis belonged in the category of devilish spiritual forces. He called their movement "the largest spiritual power which has arisen since the Reformation, . . . an embodiment of great superhuman spiritual powers in the sense of Eph. 6:12, which subject whole peoples to themselves. . . . I have seen people who went into the mass gatherings with sensible, critical, even hostile attitudes, but who came out totally changed: fanatical, prepared for any sacrifice, for any deed, even for atrocities, even to betray their next of kin."[17] The Nazis at first rejected Luther because "the nation was for him not the highest of all values." But Sasse reflected that "the great national movement of the 16th century rejected him" for the same reason, although that was the one time in history for Germany for the coincidence of both a religious renewal and a national uprising. Luther knew that he could not entrust the Gospel for his people to a national and social revolution.[18]

At first, Hitler prevented upsetting the churches unnecessarily.[19] The Nazis even curried the favor of the pastors in urging them to join the battle against Marxism, Judaism, and liberalism, while supporting national freedom, socialism, and racial purity, and accepting German mythology. One of them declared: "Our politics is Germany, our religion is Christ!" Some pastors became convinced that Nazism was Christian. But the Nazis aimed to control not only politics but also religion.[20] Adolf Hitler in his *Mein Kampf* outlined his program toward total power: "The first foundation for constructing authority presents always popularity.... In power we see the second basis of every authority.... When popularity and might unite and we are able to hold together for a while, then authority can arise on an even firmer basis, that of tradition. When finally popularity, strength and tradition are united, authority may be considered unshakable." Sasse saw through Hitler's grasp at illegitimate authority, "for what is here called authority is none at all, because such a popular might should first become authority by bowing to the authority of the [divine] right standing above it and upholding this right. Thus the present leadership is the obverse side of the decay of genuine authority."[21]

(1) The first of the six threats opposed by Sasse is that of the ancient German religion, with which the Nazis wanted to replace Christianity.[22] Indeed, Hitler fully intended to destroy the churches completely.[23] Sasse saw many people turning to the Germanic religion in enthusiasm, some of them from atheism but many from the church.[24] They were eager to believe in modern myths, especially Alfred Rosenberg's "Myth of the Twentieth Century," which was nothing other than "the faith of the powerless in fate."[25] Sasse preached during the war that these are illusions that God smashes by His wrath in the endless battlefields of Russia in winter, and in Germany's destroyed cities. In contrast to the Christian culture being one of mercy, he saw the world becoming one devoid of mercy, rejecting the grace of God.[26]

(2) Secondly, Sasse saw the threat of the Nazis assigning to the

Volk a religious value.[27] But even some Lutheran theologians taught that the people is holy as a divinely created order.[28] The so-called "German-Christians" were a pro-Nazi movement who wanted to combine the world-uniting confession to Christ with the world-separating confession to blood and race, "for the person who believes in Christ lives simultaneously in blood and race."[29]

But Sasse wrote that the church's catholicity "resides in Jesus Christ who is the one Lord over all and who has sent His church to all peoples.... If we should believe in a Christian church of German nation, ... then we must believe in the nation as eternal."[30] Moreover:

> The evangelical doctrine of original sin ... does not leave open the possibility that the German, Nordic or any other race is by nature able to fear and love God and to do His will. Rather, the new-born child of noblest Germanic descent with the best racial characteristics of mind and body is subject to everlasting damnation just like the hereditarily encumbered mongrel of two decadent races.... Further, the doctrine of the justification of the sinner *sola gratia, sola fide* is the end of the German morality as of all human morality.[31]

"The Savior also carried the sin of the Nordic race and of the German people on the cross."[32]

Sasse preached in 1938 that the grave is the end of every great human, even "the end of the 'eternal Germany.'" So in death are all alike; then every difference disappears: power, race, language, etc.[33] During the war, he preached that even in "one of the greatest wars of all times, that tears apart humanity with rage and hate, Christ is the peace of all people."[34] "What moves the Chinese Christians to preserve their church in this difficult wartime amid all needs with greatest sacrifices?"[35] Sasse's concern for his German people was like that of St. Paul for his Jewish people: The "deepest concern a person can have for his people is not about their power, room to live, inner and outer peace, but about their salvation in the Last Judgment."[36]

(3) Thirdly, Sasse clearly unmasked the threat of the *Führer* ideology.[37] Already in 1913 the motto appeared: "German race and German faith and German hero!"[38] Four hundred years ago, Sasse stated, people sacrificed everything for the sake of the Reformation, but today people are becoming martyrs "for completely different doctrines."[39] The political parties in 1932 were living movements "in

which the masses entrust themselves to a leader without even knowing his goals—'he will surely know where he leads us'—for they believe in him." Vanished are freedom and independent decisions. "One area of public life after another is being surrendered to these powers: the courts, schools, universities, science, art.... They have holy scriptures ... in which they believe.... They have confessions of faith.... Doctrines are stated that are so obvious to the believers that they need no proof.... There are orthodox, heretics, renegades; there are excommunications and genuine conversions.... Here fall the martyrs of our time.... Here is the building of new fellowship.... Old barriers are overcome: ... All are one in the miracle of a common faith in one goal, one truth, one leader." This is "substitution for the lost religion."[40] One pastor proclaimed: Hitler is "the savior of our people and our fatherland and the leader sent to us by God!" Sasse called that "secularized messianic faith.... The people are confronted by the ultimate questions of their existence. Because the church has not proclaimed them an answer ... they are no longer listening to her, ... and her great realities have lost their value."[41]

(4) Fourthly, in respect to the threat of rejecting the Old Testament,[42] Sasse preached in 1936:

> Behind the political problem of the Jewish people ... arises the question of the Bible that we share in common with the people Israel.... No one can tear apart the two parts of Scripture without destroying them both. Whoever rejects the Old Testament must ... also destroy the New Testament.... Yes, he must even reject Jesus Christ, ... who was a son of David according to the flesh.... The question of Holy Scripture is ... a real life question. For it concerns life and death. For either the assumption that the Bible is God's Word is false, ... or the Bible is God's Word; then its rejection is the rejection of God. Then what today is proclaimed in the streets and markets about the Old Testament and the God of the Old Testament is blasphemy.[43]

God chose Israel, not a people of another race.[44]

(5) Fifthly, we consider the threat of unionism. In July 1933, under pressure from Hitler and the Nazi government, the constitution of the German "Evangelical" Church was ratified by all the territorial churches and went into effect, with each church to be guaranteed its confessional integrity.[45] But within eight months, in March 1934, Bishop Hans Meiser of Bavaria could see that the Nazi state and party

and the German-Christians were aiming to eliminate the churches' independence, forming one national church with a unified confession and worship. The crisis was really over the existence of the Lutheran Church. Meiser now considered himself and his church in opposition to the state, *in statu confessionis*, that is, in suffering and brave confessing.[46]

Sasse opposed the church union under the office of the national bishop in which doctrinal power rested in the hands of one single man nominated by the Ministry of Religion, so that the government would be governing the church indirectly. He said, "the bishops of Germany's Lutheran *Landeskirchen* signed a document which ... must mean the end of the Reformation Church of the Augsburg Confession in German *Landeskirchen*."[47] Such is "the consequence for the churches of the Reformation if they sacrifice their faith and confession to the alleged interest of the nation."[48] Yet, "we do not want to make a judgment over the men who, as we presume, in difficult straits of conscience 'to prevent something worse,' by their conviction chose the lesser evil.'"[49]

(6) Sasse especially opposed the Nazis' exploitation of the church, whereby they capitalized on the Enlightenment. For this "recognized religious freedom only in the form of the freedom of the individual person to believe or not to believe. The Enlightenment did not admit on principle the freedom of the Church to proclaim her message unhindered, because it recognized no church that is to present a message from the divine Revelation, but only religious societies that represent their private religious opinions. Thus ... public teaching and the public practice of religion is a matter of the state." Of course, the state "deserves obedience from all members of the church ... if it stays within the limits of its calling." But, "according to the Lutheran Confessions, the state does not have the right to govern or to participate in governing the church."[50] Neither is the church an "institution for the religious-social education of the nation." Then she would only be "a religious society among many others. She would receive her calling from the world and no longer from her Lord."[51]

But the Nazis negotiated

> ... with the church according to the principle of *do ut des*, as in the negotiations of businessmen.... But how can a non-confessional [political] party make dogmatical demands on the church? ... The confusion of Christianity and party program, of church and state, is

clearly demonstrated by the church-political platform of the Nazi Party, ... Article 24: "We demand liberty for all religious confessions in the State, in so far as they do not in any way endanger its existence or do not offend the customs and moral feelings of the Germanic race. The party as such represents the standpoint of 'positive Christianity' without binding itself confessionally to any particular faith. It opposes the Jewish materialistic spirit within and without us and is convinced that a lasting recovery of our people is possible only from within and on the basis of: General welfare supersedes individual welfare." *This article makes every discussion with a church impossible*. . . . Evangelical theology can converse with the Nazis about all points of the party platform, even over the Jewish question and the race doctrine, . . . but impossibly about this one. . . . For her doctrine is an intentional and permanent insult to "the customs and moral feelings . . . of the Germanic race"; thus she has no right to tolerance in the Third Reich. . . . Further, we have no great interest in what is here called "Christianity," but everything depends for us on Christ who is present in Word and Sacrament. We do not want to know if the party represents Christianity, but whether in the Third Reich the church may proclaim the Gospel freely and without hindrance, whether we may continue our insults to the Germanic "moral feelings."[52]

By the time the Nazis took power in 1933, Sasse's analysis was proven right: All churches welcomed the new government, some very enthusiastically. While a few church leaders warned against cooperating too closely with Hitler (e.g., Bishop Tilemann of Oldenburg), others counseled that, "If we do not please Hitler, he will win over the pastors for his cause" (Bishop Reichardt of Thuringia). Again, "Since we must deal with the state, is it not better to have a friendly relationship with it?" (Bishop Schöffel of Hamburg). Thus, they accepted Hitler's nominee for Reich Bishop, Ludwig Müller, a superintendent of military chaplains, who also became bishop of the (union) Protestant Church of Prussia. They probably so accepted the already inflicted damage in order to prevent still greater harm.[53]

But it soon became too dangerous to speak out against the party line on church-political issues. The state even intervened massively in the churches in Prussia and Mecklenburg. When church leaders complained loudly, Hitler had an audience with three of them, namely, Bishops August Marahrens (Hannover), Meiser, and Tilemann. He specifically addressed Meiser: "I warn you against making opposition in matters of faith. It is easy to instigate a revolution, but it is hard—I say this out of experience—to stop a revolution. I see no one in the Protestant church like Dr. Martin Luther who would be able to do so." But in September and November 1933, Meiser protested against state interference in the church, once at a celebration marking Luther's 450th birthday. The Bavarian pastors announced their solidarity for Meiser, over 1,200 strong. The eyes of most church people, including laymen, were now opened to the contradiction between the Nazis and the church. Nevertheless, the Reich bishop succeeded in incorporating all the Protestant youth organizations into the Hitler Youth.[54] But out of respect for the state and afraid of reprisals, the church leaders were reluctant to confront the state directly.

Then in 1934, as it became impossible to cooperate with Bishop Müller, Bishops Meiser and Theophil Wurm (Württemberg) separated themselves from the national office. For this they were summoned to another audience with Hitler, where he gave them this warning and ultimatum: "Christianity will vanish from Germany as even from Russia. . . . The church has lost her chance. . . . You elected Müller yourselves, now you have to bear with him. . . . The church will have to get used to the doctrine of blood and race. . . . If you make opposition, you are Germany's destroyers!" They thus came to reject the government.[55] In 1937, Sasse regularly instructed a special commission of the Bavarian Lutheran Church Council and traveled throughout the province giving weekly lectures on the ecumenical movement, explaining it "as a great struggle about the church."[56] It has been observed: "The great pronouncements of the Bavarian territorial church during the Church Struggle all carried the signature of Meiser, but the writing of Sasse and the diction of [*Kirchenrat*, i.e., Vice-President] Christian Stoll."[57]

(7) Sasse was one of the few who had the insight to realize that the Nazi persecution of the church really indicated a battle in the spiritual realm. "It is the hate of Satan against Christ. . . . It is the fear before Christ the Judge; it is the rage of the mortally wounded beast; . . . he must take revenge on us."[58] Yes, this "is the time of critical fighting when we can be glad just to hold our position. . . . So the Church awaits her Lord. For she knows that to Him shall belong the victory when He comes."[59] When the End comes, "people and the peoples will be asked what they have done with the Gospel. Did they believe . . . or did they ridicule and despise it, so that the Word of rescue must

become the Word of judgment? ... Should our dear German people belong to those peoples in whom only ruins are reminders that the Church of God once experienced a great history there?"[60] Why "has our Reformation church in Germany become so weak? ... Is it not that we all ... in our own life no longer take seriously the deepest need of our soul?"[61]

B. Sasse's Lutheran Confessionalism

Both Hermann Sasse's Lutheran confessionalism and his concern for the existence of the church found expression in the *Bethel Confession* of August 1933, which became almost forgotten in contrast to the *Barmen Declaration* of 1934. But Guy Carter, in his Ph.D. dissertation about the Bethel Confession, stated that it:

> ... deserves and demands a central place in the historiography of the German church struggle and ... a corresponding place in contemporary theological discourse ... as a confession of Christian faith in the face of an anti-Christian world-view with perennial manifestations. ... A full theological confession attempting to restate the entire ensemble of the Christian faith, it deserves to be taken seriously as part of the most important legacy of the German church struggle, the legacy of faithful witness to Christ.[62]

1. Prelude to the Bethel Confession

In 1932, Joachim Hossenfelder, the leading voice of the German-Christians, published his *Guidelines*, advocating a united Reich church, positive Christianity, the spirit and tradition of Luther and heroic piety, the German spirit and nationalism, the principle that race, people, and nation are God-given orders, and denouncing Marxism, ethnic intermarriage, evangelism of Jews, ecumenism, and Freemasonry.[63] He later added that the church must listen to both the Word of God and the call of Hitler's state; the new church should use readings from German heroic legends and poetry in worship; Jewish-Christians should be separated into their own congregations and Jewish-Christian pastors excluded from the Reich church ministerium. Obviously, the aim of the German-Christians was the *Gleichschaltung* (coordination) of the churches with the Nazi state. Early April 1933 saw the enactment of the "Civil Service Reconstruction Law," whose Aryan paragraph excluded Jews from the civil service. In respect to divine orders, theologians ever since Gottlieb von Harless have spoken of the "orders of creation," often including race and nation.[64]

The errors and heresies of the German-Christians spurred many pastors into action. District assemblies, pastoral conferences and local groups of pastors issued declarations and confessions of faith in 1933 and 1934. Here, we can only summarize in passing that these declarations upheld: the Old Testament as Scripture, the Gospel that Christ died for people of all races, the independence of the church from politics and the state, and Christ as the only Lord of the church. They rejected: the so-called heroic piety, the divine origin of such orders as race and nation, the significant cultural character of the church, the exclusion of non-Aryans from the church, venerating the people and the state; if necessary, the church's ultimate means of defense is suffering and prayer.[65] Of course, there were also those who defended the German-Christians.

Even the Evangelical Lutheran Free Church of Saxony, one of the forerunners of the Independent Evangelical Lutheran Church (SELK) issued a confession, "Church, People and State" (drafted by Rev. O. Gerss of Königsberg). This was mostly in the evangelical vein, except for a pledge of allegiance to the state insofar as it upholds civil order, the family and the economy, and opposes the evils of Marxism and Bolshevism, pacifism, women's emancipation, and class struggle; for the German people have the right to shape their own life and culture in their own folk manner.[66] Superintendent Heinrich Martin, head of the Independent Evangelical Lutheran Churches in Hesse, already in 1932 criticized National Socialism and rejected Article 24 of its party program and Rosenberg's Germanic myth; even the Jewish question is a question of conscience.[67] Sasse said that the free churches were not disturbed by the Nazis because they were so insignificantly small ("*Minima non curat praetor*").[68] But because the politically and theologically conservative churches could not speak a clear word of confession,[69] they failed to take advantage of the fact that Hitler needed their support, particularly during the war.[70] Indeed, their commitment to folk, blood, and nation and their incipient anti-Semitism played into the Nazis' hands. As Sasse later explained, even confessionally Lutheran professors at first

> ... sympathized with the Nazi Movement because they did not

understand its revolutionary and anti-Christian character. They lacked the great gift of discerning spirits.... They did not know that Hitler was a criminal.... Unfortunately, some of our Free Church brethren were also blind.... Hitler would never tolerate a church which did not accept his program, including all the laws against the Jews and even faithful Jewish-Christians. But the Lutherans in Germany were blind.... Nothing has done more damage to the name of Lutheranism in Germany than this complete failure to see the realities of Nazism and to apply the eternal Law of God also to Hitler and the political powers of the world.[71]

Meanwhile, Bishop Müller published new guidelines for the German Christians, which stated: The German churches should have a German form in order to render service to the German people through the unified Reich church; the Reformation confessional basis is to be upheld; by serving God through the church one serves the fatherland. The Nazi state was trying to "portray itself as serving with the churches as the guardian and patron of traditional cultural values, [as] a populist movement which ... affirms the moral aspects and religious beliefs." This was the effect of Article 24 of the party platform, although it was really a "Delphic pledge." Many church members "saw it as an invitation to evangelize the Nazi party from within." Reacting to the German-Christians, the Young Reformation Movement ("Young Reformers") was founded, with Martin Niemöller as one of their leaders. It was becoming clear to some that "in a totalitarian state all opposition in the end becomes political opposition."[72]

In May 1933, the Protestant Church Council, under pressure from Hitler, adopted the constitution for the united *Deutsche Evangelische Kirche* (German Protestant Church). If they had not done so, as Sasse commented, "they would have been swept away."[73] Hitler's appointee as State Commissioner for the churches in Prussia, August Jäger, dismissed all church presidents in Prussian lands and the director of the Protestant News Service. Distressed over this action, conservative German-Christians declared that the state had transgressed its limits and failed to respect the confessions, frustrating the preaching and teaching ministry. This was the beginning of the end of the association of Emanuel Hirsch, Paul Althaus, and Friedrich Gogarten with the German-Christians.[74]

July 1933 saw Hitler accomplish his Concordat with the Papacy, the constitution of the united German Protestant Church go into effect, and the German-Christians win 70% of the votes in the church-wide elections to congregational councils. Thereafter the only path of resistance left was that of theological confession. The Young Reformers issued theses in early August 1933, declaring that the church's confession must be clarified by a contemporary confession in which the relationship of the three articles of the Creed would be decisive.[75]

2. Sasse's Consistent Confessionalism

Sasse called the church in 1937 to take a stand in confession to Christ: At this time of suffering, "we are called [by Christ] to a joyful confession borne by holy certainty of faith."[76] The "church of Christ ceases to be the church when she no longer dares to proclaim God's eternal commandments to the powerful of this earth!"[77] In 1942, Sasse preached: "The ancient church was right when she held that no person on this earth could have a greater blessing than . . . : 'who confesses Me before people, him will I confess before My heavenly Father' (Matt. 10:32)."[78] In "the coming spiritual battles that will follow this great war, we shall only remain if we have the same faith, loyalty and willing sacrifice as the fathers of the 16th and 17th centuries."[79] Also attuned to Christian laymen, Sasse noted that "earnest persons . . . are approaching the church with their big questions. . . . They want to know . . . what the Evangelical church teaches and confesses."[80] "The people want to be told the truth about God and about man and his sin, about judgment and salvation, about death and life. They demand it from the pastor that he commits his person and his life to what he says as true. They have a very fine sensitivity . . . to whether the minister who speaks, really believes or only believes to believe. . . . The people . . . have no interest in debate. But they have all interest in the truth, and they do not want the church to betray and surrender the truth!"[81] Sasse wrote in 1935 that the government:

> . . . would only then cease to be government when it would degenerate to raw force, when it would no longer be the protector of justice, when it would abolish the commandments of the Second Table of the Decalogue and force us to sin against God's commandments. If that would be the case, Christians would have to act according to the Word, 'One must obey God rather than men,' and then of course, according to the example of the

ancient Church, be ready to bear the consequences of such refusal of obedience.[82]

But such degeneration was already taking place.

3. Producing the Bethel Confession

A theological confession was urgently needed because the theological aberrations of the German-Christians were confusing theologically thinking people. A confession should be "a sharp, incisive weapon for the church to defend itself against the deadly danger of sinking into the mire of false doctrine."[83] The desire for a restatement and contemporary application of the Christian faith as witnessed in the Reformation confessional writings led to the Bethel Confession. Focusing especially on the church's self-determination led to the Barmen Declaration. While the German-Christians' heresies were founded upon modern liberal theology and Biblical higher-criticism, the Confessing Church reacted by advocating faithfulness to Scripture and its doctrines as taught in the churches' confessions.[84]

In early August 1933, two groups of theological students and young pastors in Berlin appealed to Friedrich von Bodelschwingh, the highly esteemed director of the Bethel Institutes, to sponsor a new confession of faith to address the crisis. Both requested as drafters Dietrich Bonhoeffer and Hermann Sasse (one group also requested Pastor Gerhard Jacobi). All three were considered loyal to the Lutheran Confessions and had spoken out against introducing the Aryan Law into the churches. Bonhoeffer, who was then only 27 years old and a lecturer at the University of Berlin, evidently influenced a group of his students to take this initiative, while young pastors and candidates in the other group were some of the Young Reformers led by Martin Niemöller.[85] Speed was essential for the promoters, for the constituting National Convention of the new church union was scheduled to take place in Wittenberg already in late September. If the confession would be accepted by the German Protestant Church, it would decisively influence the new church in its process of confessional formation. And if it would be rejected, it would still clarify the position of people in the church.[86] This confession project was extremely important for Bonhoeffer, for he sacrificed participation at a significant youth meeting of the Faith and Order Conference in Geneva at the same time, as well as canceling other appointments. A champion of internationalism and pacifism, Bonhoeffer had become ubiquitous in ecumenical circles. In the summer of 1933, he was being considered for a professorship in Berlin, but also as pastor of a German congregation in London. In his only radio address, he warned the youth not to idolize a leader, which could lead to shipwrecking the state and mocking God by confusing the state with the kingdom of God. Understandably, he was forbidden to broadcast again.[87] The most burning question for Bonhoeffer was surely the Jewish question. His personal reason to push this agenda was probably occasioned by his very close friendship with a Jewish-Christian pastor, Franz Hildebrandt.[88]

Also in April 1933, one week after the Aryan Paragraph became law, Bonhoeffer declared in a lecture:

> Where the state interferes with the essence of the church in her proclamation, for example, in the forcible exclusion of baptized Jews from our Christian congregations and in outlawing mission among Jews, here the Christian church finds herself *in statu confessionis*, and here the state finds itself in the act of self-negation. . . . The church knows that no state of the world can ever cope with the mysterious Jewish people, because God is not finished with them yet. Every new attempt to "solve" the "Jewish question" fails on the salvation-historical significance of this people. . . . The church cannot allow her activity with her members to be determined by the state. . . . Here, where Jew and German stand together under the Word of God, is church; here it is proven whether church is still Church or not.[89]

At the Wittenberg convention, Bonhoeffer distributed a flyer which declared: "To exclude out of the church organization means to interfere with the power of the Sacraments, for the Jewish-Christian was received into the Church by Baptism. . . . The Aryan Law is a heresy about the Church and destroys her substance. . . . Removing Jewish-Christians from the pastoral office contradicts the essence of the pastoral office."[90]

While Sasse was involved in the Faith and Order Conference of the Lausanne Movement, Bonhoeffer participated in the World Alliance. Together, they collaborated on a short-lived theological journal, *Vormarsch* (Marching Forward). For them confessionalism meant "deep respect toward the church's historic confession of faith as applied in a living way to the present."[91] Obviously, Bonhoeffer was the driving force behind the Bethel confession project. He met with Bodelschwingh and his theological advisor, Rev. Georg Merz, in Bethel in early August to discuss it and win their approval. Bodelschwingh arranged for Bonhoeffer and Sasse to meet in Bethel in mid-August, together with Merz and Bodelschwingh's secretary, Pastor Gerhard Stratenwerth. At Bodelschwingh's request, Wilhelm Vischer contributed a section on the church and the Jews. He aimed to recover the Old Testament as the Word of God and as witness to God's incarnate Word in Christ. A Swiss, he had just resigned as professor of Old Testament at the Bethel seminary because of loud protests from Nazi students because he had made an uncomplimentary remark about it being odd that Hitler, who came from the ethnically very impure Balkans, should stress ethnic purity.[92]

Just when the team had begun working on the confession, Bodelschwingh received a copy of a confession by pastors in the Tecklenburg area of Westphalia. This Tecklenburg Confession appears to have had an influence on the Bethel Confession, for the following concerns were dealt with by both: the politicization of Scripture; the perversion of Scripture as God's Word, of the doctrines of creation, sin, and the Trinity, and of the essence of the church; and a call for dealing with the role of the Jews and with eschatology.[93]

The work stretched from one planned week into two, Sasse not being able to stay for the second week. Bonhoeffer was able to convince the other participants to accept his treatment of the Jewish question, while Sasse's contribution is obvious in the areas of Scripture, church, and confession. The overall conception and plan was that of these two.[94] Bonhoeffer and Sasse resonated profoundly well together in Bethel as church theologians, formulating "in contemporary form the witness of the Church catholic," boldly stating what "the Church teaches."[95] Sasse called the work at Bethel "truly a joyful cooperation!"[96] Nevertheless, Bonhoeffer and Sasse ware something of an odd couple. At first, Bonhoeffer rejoiced over Sasse's confessionalism, but later disagreed with him over the function of the historical confessions. And Sasse came to consider Bonhoeffer an enthusiast for stressing, like Karl Barth, communal confessing so much that antitheses only divide theological schools.[97]

Excursus: The Content of the Bethel Confession

The sections of the Bethel Confession deal with the topics of Scripture, the Reformation, the Trinity, Creation, the Law, sin, Christ, the Holy Spirit, justification, the Church, people and state, the Jews, and eschatology.[98] In the first or so-called "August Version," the confession repudiates errors of both liberal higher-critics and enthusiasts. But in respect to errors of the German-Christians and Nazis, only the following excerpts will be noted here:

> **I. On Holy Scripture**: The Holy Scripture of the Old and New Testaments is alone the source and norm of the Church's doctrine. It testifies ... that Jesus of Nazareth ... is the promised Messiah of Israel, the King of the Church, the Son of the living God. ... Holy Scripture is a whole. Its unity is Jesus Christ, the Crucified and Risen, who speaks through the entire Scripture. ... We reject the error that tears apart the unity of Holy Scripture by rejecting the Old Testament or even replacing it with non-Christian documents from pagan antiquity.[99]

> **II. What is the Reformation?** ... Martin Luther is the Church's teacher, obedient to the Word of Holy Scripture. To understand his accomplishment as penetration by the Germanic spirit, or as the source of the modern concept of freedom, or as the founding of a new religion clashes against his own word. He struggled against the blind over-evaluation of human reason and rejected man's dream to come to God by one's own spirit without the divine Word as devilish seduction. But as he knew himself sent to help the German nation to improve their Christianity, so he also served and serves today, too, all peoples in the office of evangelist.[100]

> **IV. On Creation and Sin**: ... Natural reason never recognizes God as the living Lord who calls and makes demands of people in their thinking, willing and doing. Faith proceeds from God and His Word. ... Only through obedience to the Word of God from Scripture do we recognize the Creator, not out of some interpretation of events in the world. ... We reject the error that conflict is the basic law of the original creation and that an aggressive attitude is thus a command of God since the original creation. ... We reject the error that God speaks to us directly through a certain "historical law" ... for it is enthusiasm to want to determine the will of God without the outer Word of Holy Scripture. ... We reject the error that the people's voice is God's voice as enthusiast interpretation of history. ... The human race is a unity in its origin and in its goal. ...

Neither the Bible nor the Confessions speak of the modern concept of race.... "The stranger ... shall live with you as a native and you shall love him as yourself ... for I am the LORD" (Lev. 19:34).... We reject the error that there are in the fallen world some final orders which were not placed under God's curse by the Fall and which as unbroken orders of creation can be recognized and accepted in their originality. For here people would be enabled to return to a sinless world and Christ's death on the cross is made superfluous.[101]

V. On Christ: ... We reject the error that the appearance of Jesus was the flaring up of Nordic kind in a world suffering from signs of decadence. Christ is the shining of the glory of God (Hebr. 12) in the world and the Son of David, sent to the lost sheep of the House of Israel.... We reject the error that we commit ourselves to Jesus as our Lord because of His heroic piety. Only as the One sent from the Father, the Son and Savior crucified and risen for us, is He our Lord. With the Confessions we here reject the error of the new Arians.... We reject the error that the crucifixion of Christ was the guilt of the Jewish people alone.... All peoples and races, even the highest, share the guilt of His death and daily make themselves guilty anew when they revile the Spirit of grace (Hebr. 10:29; ... Isa. 53:6).[102]

VI. On the Holy Spirit and the Church: ... We reject the attempt to extend the modern concept of *Führer* to the Preaching Office, for this is service with the Word of reconciliation and thus stands in contradiction to any *Führer* magic.... The Church ... can become, after the example of the Apostle, "to the Jews a Jew, to the Greeks a Greek," to the Germans a German, to the Chinese a Chinese, "in order to win some." ... The fellowship of the confessing church goes beyond the people's limits. Never do the boundaries of the people coincide with those of the church.... In every people to which the message of the Church has come, the church lives. The people is not the church; but those who belong to both are bound to both in indissoluble solidarity. They participate in the guilt of their people. They are also members of the people of God whose citizenship is in heaven.... Earthly government, ... through the proper proclamation of the church, is directed to the limits of its own order so that it may not become the tool of the devil, who seeks disorder to destroy life, ... and wants to have people revere an unlimited government as the source of life and salvation.[103]

VI:6 The Church and the Jews: ... Among all the peoples of the earth, God chose Israel as His people.... Through the crucifixion and resurrection of the Christ Jesus, the wall between Jews and Gentiles was broken down (Eph. 2). In the place of the Old Testament covenant people there appears not another nation, but the Christian church from and in all peoples. God exhibits His faithfulness generously even after the crucifixion of the Christ by remaining faithful to Israel according to the flesh, from whom Christ was born according to the flesh. . . . He preserves from Israel according to the flesh a holy remnant that . . . cannot be destroyed through Pharaoh-like means. . . . The church has received from her Lord the task to call the Jews to repentance and to baptize the believers . . . (Matt. 10:5f; Acts 2:38ff; 3:19-26). . . . The fellowship of those belonging to the church is determined neither by blood nor by race, but by the Holy Spirit and Baptism. . . . It can never, ever be the task of a people to take revenge on the Jews for the murder at Golgatha. . . . (Deut. 32:35; Hebr. 10:30). . . . We oppose the undertaking to rob the German Protestant church of her promise by transforming her into a Reich church of Christians of Aryan race. For thereby a racist law would be erected before the entrance to the church . . . We thus reject the building of Jewish-Christian congregations, for the false precondition for that . . . is that Christians from Judaism would have to develop a Christianity appropriate to their kind. But what is special for the Jewish-Christian is not founded in his race or kind or history, but only in the special faithfulness of God to Israel according to the flesh. . . . The Christians from the Gentile world must rather expose themselves to persecution than freely or by force surrender even in a single relationship the ecclesial fellowship of Word and Sacrament with Jewish-Christians. . . . We reject the concept of the thousand-year Reich, which would recognize in certain historical events the beginning of the visible rule of Christ on earth.[104]

The hope of Bonhoeffer and Niemöller for a quick, definitive confession was torpedoed because the other participants had different agendas. Sasse's main interests were that the Nazis were challenging the lordship of Christ in His church, and that confessional integrity must be protected against unionism. It was important for Bodelschwingh to avoid a confrontation at the Wittenberg Convention, to give advice to struggling clergymen, and to bring all groups in the church together, including the German-Christians. Therefore, he sent out the first prepared draft for the confession to about twenty other theologians, without first gaining approval from Bonhoeffer and Sasse as to either the choice of persons or the resultant time delay. The twenty commentators who are known included Paul Althaus, Hans Asmussen, Karl Barth, Adolf Schlatter, Theodor Schlatter, Wilhelm

Trillhaas, and Wilhelm Zoellner.[105]

Thus, the original purpose of the confession was eliminated. Instead, the desire to initiate an inner-church dialogue process and to speak for possibly all people of the church led to many changes, which especially altered parts dear to Bonhoeffer. Therefore, he refused to cooperate in the further work. Niemöller pleaded with Bodelschwingh in September to deliver whatever text of the confession the group had prepared in order to present a confessional protest to the National Convention and provide encouragement to hundreds of thousands of confused pastors and church people. He later continued to press Bodelschwingh for publication. After the suggestions of the twenty theologians were received, Sasse, Merz, and Professor Walter Künneth worked on revising the text in Bethel in October.[106]

The German-Christians took advantage of doctrines derived from general revelation, that fundamental moral law is indigenous to each folk or racial type, that folk and race are divinely created orders, and that the duty of obedience is divinely commanded, including full obedience to the state. Thus, the original Bethel Confession ignored general revelation in favor of revelation only through Christ. However, mainly due to objections from Adolf Schlatter, general revelation in history was introduced along with the idea that obedience to Scripture may perceive revelation of the Creator in nature. Schlatter was not so much interested in theological formulations for theologians as in evangelical witness that would draw Nazis to faith in Christ, wanting to come to grips with a secular theology on its own terms.[107]

Protests against the totalitarian state were removed with the excuse that the immediate struggle was with the German-Christians. It was yet too early for most theologians to realize that it was high time to protest against the Nazi state. Although the Bethel Confession is chiefly remembered for the section on the church and the Jews, much of this was deleted or strongly rewritten. The objections to the Aryan Law were omitted, so solidarity with Jewish Christians was no longer apparent. The drastic editing prompted Karl Barth's question: "Is the *civil* treatment of the Jews, as systematically permitted in present-day Germany, something that 'we' do not have to notice, which 'we' accept and support as willed by God because it is ordered by the state?"[108]

Sasse's concern for a truly Lutheran confession was altered by seeking a wider appeal, as Merz and Stratenwerth weakened some of

Sasse's pointedly Lutheran emphases and included some Reformed concepts. So he refused to sign it. Further, Bodelschwingh's introduction changed the character of the confession into merely a catechetical tract recommended to pastors "for consideration." Bonhoeffer angrily rejected the final version out of hand and privately circulated a copy of the earlier version. Sasse had written to Bonhoeffer in September, suggesting to use the Bethel Confession as the basis for a free Lutheran church independent of the German Protestant Church. He also advised Bonhoeffer to go to London, for "I saw in him one of Germany's best theologians and did not want to see him go under in the petty war against the Gestapo and Rosenberg." Bonhoeffer did accept the call to London, where he stated in November that the confession had been frustrated by Bodelschwingh and thwarted by a few pastors.[109]

Bodelschwingh was advised out of personal and political considerations not to sign it himself, so this was left to Niemöller, although he never participated in its formulation, but was glad to get the confession in any form. It was sent to the printer just before Christmas and appeared in January 1934 under the title, "Das Bekenntnis der Väter und die bekennende Gemeinde [The Confession of the Fathers and the Confessing Community]." Its 10,000 copies wore immediately sold out and it was reprinted in April. At least the *Reformierte Kirchenzeitung* (Reformed Church Magazine) rejoiced over the strong bond between confessional Lutherans and Reformed in the substance of faith. But otherwise, the Bethel Confession soon became forgotten: too little, too late.[110]

The Bethel Confession attempted to present an outline of Christian doctrine in conformity to the confessions of the ancient and Lutheran fathers. Its basis "is the doctrine of revelation, . . . the point on which the entire theological struggle with Nazi ideology hinged." But it is not properly a confession, lacking the consensus of the entire church in Germany, even of only the Lutherans. Yet, it indeed retains remarkable value at least as the first significant effort by theologians before the organizing of the Confessing Church to counter the errors of the German-Christians, and as a precursor to the theologically greatly inferior Barmen Declaration of the Confessing Church in 1934. And in its original form as worked out by Bonhoeffer, Sasse, and Vischer, it was the first theological document to defend Jewish-Christians and

Jews against the Nazi anti-Semitic laws.[111]

However, "the overall effect of the revision process was a disaster for this attempt to speak a timely word of confession on the basis of Biblical and confessional witness," especially on the Jewish-Christian question. Too many participants failed to recognize the "radical challenge to the Gospel" presented by "the Nazi state and the German-Christians." Thus, "the German Church of the Reformation" failed to issue a decisive protest "at precisely the time and at the only time when a clear cry of outrage would have had a chance to shape the course of events."[112] As Hitler himself said to Bishop Meiser a couple of weeks after the Bethel Confession was published: "The church has lost its chance."[113]

4. The Barmen Declaration, 1934

Hermann Sasse later reported:

> In the beginning of 1934 I offered, on behalf of [1000 Lutheran pastors in] the 'Confessional Movement' in northern Germany, to [Werner] Elert the leadership of this movement. They were at that time prepared to follow him on the basis of the Augsburg Confession. He declined. He replied: "Do you know where this will end? Are you prepared to sacrifice your professorship, your salary, etc.?" I could only answer: ". . . Perhaps God would help me. He had given strength to your [Lutheran] fathers in Prussia . . . to resist [the union church enforced by] the King of Prussia." His reply was: "They were wrong. They should have followed the commands of the king and accepted the union." And he was the strongest of the Lutherans. The few Lutherans who could not be bribed were the adherents of old [August] Vilmar, men like F. W. Hopf.[114]

The Confessional Movement "was originally a Lutheran enterprise. . . . Elert could not see a possibility of fighting the Nazi party. How different would the course of the history of German Lutheranism have been, had not the leaders of the Lutheran church and theology refused to oppose Hitler."[115]

Because the confessional Lutherans failed to produce a united opposition and their own confession, the initiative in the Church Struggle passed to those committed to a united church, whose leading theologian was Karl Barth. His reply to the Bethel Confession was: Is a Lutheran confession sufficient, or is it not necessary "to work through the draft together so that it . . . could appear before the public as a [united] Protestant confession of faith?"[116]

Sasse saw that, because the heresy of the common enemy appears "as pseudo-Lutheran, it confuses the Lutheran church more than the Reformed. . . . The battle for confessionally loyal Lutheranism is in many ways other than that of the Reformed: a battle about the right understanding of the doctrine of our confessions on the debated questions. As such, . . . we must fight it alone." Has the time "come when the common opponent is so powerful . . . that the historical points of disagreement between the Lutheran and Reformed churches have become questions of secondary importance? . . . The Lutheran church cannot survive when her confessions are set aside."[117] If the church, perhaps "in order to avoid conflict, should not refuse its agreement to such legal forms, she would deny before the world her own doctrine as the right interpretation of the Word of God and so destroy herself as church."[118]

Sasse had consistently spoken out against the new church union of all *Landeskirchen*, the German Protestant Church. He distributed his opposing view in writing ("Die Deutsche Union von 1933") to the church leaders who assembled at the National Convention in Wittenberg in September 1933. He argued that, to accept the union church's constitution was "contrary to the Lutheran Confessions and constitutionally invalid," for the result would be the merger of all confessions.[119] At the Barmen Synod, he concluded his protest: "I deeply regret that the great hour of a confederation of the confessional churches in Germany has been missed, and that thereby steps were taken toward a new union which will efface and dissolve the Confessions of the Reformation."[120] He later commented: "No Lutheran was any longer prepared to listen to that warning. The tragedy was that the Lutherans obeyed Hitler rather than the confession of their church."[121]

The Confessing Community had named Barth, Hans Asmussen, and Thomas Breit to the "Nürnberg Committee" to draft a declaration. In May 1934, Bishop Meiser, evidently persuaded by Althaus and Elert, added Sasse to the committee to safeguard the declaration's Lutheran character, warning: "It would he fatal to draft a joint confession." Sasse had just published an anti-unionistic article ("*Union und Bekenntnis* [Union and Confession]") in March as a reply to

Barth's position. The latter held that the crisis demanded a common Protestant statement by Lutheran, Reformed, and united churchmen, claiming that "the Church Struggle is . . . over the First Commandment and we have to 'confess.' . . . The serious opposition between theological schools must no longer be divisive and schismatic." Sasse replied: We should "as good Lutheran and Reformed churchmen confess the faith of the fathers in common where we *can*, but divided where we *must*." He also held that, in acknowledging the theological basis for the union of churches in the German Protestant Church constitution, one would accept a false basis, for according to the Lutheran confession, that is no church, but "an artificial religious coalition standing for no definite doctrine or church confession before the world."[122]

Sasse's precedent for his stand was the constitution of the German Protestant Federation of 1922, which stated: "Everything that touches on confessional matters is reserved . . . for the respective *Landeskirchen*." Sasse hoped for discussions in one body, with separate confessional caucuses and separate votes. He insisted on rewriting the preamble of the draft declaration to stress the clear confessional distinction between the Lutheran and Reformed churches so their confessional groups would be the sole authorities empowered to expound on a joint declaration. But when Asmussen took this "Erlangen draft" to Barth, he convinced him to reject it.[123]

Sasse appeared briefly at Barmen, where he rejected the declaration, saying: "These statements should in no way be accepted by the synod, because it thereby assumes the teaching office over Lutheran and Reformed congregations. What is pure and false teaching can . . . only be said by a Lutheran synod for Lutherans and by a Reformed synod for Reformed. . . . The Lutheran Confessions do not know of a church above the confessions."[124] This is the historical Lutheran view. But those in charge of the synod wanted to hear no more from Sasse. So, when he was denied the opportunity to expound his position to either the Lutheran caucus or the synod plenum, after an excited conversation with Bishop Meiser, he delivered a written statement to the president of the synod, Karl Koch, and left for home on the next train.[125]

On the one hand, Sasse did not appear to oppose the Barmen Declaration. He declared: "There is today a common enemy against which both Reformation confessions must fight shoulder to shoulder, against the great heresy that has appeared.... Both Lutherans and Reformed battle against the false teaching that threatens the uniqueness of the divine revelation in Scripture, against the Marcionite destruction of the Bible, against [the rejection of original sin], against falsifying the doctrines of the Person of Jesus Christ and of God's Trinity.... Enthusiasm wants to complete the Reformation."[126] Thus, Sasse agreed with the Biblical truths and the rejection of false teachings as stated in the Barmen Declaration, envisioning them as a "basis for the further work of theological conferences to clarify which false teachings are to be rejected by the Protestant churches."[127] It was "a necessary word of defense against the German-Christians and their errors.... Limits were set that had to be set."[128] However, Sasse was "compelled to make a solemn protest against the resolutions of the Free Synod in Barmen as being a violation of the Evangelical Lutheran Church."[129] Barmen failed because of its pan-confessional intention.[130]

Sasse also questioned the text because it could be interpreted differently by Lutheran and Reformed theologians.[131] He later said: "The Barmen Declaration ... was not born out of the consensus of the true church, ... [for] it lacks the consensus of the fathers." The statements that follow the Scripture quotations are not proper expositions: "Scripture is misused in order to force a compromise artificially." Soon afterwards, Bishop Meiser rejected the Barmen Declaration as a binding confession for the Bavarian Church.[132]

Sasse's contributions to Bethel and Barmen faded into "an embarrassed silence," although Hans Asmussen had reminded the Barmen Synod about him: "We know him as one of the very few university professors who has supported us by word and deed in the Church Struggle and at the risk of our lives." This was greeted by applause.[133] But later historians accused Sasse "of the blindness of a strict Lutheran who excluded himself from the most important confession of his time,"[134] and concluded that his "narrow Lutheran confessionalism ... greatly weakened the church's opposition to National Socialism."[135] However, it was the unionists who took advantage of the Nazi pressure to defeat the confessionalists.

Sasse later remarked:

The Lutherans in Germany ... were believing in the nation more than in the Church.... That the Protestant churches survived Hitler's attempts to subjugate them is the real result of the awakening in the Twenties. The

> "Confessing Church" ... was strong enough to frustrate the attempts to smash the church.... Unfortunately, the endeavour to save the German churches was bound up with the desire to unite them.... While the Lutherans within the Confessing Church demanded the maintenance of the old confessions, the Reformed minority with the union churches stood for a real unification, expressed in a new common confession.... This was the aim of Karl Barth. He renewed the old Reformed concept of the one Church of the Reformation, based on *sola scriptura*, in which Lutherans and Reformed could exist as different theological schools.... He developed [since 1925] a concept of the confession in which the actual act of confessing was dominant and overshadowed the doctrinal content of the confession.... Thus the famous "Theological Declaration of Barmen" was formulated after the resistance of confessional Lutheranism had been smashed. The Lutherans who remained at the synod accepted the declaration with the proviso that it should not be regarded as a confession. [But] soon after this synod, a Prussian confessing synod declared the border between Lutherans and Reformed obsolete and proclaimed general intercommunion between all Protestants. Thus from the beginning a lack of truthfulness robbed the Confessing Church of its spiritual authority. After the war this Confessing Church took over the reorganization of the German churches. The result was the "Evangelical [Protestant] Church in Germany," whose definite unionistic character became more and more obvious.[136]

Already in 1933, Sasse denounced the German Protestant Church as the attempt to unionize all Germany. The later development proved him right. Ironically, "the idea of the national church is a product of the Nineteenth Century ... , demanded by liberalism ... ; but this old liberal demand has been realized by a movement [Nazism] that wants to destroy liberalism. The Reformation church understood the Church as a confessional fellowship beyond the limits of peoples ... (Ap 7-8)."[137] The "national question hardly plays a role in the Confessions" because "they are concerned about the reformation of the *church*. They are not interested in portraying the foundation of a German national church, but they want to proclaim the pure doctrine of the Gospel that should be the same for Christianity in all peoples."[138]

Sasse later stated:

> It was not Lutheranism as such, but a sick Lutheranism that gave Nazism an open door into the Church. It had fallen asleep. It had lost the power of distinguishing between spirits. Christians of all persuasions were carried

away, including Lutherans of all complexions.... Lutheran theology was greatly influenced by the concept of the absolute state. Under the philosophical precepts of Fichte and Hegel, reverence for the state became a sort of secret religion. As for the average German, the state took the place of the church.... People picked out of Luther's teachings those statements about governmental authority which they wanted to hear, but what Luther said about the sins of governmental authority and the boundaries of obedience was not mentioned. So they supplemented Luther with Robespierre.... On the other hand, it was the churches of Prussia, having long before ceased to be Lutheran, who succumbed in large measure to the German-Christian movement, whereas it was the very Lutheranism in the churches of Bavaria, Württemberg and Hannover [Lower Saxony] which prevented a similar collapse from occurring there.[139]

Sasse offered himself willingly as an advisor to church bishops and presidents,[140] cooperating closely with Vice-Presidents Christian Stoll and Wilhelm Bogner in Bavaria. It was about the time of the Barmen aftermath that Sasse published *Was heißt lutherisch?* (Was Does Lutheran Mean?) Here, he clarified the doctrines of Law and Gospel, justification and predestination, incarnation and real presence.[141]

Sasse also played a significant role in the Schwabach Conventicle, a colloquium of pastors chaired by Stoll to activate confessional strength and theological study. At the end of the war in 1945, with the singular opportunity for the Reformation churches to reorganize themselves independently from state influence according to their respective confessions, Sasse led the Schwabach Conventicle to work out and present detailed plans. However, the errors of 1933 that had been made under Nazi duress were repeated in 1945 and 1947 without Nazi pressure.[142]

C. Did Sasse Fail to Profess His Faith Clearly Enough?

1. Did He Merely Silence His Own Critique of the Nazis to Save Himself?

An example of the bottom line for what the Nazis would tolerate was the statement of a Nazi judge in 1934 to the Swedish Bishop Anders Nygren: The Nazi party has no interest in attacking Christianity, but will tolerate "nothing against the nationalist ideology." Thus, Sasse's stand in 1932 was impermissible, for he blatantly attacked the party's program publicly.[143]

It was probably a professor at the University of Erlangen in whose theological faculty Sasse was to receive an appointment, who denounced him to the Bavarian Ministry of Culture, thereby placing his offered professorship in jeopardy. When questioned by the Deputy Minister of Culture, Sasse evidently replied with a declaration of loyalty. Also summoned by the Minister of Culture himself, Sasse must have been able to reassure him of his trustworthiness, for the minister declared: "What one has written against us before 1933 is forgotten and forgiven, if he only stands loyal now."[144]

A colleague, Wilhelm Trillhaas, once said that he stood "superficially loyal, . . . although he never ceased to criticize the Third Reich." Yet, Sasse also suffered deprivation under the Nazis: he only received the appointment of an assistant professor although having to fulfill all the duties of a full professor. His colleagues complained that he spent too little time on scholarly research, for he sacrificed much time for the cause of the Church Struggle. His students joked that he was able to remain in office because he always had the SA and SS (plus E for Evangel) with him. Obviously, Sasse attempted to maintain a low profile. He became more subtle in his opposition, once admitting to lecturing against the religion of Hitler, but his topic was "The Religion of Robespierre."[145]

As a professor under the employ of the state, Sasse was denied an exit visa to attend the ecumenical Commission of the Church and the Word in Denmark in 1935, although he had become its secretary the previous year.[146] Also in 1935, Sasse was to present one of the major lectures at the Lutheran World Council meeting in Paris, but his trip was canceled by the government on only two weeks' notice.[147] Likewise, Sasse could not attend the Faith and Order Conference in Edinburgh in 1937. The Nazis wanted to isolate Christians of Germany from ecumenical contacts.[148]

Sasse could have accepted a call to Wartburg Seminary (Dubuque, Iowa) in about 1936 through the auspices of J. Michael Reu, but he felt that such a move then would appear as a desertion from the Church Struggle. In 1946, he wrote in a private letter that not following that call "would have been the worst mistake of his life if experiencing the powerful divine judgment that came over Germany and helping to carry the guilt and the suffering of his people had not been the most powerful school of a 'theology of facts.'" But now he would be ready with this experience to serve in America.[149]

Sasse was the object of heavy attacks from Nazis, especially from the ideologist Alfred Rosenberg. He became completely isolated in his own faculty. By 1938, Sasse's situation appeared hopeless, so he decided to emigrate to the U.S.A., but that was hampered by difficult negotiations with the immigration officials until it was declared to him: "You can emigrate; we can do without you; but your wife and two sons must stay here!"[150] The next year, Sasse agreed with Theodore Tappert of Lutheran Seminary, Mt. Airy [a Philadelphia neighborhood], Pennsylvania, that he should emigrate for a position there. But on the day of his agreement with Tappert, World War II broke out, and it was no longer possible to emigrate to the U.S.[151]

After assuming power, the Nazi state and party intervened ever more massively in church life. They destroyed youth work, forbade church events outside of divine services, throttled freedom of movement, including a pastor's accepting a call to a different position, and canceled the church press.[152] Sasse wrote in 1935 that much that previously belonged to the individual was declared to belong to the people and subjected to the rule of the state, including science and art, so religion is no exception. That "religion is a private matter" makes no sense in a lost world.[153] At one meeting, a pastor declared: "Now is church struggle, so we all should wear the uniform of the confessions!" But Sasse replied: "The confession is not a uniform, but the weapon in the struggle against heresy!"[154]

Sasse preached in wartime: "In these days it has been made brutally clear to our theology students how superfluous they are!"[155] "Never have people suffered so much as in the great persecutions of the Church.... The greatest persecution of Christians in history began exactly 25 years ago in Communist Russia.... Alone in Turkey about 6,000,000 Christian Armenians were killed.... How harmless were the Christian persecutions of ancient time in comparison with those of our time! ... There was never this systematic destruction, ... and that under the hypocritical mask of religious freedom."[156]

"It is not so easy today to confess Jesus Christ and His Church publicly...," as a student of theology or as a faithful churchgoer. "Churchgoing has become ... a confession, and the Christian faith the faith of manly character. Thus, such times do not harm the church, as

one sees that respect for the churches in Germany among the people...
is much greater than 25 years ago.... The church is ridiculed and all
kinds of evil are spoken against those who hold to their Christian
faith." For you belong to those permitted to carry the dear holy cross,
"rejoicing that they were worthy to suffer shame for His name" (Acts
5:41). "Only that church is the right church of Christ which is not a
church of glory but one of the Cross."[157]

Did Sasse nearly silence his criticism of the Nazis in order to save himself? No. Instead, he continued to speak out in opposition, in more muted tones, but still clearly enough that he was continually harassed. It could only be asked whether he might have been more outspoken. However, we who have not experienced such persecution cannot rightfully judge him or others whether their opposition was great enough. Should we say that anyone who survived the Nazi period without having been shot for treason, or sent to the front lines to be killed or to waste away in a Russian concentration camp, must have been something less than a confessional Christian? We know of some, like the pastors Paul Schneider and Richard Hofmann and the Austrian peasant Franz Jägerstätter, who suffered such fates. Schneider persisted in vocal opposition, even after he was interred in a concentration camp, denouncing Nazi racist crimes until he himself died of torture in 1938, "the preacher of Buchenwald."[158] Hofmann was sent to death in the front lines for refusing to accept an officer's promotion, which would have forced him to take and give orders against his conscience. Jägerstätter, who, against the prudent advice of his parish priest and even his bishop, refused to swear obedience to Hitler in the German army because he realized the Nazi movement was diabolical, was executed in prison.[159] It appears that Sasse was loyal to his healthy Christian conscience in the degree of his opposition. According to the principles of Lutheran ethics, that we must respect.

2. Did Sasse Fail to Oppose Nazi Anti-Semitism Sufficiently?

Sasse was adamant in his defense of the Old Testament as true Word of God for Christians. However, it appears that Sasse was ambivalent toward the Nazi persecution of Jews, even of Jewish-Christians. After agreeing to remarkable statements by Bonhoeffer and Vischer against such persecution, he was willing to let many of them be eliminated from the Bethel Confession when they were opposed by other theologians. He was one of few theologians in 1933 who realized that the time to speak softly to the Nazis in compromising ways, hoping to win them over to the church, was already past. Instead, he knew that they must be confronted directly and forcefully wherever they endanger the Gospel and the church's doctrine.[160] Why, then, was he so indecisive on the Jewish question? Why did he fail to see that, when racism rears its ugly head against the people of our Lord Jesus Christ according to the flesh, it blasphemes the incarnation and the person of Christ Himself? On this major point, Sasse failed to recognize an essential *casus confessionis*.

Rather early on, Hitler's control of the media and legal system was so complete that objection or protest against any state action was impossible or immediately crushed. When the Confessing Church finally took a strong stand against racism in 1935, 700 of their pastors were briefly arrested. Yet, "for several years, the Confessing Church helped Jewish-Christians flee abroad through the 'Office Grüber' in Berlin, until the Nazis closed it in 1940. . . . A few pastors dared speak out against Nazi anti-Semitism in sermons. But if they persisted, they endangered themselves and their families."[161]

Had Christians protested the Nazi persecution massively at least by the mid-30s, it might have been effective. But the Christian aversion to injustice was checkmated by incipient anti-Semitism and reverence for the state. Church officials were generally too preoccupied with saving what they could of their programs and structure to be concerned with the Jews until it was too late. Hitler was forced to stop his euthanasia program against the mentally retarded because of a massive public outrage. But neither within nor outside Germany did any outcry deter his systematic persecution and annihilation of Jewish people.[162] Christians in general, even in North America, failed to acknowledge their common roots with the Jewish people and that our crucified and glorified Lord Jesus Christ is fully a Jew. Thus, any expression or act of prejudice and animosity toward any Jew as a Jew amounts to a grievous sin against Jesus Himself.[163]

3. *The Lesson of Absolute Loyalty to Be Learned from the Church Struggle*

When the churches fell under state persecution, the overriding concern of the church leaders and pastors was to save the structure of the church at all costs so that it could at least continue to function as church. This meant that compromises and concessions had to be made so that the church leaders might retain their positions, church property might not be confiscated, worship services might still be held, and pastors might not be imprisoned or sent to the front lines.

But other things could be sacrificed: youth work, the church press, theological students to the front, and pastors, theological professors, or church leaders who too loudly opposed the regime, to concentration camps; only those could be appointed to church positions who were obedient to the state; Jews and even Jewish-Christians could lose their jobs, be ostracized from society and the church, and even disappear completely. All this could be sacrificed, but not the church organization nor whatever one regarded as the minimum of church life, especially the Sunday morning divine service.

Sasse rightly spoke out definitively in 1932 against the Nazi church program on the point that implied control of the church. However, should there not have been massive protests in 1933 to prevent the persecution of Jews and the loss of the youth work? These early actions by the Nazis were allowed to proceed with impunity, although they struck deep at the heart of the church's doctrine and life. But the churchmen were afraid, as Sasse himself once said in suppressed sarcasm against the Lutheran bishops who buckled under to Nazi pressure to accept the unionistic German Protestant Church: they did so "to prevent something worse." But what could be worse than to blaspheme the incarnation of Christ by permitting the racist persecution of Jews? What could be worse than to sacrifice the church's youth to the heathen idolatry of Nazism? Is it indeed more valuable to save the church's offices and worship services for apparent normality than to save the truth?

In the early church persecutions the Christians readily risked everything: their lives, their church leaders, their worship services, rather than make any concessions. In China in the 20th century, whether Christians wanted to give it up or not, everything was taken away from them: pastors, churches, worship services, and Bibles. But that was by no means the end of the church: from about three million Christians before the Communist persecution, less than fifty years later, there are now probably no fewer than sixty million. This is proof that, when it comes to giving ground confessionally or doctrinally, there is no bottom line. We must be ready to sacrifice everything else whatsoever for the sake of loyalty to Jesus Christ our Lord. Today, Germany also has about sixty million Christians; but about 95% of them are merely nominal, while most of China's Christians are vibrant.

The lesson, therefore, is that it is better to give up everything else in faithfulness to our Lord without retreating an inch, for our faithful Lord will never allow "the gates of hell to prevail against" His Church (Matthew 16:18)!

Hermann Sasse was quite right on most of his standpoints on the Nazi threats to the church. He is greatly to be admired for his exemplary courage in speaking out against them continually. May we, who profess that the Lutheran confession is faithfully Biblical and Christian, endeavor with the help of Christ to follow his example of outspoken loyalty to His Lord at the expense of personal comfort and even martyrdom. As Hermann Bezzel stated nearly one hundred years ago: "God grant that our confession be life and our life be confession!"[164]

Notes

[1] Feuerhahn, *EC*, 1.

[2] In presenting Sasse here, he will often be allowed to speak for himself through his articles, lectures, sermons and letters, the translation provided mainly by this writer.

[3] "Geleitwort des Verfassers," *ISC* I:10; my trans. See Friedrich Wilhelm Hopf, "Wer war Hermann Sasse?", Z, 18; Ronald R. Feuerhahn, "Hermann Sasse on Law and Gospel" (Lecture to "Confessional Lutherans," 21 April 1995), 2.

[4] "Aus Treue zum Bekenntnis: Hermann Sasses Vermächtnis," *Lutherisches Monatsheft*, 6.1 (1977): 7; ET in *EC*, 7.

[5] "Die Botschaft der Reformation in der Zeitenwende" (1942), Z, 224.

[6] Huß, 90; my trans.

[7] "Zur Lage der lutherischen Kirchen in der Welt," *Briefe an lutherische Pastoren* 1 (1 Dec. 1948): 93; my trans. See Ronald R. Feuerhahn: "Hermann Sasse: Confessional Ecumenist," *Lutherische Theologie und Kirche* 19.3 (November 1995).

[8] Hans-Jörg Voigt, "Von der Kartographie der Kirche: Hermann Sasse und 60 Jahre Barmer theologische Erlkärung," *Lutherische Kirche* 25.11 (Nov. 1994): 5.

[9] Hermann Sasse, *Kirchenregiment und weltliche Obrigkeit nach lutherischer Lehre*, Bekennende Kirche 30 (München: Chr. Kaiser Verlag, 1935), 258.

[10] Erich Beyreuther, "Die Vorgeschichte des Kirchenkampfes zwischen 1918 und 1933," in Paul Rieger und Johannes Strauss, eds., *Kirche und Nationalsocialismus; Zur Geschichte des Kirchenkampfes, Tutzinger Texte* I (München: Claudius, 1969), 20, 23.

[11] Helmust Baier, "Die bayerische Landeskirche im Umbruch 1931-1934," in Rieger and Strauss, *Kirche und Nationalsozialismus*, 34.

[12] Sasse, "Die unbegreifliche Osterbotschaft" (1938), Z, 66; and "Reformationsfest: Bußtag der Kirche" (1943), Z, 180.

[13] Beyreuther, in Rieger and Strauss, *Kirche und Nationalsozialismus*, 26.

[14] "Eine Adventsfrage aller Zeiten" (1933), Z, 34; my trans.

[15] "Geleitwort," Z, 10; my trans.

[16] "Die Gemeinde der Erlösten" (1937), Z, 58-61.

[17] Letter to Ludwig Fuerbringer (1 Feb. 1936), qtd and trans. Feuerhahn, "Law and Gospel," 5; see 4.

[18] *Das Volk nach der Lehre der Evangelischen Kirche, Bekennende Kirche* 20 (München: Chr. Kaiser Verlag, 1934), 6-7.

[19] Adrian Hastings, *A History of English Christianity 1920-1990*, 3rd ed. (London: SCM Press, 1991), 365; Georg Kretschmar, "Die Auseinandersetzung der Bekennenden Kirche mit den Deutschen Christen," in Rieger and Strauss, *Kirche und Nationalsozialismus*, 121; Gene Edward Veith, Jr.: *Modern Fascism: Liquidating the Judeo-Christian Worldview* (St. Louis: Concordia, 1993), 66.

[20] Baier, in Rieger and Strauss, *Kirche und Nationalsozialismus*, 42-44.

[21] "Die Kirche und die politischen Mächte der Zeit," *Kirchliches Jahrbuch für die evangelischen Landeskirchen Deutschlands* 59 (1932), *ISC* I:252f., n. 1; my trans.

[22] Baier, in Rieger and Strauss, *Kirche und Nationalsozialismus*, 34; Sasse, *Kirchenregiment*, 91.

[23] Veith, *Modern Fascism*, 66.

[24] Sasse, "Adventsfrage," 39; *Volk*, 13.

[25] "Im neuen Kirchenjahr" (1936), Z, 24; "Die Kirche Gottes in ihrer Bewegung" (1937), Z, 155; and "Reformationsfest," Z, 180; my trans. See also Veith, *Modern Fascism*, 68-69.

[26] "Reformationsfest," Z, 179; "Die Botschaft der Reformation," Z, 219; and "Luthers Glaube an die Eine Heilige Kirche" (1943), Z, 240.

[27] "Die Kirche und die politischen Mächte der Zeit," *ISC* I:253.

[28] Baier, in Rieger and Strauss, *Kirche und Nationalsozialismus*, 32.

[29] Kretschmar, in Rieger and Strauss, *Kirche und Nationalsozialismus*, 122-23; my trans. This movement "articulated a highly politicized and secularized theology that subverted scripture and the inherited Lutheran and Reformed confessions with führer-worship, German völkischness, and explicitly racial anti-Semitism." Shelley Baranowski, *The Confessing Church, Conservative Elites, and the Nazi State* (Lewiston, NY: E. Mellen Press, 1986), 58. See Veith, *Modern Fascism*, 57-58.

[30] *Volk*, 12-14.

[31] "Die Kirche und die polititischen Mächte der Zeit," *ISC* I:262-63.

[32] Qtd by Hopf, "Wer war Hermann Sasse?" *Z*, 21; my trans.

[33] "Osterbotschaft," *Z*, 73; "Die Frage nach der Kirche" (1943), *Z*, 103.

[34] "Luthers Glaube," *Z*, 204; my trans.

[35] "Das Pfingstwunder" (1940), *Z*, 101f.; my trans.

[36] Qtd by Hopf, "Wer war Hermann Sasse?" *Z*, 21.

[37] *EC*, 45.

[38] Beyreuther, in Rieger and Strauss, *Kirche und Nationalsozialismus*, 13-14; my trans.

[39] "Die Botschaft der Reformation in der Zeitenwende," *Z*, 206; my trans.

[40] "Die Kirche und die politischen Mächte der Zeit," *ISC* I:253f; my trans.

[41] *ISC* I: 255f; my trans.

[42] This was demanded by many German-Christians, e.g., at the infamous sport stadium rally in Berlin in November, 1933; see Veith, *Modern Fascism*, 58.

[43] "Im neuen Kirchenjahr," *Z*, 25-27; my trans.

[44] "Das Geheimnis der letzten Dinge" (1938), *Z*, 186; see below the section on Scripture, Excursus on the Bethel Confession.

[45] Baier, in Rieger and Strauss, *Kirche und Nationalsozialismus*, 51, 53.

[46] Baier, in Rieger and Strauss, *Kirche und Nationalsozialismus*, 43f., 65.

[47] "Die deutsche Union von 1933," *Theologische Blätter* 12 (1933), repr. *ISC* I:271, 265; my trans.

[48] "Letter to J. A. O. Preus" (31 Oct. 1968; *CTS*).

[49] "Die deutsche Union von 1933," *ISC* I:265; my trans.

[50] *Kirchenregiment*, 76-77, 89f.; my trans.

[51] "Die Kirche und die politischen Mächte der Zeit," *ISC* I:257; my trans.

[52] Ibid. I:259, 262-63; my trans.

[53] Baier, in Rieger and Srauss, *Kirche und Nationalsozialismus*, 96-97, 100.

[54] Rieger and Strauss, *Kirche und Nationalsozialismus*, 45, 57-61, 88-91, 95, 99.

[55] Ibid., 111-13, 115; my trans.

[56] Qtd Feuerhahn, *EC*, 39-40.

[57] Huß, 78.

[58] "Der Höhepunkt der Seligpreisungen" (1942), *Z*, 134; my trans.

[59] "Gottes kämpfendes Heer" (1936), *Z*, 148; my trans.

[60] "Die Kirche Gottes in ihrer Bewegung," *Z*, 157f; my trans.

[61] "Reformationsfest," *Z*, 177; my trans.

[62] Guy C. Carter, *Confession at Bethel, August 1933, Enduring Witness: The Formation, Revision and Significance of the First Full Theological Confession of the Evangelical Church Struggle in Nazi Germany*, Ph.D. Dissertation (Milwaukee: Marquette University, 1987), xi.

[63] Carter, *Confession at Bethel*, 19-20; Kretschmar, in Rieger and Strauss, *Kirche und Nationalsozialismus*, 128-30.

[64] Carter, *Confession at Bethel*, 7, 9-10, 27-28.

[65] Ibid., 19-51.

[66] Ibid., 33-35. Although some free Lutherans saw strong dangers in National Socialism, Hitler's promises of freedom for the churches were accepted at face value, and they reiterated their ideal of the separation of church and state. Rosenberg's Germanic myth was clearly rejected as pagan and atheistic, and the German-Christians were opposed because of their rejection of the Old Testament and the Cross of Christ. However, political action against imagined negatively socio-economical influences of Jews was greeted, though it should not go beyond the limits of God's commandments; the proper solution to the Jewish question is mission among Jews, for they are included in the Church of all nations. The pastors of the Evangelical Lutheran Hermannsburg-Hamburg Free Church rejected the Aryan Paragraph and supported one of their pastors, Erwin Horwitz, whose father was Jewish, so that he was spared deportation. Some greeted warmly Sasse's clear presentation of the situation and his stand against unionism. Some also admired the Confessing Church for its Biblical and confessional stand, but criticized the Barmen Declaration for its Reformed tendencies. The Evangelical Lutheran Church in Prussia, which kept close contacts with the Lutheran *Landeskirchen*, joined their recently constituted Lutheran Council in 1936. But this left it less free than the other free churches, for its leadership felt constrained to support the Nazi government consistently, even requiring their pastors to swear the required

allegiance to Hitler in 1938 (which the others rejected), and allowing a Jewish-Christian deaconess and some of the mentally retarded in their institution to be deported; *Bericht: Geschichte der Lutherischen Freikirchen im Dritten Reich, Kirchensynode* [Church Convention], Selbständige Evangelisch-Lutherische Kirche (SELK; Hannover, 1987), 11-22, 33-39, 57-63, 67-72, 79.

[67] *SELK Bericht*, 87-89.

[68] Letter to Michael Reu (29 Dec. 1935); copy provided by R. Feuerhahn.

[69] Carter, *Confession at Bethel*, 40.

[70] Hastings, *History*, 365.

[71] Letter to Kurt Marquart (10 Sept. 1967); collection of Prof. Kurt Marquart.

[72] Carter, *Confession at Bethel*, 4f., 5, 7, 9, 41, 43-45.

[73] Letter to Reu.

[74] Carter, *Confession at Bethel*, 16f., 47f.

[75] Ibid., 7, 9, 17, 49-51.

[76] "Im neuen Kirchenjahr," Z, 27-28.

[77] "Adventsfrage," Z, 36. Luther held that pastors must protest against politicians' injustice (*AE* 13:49); "I shall not give up my snout [tongue] lest I consent to injustice"; *WA* 28:283. See Uwe Siemon-Netto, *The Fabricated Luther: The Rise and Fall of the Shirer Myth* (St. Louis: Concordia, 1995), 78-79.

[78] "Der Höhepunkt der Seligpreisungen," Z, 131; my trans.

[79] "Luthers Glaube," Z, 225; my trans.

[80] "Die Kirche und die politischen Mächte der Zeit," *ISC* I:257; my trans.

[81] Cited by Hopf, "Wer war Hermann Sasse?" Z, 21; my trans.

[82] *Kirchenregiment*, 77; my trans. Luther taught that, because the Christian owes more obedience to God than to man, he must refuse to execute evil commands, even at the risk of losing all he has and his life (*WA* 11:277; 19:656). On this principle, Bishop Eivind Berggrav of Oslo led the resistance of Norway's Lutheran state church against the pro-Nazi Quisling government (Siemon-Netto, *The Fabricated Luther*, 65, 72). Similarly, the 15-year-old free Lutheran, Gerhard Großmann, who with the Hitler Youth had to help defend Berlin in April, 1945 (whoever refused was hanged from a lamppost), gave his rifle to a comrade without one "so I could not kill anyone" (he was later mortally wounded by a grenade).

[83] Carter, *Confession at Bethel*, 19, 64.

[84] Veith, *Modern Fascism*, 56-63.

[85] Christine-Ruth Müller, *Bekenntnis und Bekennen: Dietrich Bonhoeffer in Bethel (1933)* (München: Chr. Kaiser Verlag, 1989), 9-10.

[86] Carter, *Confession at Bethel*, 64, 93.

[87] Ibid., 74-76.

[88] Müller, *Bekenntnis und Bekennen*, 11-13; Eberhard Bethge, ed., *Dietrich Bonhoeffer: Gesammelte Schriften*, Vol. 2, *Kirchenkampf und Finkenwalde* (München: Chr. Kaiser Verlag, 1959), 131.

[89] Bethge, *GS* II:46, 48-51, 53; my trans. See Bonhoeffer's letter to Karl Barth, *GS* II:126-28.

[90] Ibid., II:62-67; my trans. The German-Christians rationalized the removal of Jewish-Christian pastors from the ministry as an *adiaphoron*, for there were only 19 of them out of a total of some 18,000 (Siemon-Netto, *The Fabricated Luther*, 93).

[91] Carter, *Confession at Bethel*, 77-79.

[92] Carter, *Confession at Bethel*, 71-73, 79-82; Müller, *Bekenntnis und Bekennen*, 15, 18.

[93] Carter, *Confession at Bethel*, 156-57; Bethge, *GS* II:82-83.

[94] Müller, *Bekenntnis und Bekennen*, 15, 18-21; Bethge, *GS* II:82.

[95] Carter, *Confession at Bethel*, 164, 166.

[96] Bethge, *GS* II:83.

[97] Feuerhahn, *EC*, 110-11.

[98] Müller, *Bekenntnis und Bekennen*, 82.

[99] Ibid., 82, 83, 85; my trans. For Sasse, Holy Scripture was always the Word of the living God over-against both emptying it through lack of commitment and distorting it through a false doctrine of inspiration; see Hans-Siegried Huß, "Bekennende Kirche: zum Gedenken an Hermann Sasse (1895-1995)," *Lutherische Kirche* 27.7 (1995): 14.

[100] Müller, *Bekenntnis und Bekennen*, 87; my trans.

[101] Ibid., 88-94; my trans. Cf. Carter, *Confession at Bethel*, 182, 204-8, 210-12, 214.

[102] Müller, *Bekenntnis und Bekennen*, 98-100; my trans.

[103] Ibid., 108-12; cf. Carter, *Confession at Bethel*, 236, 241-42, 246-47, 250-51, 253-55.

[104] Müller, *Bekenntnis und Bekennen*, 112-15, 117; my trans. Cf. Carter, *Confession at Bethel*, 255, 258, 262-65.

[105] Carter, *Confession at Bethel*, 90, 92, 269.

[106] Ibid., 149-50; Müller, *Bekenntnis und Bekennen*, 70-75; Feuerhahn, *EC*, 50-56.

[107] Carter, *Confession at Bethel*, 115, 117, 181f., 185, 202, 204, 212, 241, 247, 255; Müller, *Bekenntnis und Bekennen*, 174, 176.

[108] Carter, *Confession at Bethel*, 211, 236, 253-55, 258, 262; Müller, *Bekenntnis und Bekennen*, 194.

[109] Carter, *Confession at Bethel*, 170, 228, 265-67; Letter to Eberhard Bethge (28 Sept. 1956, quote provided by R. Feuerhahn).

[110] Carter, *Confession at Bethel*, 153; Bethge, *GS* II:86-88.

[111] Carter, *Confession at Bethel*, 189.

[112] Ibid., 189, 268-69.

[113] Helmut Baier, "Das Verhalten der lutherischen Bischöfe gegenüber dem nationalsozialistischen Staat 1933/34," in Rieger and Strauss, *Kirche und Nationalsozialismus*, 112.

[114] Letter to Kurt Marquart.

[115] Letter to Ralph Gehrke (16 Jan. 1955); collection of Dr. Ralph Gehrke.

[116] Feuerhahn, *EC*, 56.

[117] "Union und Bekenntnis," *Junge Kirche* 2 (1934), repr. *ISC* I:276-77; my trans.

[118] *Kirchenregiment*, 10; my trans.

[119] Feuerhahn, *EC*, 61.

[120] "Erklärung an den Präses der Barmer Synode" [Karl Koch, President of the (United) Church of Westphalia] (31 May 1934), *ISC* I:281; my trans.

[121] Letter to Herman A. Preus (27 Mar. 1963), Preus Collection, ALC Archives, Luther Seminary, St. Paul.

[122] Feuerhahn, *EC*, 56-57, 61; Huß, 79.

[123] *EC*, 57-59.

[124] "Das Bekenntnis der lutherischen Kirche und die Barmer Theologische Erklärung," *ISC* I:281; my trans.

[125] Feuerhahn, *EC*, 60, 66. He refused to make his statement public in order not to strengthen the German-Christians against the Confessing Church (Voigt, art. cit.).

[126] "Union und Bekenntnis," *ISC* I:275f.; my trans.

[127] "Das Bekenntnis der lutherischen Kirche und die Barmer Theologische

Erklärung," *ISC* I:281; my trans. See Veith, *Modern Fascism*, 59-61.

[128] "Thesen anläßlich einer theologischen Arbeitstagung des Rates der Evang.-Luth. Kirche Deutschlands in Bethel" (22-25 Oct. 1936), repr. *ISC* I:282, 285; my trans.

[129] "Das Bekenntnis der lutherischen Kirche und die Barmer Theologische Erklärung," *ISC* I:281; my trans.

[130] Feuerhahn, *EC*, 6, 60.

[131] Ibid., 60. The text: K. Koch, ed., *Zeugnisse der bekennende Kirche*.

[132] "Thesen," *ISC* I:282-83, 285; my trans.

[133] Feuerhahn, *EC*, 62.

[134] Klaus Scholder, *The Churches and the Third Reich*, vol. 2 (London: SCM, 1978),144, qtd by Feuerhahn, *EC*, 63.

[135] Arthur C. Cochrane, *The Church's Confession under Hitler* (Philadelphia: Westminster, 1962), 36; qtd by Feuerhahn, *EC*, 63.

[136] Letter to Prof. Leiv Aalen (21 June 1974), qtd by Feuerhahn, EC, 64f. See Matthew Harrison, "Hermann Sasse and EKiD—1948: The Death of the Lutheran Church," *Logia* 4.4 (1995): 42-44.

[137] "Die deutsche Union von 1933," *ISC* I:268; my trans.

[138] *Volk*, 8, 11; my trans.

[139] Letter to Herman A. Preus (provided by R. Feuerhahn).

[140] Huß, "Bekennende Kirche," *Lutherische Kirche* 27.7:14; Huß, 78-80.

[141] Huß, 78-80. This booklet was sold out immediately, expanded and reprinted in 1936 and again quickly sold out, but a third edition was prevented by the Nazis. It was later translated and published in English as *Here We Stand*.

[142] Huß, 83; Huß, "Bekennende Kirche," Lutherische Kirche 27.7:13.

[143] Feuerhahn, *EC*, 48.

[144] *EC*, 47.

[145] Ibid., 47-50.

[146] Ibid., 35-36.

[147] Huß, 74.

[148] Feuerhahn, *EC*, 38.

[149] Letter to H. A. Preus (13 Jan. 1946), provided by R. Feuerhahn.

[150] Ibid.; Huß, 76.

[151] Letter to H. Preus (1946).

[152] Huß, 82.

[153] *Kirchenregiment*, 90.

[154] Huß, 83; my trans.

[155] "Gleichheit aller Menschen?" (1939), *Z*, 125; my trans.

[156] Ibid., 132f.; my trans.

[157] Ibid., 129-31, 136; my trans.

[158] Heinrich Vogel, ed., *Der Prediger von Buchenwald; Das Martyrium Paul Schneiders*, 2nd ed. (Berlin: Evangelisches Verlagsanstalt, 1958).

[159] Hastings, *History*, 366.

[160] So Flacius: "The greatest fool is he who believes that one can avoid war and destruction by pacifying godless people who are but dirt and Feces" (qtd by Hans Christoph von Hase, *Die Gestalt der Kirche Luthers: Der Casus Confessionis im Kampf des Matthias Flacius gegen das Interim von 1548*, [Göttingen: Vandenhoeck & Ruprecht, 1940], 39; qtd by Siemon-Netto, *The Fabricated Luther*, 95).

[161] John R. Wilch, "The Jewish Holocaust: A Christian Response" (Board for Evangelism Services, LC-MS, unpublished, 1989), 9f.

[162] Ibid., 9-11; see Veith, *Modern Fascism*, 64.

[163] See Wilch, "The Jewish Holocaust," 28-31.

[164] Cited by Huß, "Bekennende Kirche," *Lutherische Kirche* 27.7:14.

Sasse on Worship

John W. Kleinig

Dr. Sasse repeatedly asserted, as only he could, forcibly and passionately, that every great theologian was also a great liturgist.[1] And yet he himself was no liturgical scholar. He did not teach liturgics, nor did he, as far as I can ascertain, ever sit on any liturgical committee either in Germany or in Australia. He did not compose any new liturgy, nor did he write any hymns, even though his last years coincided with the production of *The Lutheran Hymnal* in Australia. True, he did make one very decisive and distinctive contribution to the "Service with Communion" for that hymnal in 1973. At his insistence the phrase "in true faith" was replaced with "in body and soul" in the formula of dismissal. His essays on "The Joyful Season of the Church" (1955) and on "Concerning the Origin of the Improperia" (1957) did pave the way for the eventual production of the services for the Easter Triduum in the Lutheran Church of Australia.[2] But apart from that he was not responsible for any major liturgical innovation.

Yet I would maintain that he was a liturgist, and a great one at that. As a historian he knew the liturgical history of the western church extremely well. So too the heritage of Lutheran liturgy. He constantly mentioned the liturgy in his lectures and went so far as to claim that the history of the liturgy was the core of church history.[3] He held that the liturgical movement was one of the great movements in the modern world and was most impressed by its contribution to the reform of the Roman Catholic Church.[4] Yet, for all that, he was not a liturgical historian. Rather, he was a liturgical theologian, for his whole theology was steeped in the liturgy and was concerned with the liturgy.

In my use of the term "liturgical theologian," I quite consciously recall the recent challenging book by David Fagerberg entitled *What is Liturgical Theology?*[5] In it he examines the work of Regin Prenter and Peter Brunner to discover whether they do justice to the liturgical character of all true theology. Now I do not intend to discuss this important book, nor do I wish to analyze Sasse in its light. But I do contend that Sasse was a liturgical theologian, a rare bird among modern Lutheran teachers of theology. From him I learnt to do theology liturgically, for he emphasized that the angelic praise of the Holy Trinity was "primary theology."[6]

Even though he reflected long and deeply on the liturgy, he did not produce any major works on liturgical theology. Apart from frequent references to the liturgy in his three main books on the sacraments, *Church and Lord's Supper* (1938), *This Is My Body* (1959) and *Corpus Christi* (1979), he wrote eight major essays on liturgical theology. They cover the following topics:

1. "The Lord's Supper in the Life of the Church" (1939)[7];
2. "The Lutheran Church and the Liturgical Movement"(1948);
3. "The Church of Prayer" (1949)[8];
4. "The Lutheran Understanding of the Consecration" (1952)[9];
5. "Word and Sacrament, Preaching and the Lord's Supper" (1956)[10];
6. "Consecration and the Real Presence" (1957)[11];
7. "The Remembrance of the Dead in the Liturgy" (1957)[12];
8. "Liturgy and Confession" (1959).[13]

While this represents only a fraction of his whole life work, I would maintain that these writings sketch out, all too briefly and piecemeal, what lay at the heart of his theological enterprise. Here we see Sasse at his most winsome. When he as a lecturer spoke on the theology of worship, or on its practice, or even on liturgical piety, his whole manner would change. The stern passion for truth and polemical edge to his teaching would give way to a sense of joy and sparkling wonder at the mystery of it all. As he spoke with unutterable and exalted joy on these topics, he won me over to his vision of heavenly worship and his conception of liturgical theology, unfashionable though it was. And this is what I would like to explore rather tentatively in this tribute to my late teacher at the anniversary of his birth.

I. The Real Presence as the Heart of the Liturgy

In 1939 Sasse addressed a rally at Nuremberg on "The Lord's Supper in the Life of the Church." In this address he maintained that the liturgy grew out of the Lord's Supper.[14] Now, while this may appear to be a sweeping historical generalization, such as he was often wont to make, it should rather be taken as a foundational theological assertion. Sasse knew that, historically, the Service of the Word was derived from the synagogue, just as the Lord's Supper had its antecedents in the sacrificial liturgy with its banquets at the temple. Yet, theologically, the liturgy was not an accidental conjunction of these two services. Rather, it was created by Christ's institution of the Lord's Supper and Christ's words about the presence of His body and blood in it.

While Sasse acknowledged that the church has had, and could have, many different services,[15] he held that the Lord's Supper was the Divine Service par excellence.[16] In fact, the Lord's Supper lay at the heart of Christian worship.[17] Without it every other act of worship was partial and incomplete. Every other act of worship gained its significance from its connection with the Lord's Supper, even when it was conducted apart from it.

If the Lord's Supper constituted the heart of Christian worship, the heart of the Lord's Supper was the presence of the risen Lord physically with His disciples in it. Like the sun with the planets in our solar system, the real presence of Christ shaped the liturgy, illuminated everything in it, and galvanized its operation. Apart from the real presence the liturgy no longer worked properly, nor did it make sense any more.[18] Apart from the real presence there was "no true liturgy."[19] Nor could there be, for the liturgy gained its life and power from Christ present and at work in it.

The Lord's Supper was indeed a ritual commemoration of Christ, but a commemoration with a difference in the history of ritual and religion. By its actual enactment it did not merely remember what Christ had done or would do; it did not merely represent what He had done or what He would do. Rather, it presented the risen Lord Jesus in His humanity and divinity entirely to the congregation.[20] So, even though the eucharistic liturgy recalled the past words and deeds of Jesus and anticipated His return in glory and the celebration of the messianic banquet in the age to come, the liturgy was not created either by remembrance or by hope. It was shaped by the presence of the risen Lord with His disciples and their faith in His presence with them. That came first. That gave shape and content to the Divine Service. Christ's real presence made Christian worship radically different from all other ritual enactments.[21] It gave the liturgy its unearthly beauty and its attractive power.[22] Apart from Christ's presence in the sacrament, the liturgy was an empty shell, a palace without a king. Those churches, therefore, which denied the real presence of Christ according to His humanity and divinity, could no longer understand and pray the liturgy properly.

Throughout his writing and teaching, Sasse never tired of drawing out the implications of this simple, and yet profound, mystery. Christ's real presence in the Sacrament alone accounted for the rise of Sunday as the Christian day of worship and the creation of a new liturgical calendar. Because the early Christians believed that the risen Lord had promised to give them His body and blood in the Sacrament, they assembled to celebrate the Lord's Supper on the first day of the week rather than on the Sabbath, or even on Thursday night, as precedent would require. Since the Sacrament was celebrated every Sunday, every Sunday was an Easter Sunday. The weekly celebration of Christ's resurrection was unthinkable without the enactment of the Sacrament.[23] And rightly so!

Sasse maintained that the earliest fragments of the eucharistic liturgy in the Scriptures and the references to it testified to the centrality of the real presence in Christian worship.[24] Already the pre-Pauline Aramaic church, as it gathered to receive the Sacrament, prayed: "Maran atha! Come Lord Jesus." By doing so, it acknowledged that the Christ who had come and who was to reappear in glory came to His own in the eucharistic meal.[25] So too did the holy kiss, the anathema and the salutation which are already found at the end of Paul's First Letter to the Corinthians.[26] The same applies to what we know about the liturgy from the apostolic fathers. It acclaimed the presence of the risen Lord with the Sanctus, Benedictus, and Agnus Dei. Most significantly, the faith of the early church in the real presence is evident in the great eucharistic prayers as well as the hymns of thanksgiving and praise which arose out of it.[27] These were prayed by the celebrant at the altar; they and everything else which happened in the Divine Service gained their significance from Christ's presence there.

Just as the real presence of the whole Christ in the Lord's Supper determined what happened in the liturgy, so it also established the eschatological significance and power of the Sacrament. Since the glorified Lord Jesus was physically present with His body and blood, He bridged the gap between heaven and earth and transcended the limits of time and space. By its participation in the Sacrament the church therefore stood together with the angels, as described in Rev. 4-5 and Heb. 12:22-24, and joined them in singing the Sanctus before the Triune God.[28] This needs to be understood in the light of the Jewish tradition which held that Israel would only join the angels in singing the heavenly Sanctus in the age to come. Through its risen Lord the church on earth, already now in this age, was united with the angels in heaven. Through His body and blood the faithful had access to heaven on earth, for, if Christ who was seated at the right hand of the Father was present in the Sacrament, then "the Lord's Supper is truly our heaven on earth until we enter heaven."[29] Because Christ is present there, "the altar of the church stands at the intersection between heaven and earth, time and eternity."[30]

Since the real presence of Christ with His humanity and divinity was presupposed by the liturgy, loss of faith in that teaching led, inevitably, to neglect of the traditional liturgy and its rejection for other less sacramental forms of worship. On the other hand, liturgical renewal had to begin with the rediscovery and recovery of the real presence and its significance in the Lutheran Church, as it had with the Roman Catholic Church in the first half of this century.[31] Unless it built on this foundation, it would accomplish little of lasting worth and fail to exercise spiritual power over modern people with their secular mentality.[32] In fact, any church which neglected the Sacrament would itself become secularized.[33] The restoration of the Sacrament to its proper place in the Divine Service was therefore a matter of life and death for the Lutheran Church.[34]

II. The Proclamation of the Gospel in the Liturgy

At a conference for pastors in Australia a paper was given on preaching. The discussion which followed focused on whether it was always necessary to preach both Law and Gospel in every sermon. A seminary professor declared, rather vehemently, that he always preached about the Gospel in every sermon. At this Sasse got up, shuffled to the microphone and stunned the audience by saying:

> Never in all my life have I preached about the Gospel in any sermon. And I will never preach about the Gospel as long as I live. I have always and will always proclaim the Gospel.

That for me sums up Sasse's understanding of the Gospel. The Gospel was, for him, always an enactment, a performative utterance. And so, even though he often taught as he preached, he always spoke in such a way that Christ spoke through him to grant forgiveness and all His gifts to the faithful.

For Sasse the liturgy was rooted and grounded in the Gospel.[35] It existed to enact and proclaim and confess the eternal Gospel of Christ. The right understanding of the Gospel was therefore the criterion by which the Lutheran Church, beginning with Luther himself in his reform of the Mass and the creation of the German Mass, has always evaluated the liturgy and all liturgical innovations.[36] The concern for the Gospel led Sasse, like Luther before him, to reject the inclusion of the words of institution as a subordinate clause in the eucharistic prayer and to criticize any eucharistic prayers which did so.[37] The liturgy depended on the Gospel. Without the Gospel it could not possibly survive, because it drew its life from the Gospel and existed entirely for the Gospel.

It is true that the Gospel could exist and did exist apart from the liturgy as a word of witness and as missionary preaching to the world.[38] But all such proclamation of the Gospel in evangelism reached its fulfillment and goal in the baptism of its hearers and their incorporation into the liturgical assembly. Apart from the Sacrament of Baptism the message of the Gospel would be taken by its hearers as a new kind of religious philosophy and lead at best to the creation of societies for spiritual self-development.[39] The proclamation of the Gospel did not merely initiate people into the Divine Service of the church but found its proper place in the service of the church. Sasse drove this point home dramatically to us on one occasion by referring to the location of the pulpit between the font and the altar in the church. In preaching, he said, the pastor led people first to the font and then from the font to the altar. Preaching was therefore not an end in itself but a means to an end. In the sermon the pastor spoke from God's presence in the sanctuary. He brought Christ to the people and the people to Christ. The preaching of the Gospel therefore took place in the liturgy, because it could not be separated from what happened in baptism or the absolution or the Lord's Supper.

For Sasse, as for Luther, the Gospel was always pluriform. It was proclaimed in a number of different ways in the liturgy. It was not just the message about what God had done or what He would yet do but was also the announcement of what the Triune God was actually doing for the faithful in the liturgical assembly. The Gospel was always enacted and proclaimed in the presence of the risen Lord. It could not exist apart from His presence with His people, for He made Himself and His gifts available through the Gospel. So the Gospel was pluriform, because it proclaimed Christ's varied activity in worship.

The Gospel came to the faithful in a twofold way, verbally through the pronouncement of the absolution, the reading of the Scriptures, and the preaching of God's Word in the sermon, and sacramentally through the enactment of Baptism and the reception of Christ's body and blood in the Sacrament.[40] Sasse went so far as to claim that the risen Lord Jesus continued His ministry of word and deed through the preaching of the Gospel and enactment of the sacraments. He says:

> As the church's preaching of the Word, if it be the preaching of the pure simple Gospel, is nothing else but the continuation of Jesus' preaching, so his saving activity also continues in the right administration of the sacraments.[41]

In the liturgy Christ therefore ministers to both body and soul, for He came to save both, and both are destined for resurrection to eternal life.

Sasse often dealt with the essential connection between the preaching of God's Word and the celebration of the Sacrament in the liturgy. Both illuminated and empowered each other. If either was divorced from the other, or malformed in any way, both were distorted and disempowered. Both then ceased to proclaim the Gospel; neither communicated Christ as Savior to the faithful.[42] The Gospel could only be taught purely and proclaimed effectually where the Sacrament was celebrated rightly in connection with it.[43] Apart from the Lord's Supper the preacher could all too easily forget Christ and cease to proclaim salvation through His death on the cross.

On the one hand, there could be no true preaching of the Gospel apart from the Lord's Supper. Wherever the Gospel is proclaimed apart from the Lord's Supper, it is dissociated from the presence of the incarnate, crucified, and exalted Lord. Without the Sacrament Christ becomes a figure of ancient history whose teachings must be observed, and whose example must be emulated; the great Christological doctrines cease to affirm realities and become concepts instead; the sacrifice of Christ for our justification and reconciliation becomes an idea to be grasped rather than an event in which we were, and still are, involved. Without the regular celebration of the Sacrament, preaching degenerates into speculative religious discourse or the sharing of religious experiences.[44] Through such preaching people hear about redemption without participating in it.[45] The sermon no longer proclaims the Gospel,[46] but propagates a Christian ideology.[47] Without the Lord's Supper the Gospel becomes just another religious message, one option among many, without anything unique about it.[48]

On the other hand, the Lord's Supper could not exist apart from the preaching of the Gospel. It was in fact instituted to proclaim Christ and the Gospel,[49] for its content is the Gospel of Christ crucified for our sins and raised for our justification.[50] The sermon is meant to proclaim who is present in the Sacrament and what He offers there. It initiates the faithful into the mystery of the Sacrament and unfolds its riches. Without the right preaching of the Gospel the Lord's Supper becomes an incomprehensible, obscure, and misunderstood rite.[51] Unless the celebration of the Sacrament is accompanied by the preaching of the Gospel, it readily ceases to be understood evangelically as God's gracious gift to sinners and is instead regarded as a human offering to God, as in the Roman Catholic Church and in some branches of liberal Protestantism. Right preaching prevents the degeneration of the Sacrament into cultic mysticism and Christian magic.[52] So then, the Sacrament must be accompanied by preaching if it is to be celebrated evangelically and received eucharistically by the faithful.

Both preaching and the Sacrament of the Altar are properly conjoined in the divine service.[53] They accompany each other, just as the preaching of Jesus was accompanied by the performance of signs and wonders.[54] In both the same Christ is present and active in different and yet complementary ways. Both together proclaim the same Gospel and confess the same faith in the whole Christ present with those who assemble around His altar.

III. Liturgy as Prayer

Sasse held that the ancient world differed from modern western societies in its attitude to prayer. Everybody prayed in the ancient world, but we live in a world which no longer prays, because it no longer believes in the power of prayer. Indeed many people can no longer pray.[55] And that has affected the church profoundly. It has created a crisis in modern Christianity, for we now have Christians, pastors and even churches which no longer pray. Unless that changed, all the many attempts to renew the church would accomplish nothing.

In the book *Corpus Christi* Sasse notes that people have always asked and still ask: "What does the church actually do?" He answers the question most simply: "The church prays."[56] That is its main calling.[57] By praying for itself and the world it makes its unique contribution to the world. By praying in the name of Jesus, it does what it alone can do.[58] The church is nothing else than the assembly of the faithful as they gather in prayer around the Lord's table.[59] At the altar the faithful not only prayed the Marana tha, the Sanctus and the Eucharistic Thanksgiving but also brought before their heavenly Father their intercession for the church and the world. All unbelievers and even the candidates for baptism were excluded from this part of the service, because it was the prayer of the faithful; it could be done only by them.[60]

The church is a liturgical community.[61] As a liturgical community it prays. And the whole community is involved in its praying. That is how it was right from the beginning of the church.[62] After the ascension of Jesus the believers joined together in constant prayer (Acts 1:14). After Pentecost those who were baptized devoted themselves with the faithful to the apostles' teaching, to the offering of gifts, to the breaking of bread in Holy Communion and to intercessory prayer (Acts 2:42). Intercessory prayer was therefore one of the four main parts in the liturgy.[63] The early church was a church at prayer. As a praying community it made such impact on its social environment that all people were filled with awe at it (Acts 2:43).

The early church dealt with the problems before it by praying. When it was faced with the challenge of evangelizing to the whole world, it did not establish missionary societies or organize a program for the systematic evangelization of each nation in turn; nor did it write tracts on evangelism to encourage its members to be evangelists. Instead, it celebrated the Sacrament and engaged in constant prayer. As a result, the Lord added daily to their number (Acts 2:47). It did the same when Peter was imprisoned (Acts 12:5). And how did it deal with the pressing political problems of its day, such as the Roman occupation of Palestine and the later threat to the security of the Roman Empire from barbarian invasions? It did not organize seminars and conferences to discuss the role of the church in the world; instead it prayed without ceasing and sang its hymns of praise. And none of these prayers was in vain. They reached heaven and changed the world.[64] By praying, the church made its unique contribution to the world. And it still does so!

In his splendid essay, "Ecclesia Orans" ("The Church of Prayer," 1949), Sasse spells out in some detail the liturgical practice and theological significance of the service of intercession in the liturgy. First, he emphasizes that it is the prayer of the whole congregation.[65] Since all Christians have received the gift of the Holy Spirit in Baptism and are therefore all saints, they all equally stand in the presence of the Triune God and are all equally involved in the act of intercession.[66] The oldest fragments of these prayers, which have come down to us from the early church, show us how the whole congregation was quite deliberately involved in the prayer of the church. Commonly, a deacon would announce a topic for prayer and invite all to pray. This was followed by a period of silence for personal prayer. Then the celebrant would lead the whole congregation in intercession and the congregation would affirm it as its prayer by a final Amen. It was therefore not considered the prayer of the celebrant for the congregation but the prayer of the congregation for the world. And nothing was excluded from its scope. By it the church brought the whole human race with all its varied needs and sins before the Triune God. In it the faithful people of God prayed for all branches of government, the whole church throughout the world, and the needs of all people including themselves. The prayer of the church was therefore always corporate and inclusive.

Secondly, the prayer of the church was connected with its faith in Christ.[67] It was prayed in the name of Jesus. That alone distinguished it from the prayer of the synagogue. That gave the prayer of the church such power that it shook the world. Well, what is meant by prayer in the name of Jesus? It presupposes that the risen Lord who has received all power in heaven and earth is present in the liturgical assembly.[68] As the high priest who intercedes for the faithful before his Father, He joined them in their worship and led them in their prayers. Christ then was their chief liturgist. Through Him and together with Him they approached God the Father in petition and intercession, in thanksgiving and adoration. He prayed for them and with them. As they joined with Him in prayer, He took up their prayers and made them His own.

This reality is best expressed by the salutation in the liturgy.[69] Here is how Sasse explains it:

> "The Lord be with you": this introductory salutation of the bishop expresses the wish of the congregation that the Lord Jesus may now pray with it and make its prayer His own. The Head of this Body prays together with the Body. The response "And with thy spirit" expresses the wish of the congregation to the minister who leads the prayer that the Lord may pray together with him, make his prayer His own, so that the prayer rises up before God's throne "through Jesus Christ our Lord."[70]

The Father cannot but hear and answer such prayer, for it comes from and reaches into the Trinity. It is not only offered by the Son to the Father; it is also empowered by the Holy Spirit who prays within the saints. So, when prayer is made in the name of Jesus, the whole congregation, led by the celebrant, joins its risen Lord in His intercession for the church and the world. Such prayer is truly evangelical. By it the church recognizes that it is not as it should be and relies totally on the mercy of God for its life and for the salvation of the world. It even depends on the Lord Jesus and the Holy Spirit to bring its prayer to the heavenly Father.[71] By its prayer the church confesses its faith in the Triune God, practically and concretely.

The prayer of the church is today even more misunderstood and neglected than when Sasse wrote his powerful essay on it in 1949. We would therefore do well to heed his impassioned plea:

> Fear has not come upon one single soul because of Amsterdam, Bethel, and Leipzig, because of the Ecumenical Council of Churches, the EKiD and the VELK, and not because of the College of Cardinals either. For only the praying Church which moves heaven and earth with her prayer, even when outwardly she has to go down in defeat in the process, could

and might effect truly world-shattering changes in this century. The praying Church . . . is a power which shakes the social and political world of our century, because in her and in her alone He is present unto whom all power in heaven and earth is given. The life of the Lutheran Church in this century depends on this, whether she again will become a praying Church . . . in the sense of Luther and the Lutheran Reformation.[72]

We still have a long way to go before that is so! The stress on the presence and work of Christ in Word and Sacrament as the heart of our liturgy will accomplish little unless we again learn to pray the liturgy and use the liturgy to intercede for the world.

IV. Conclusion

In many respects Sasse, like Luther, could be regarded as a liturgical conservative out of touch with the temper of his time. While he repeatedly argued for the freedom of the church from all kinds of liturgical legalism, he had no time for liturgical experimentation.[73] He always taught us that we should use our freedom in a catholic way to retain the best of the past and affirm our continuity with the church of all ages.[74] In contrast to most modern church men and women, he maintained that the oldest liturgies were the best.[75] Paradoxically, the greatest freedom for individual Christians lay in the use of the old forms, because they were catholic and not idiosyncratic; they did not demand uniformity of experience or piety. Just because they were objective and because they expressed what all Christians had in common, they were capacious and inclusive.

Sasse regarded the liturgy as the common property of the whole church. I still remember one occasion when a student argued that each pastor and congregation was free to adapt the liturgy to local circumstances. In response to this suggestion Sasse thundered in full fury that the liturgy did not belong to any pastor or any worship committee or any congregation; it was the liturgy of the church. Since it belonged to the church, only the church could change it. And then only for some good reason.

In making assertions such as these, Sasse was, however, not motivated either by blind conservatism or high church romanticism. No one could be more contemptuous of both these movements than Sasse himself. Rather, the reason for his reverence for the liturgy lay in his conviction about the connection of the liturgy of the church to its confession of faith.[76] For him they were as inseparable from each other, as husband and wife in marriage. In both cases divorce was equally disastrous. What the church confessed as its faith determined how it worshipped. And vice versa! Dogma was always prayed before it was formulated abstractly.[77] By its worship the church therefore expressed and confessed its faith before the world. Since the liturgy of the church was determined by its confession of faith, contempt for the liturgy and disregard of it usually stemmed from the rejection of what was confessed in it.[78] The most serious charge that could possibly be laid against any theologian was the lack of understanding for liturgy.[79]

Now, if Sasse was right in this, and I believe that he was, we, like most confessional churches in the English-speaking world, are in deep trouble. Many Lutheran congregations are no longer at home in the Lutheran liturgy which is, as Sasse so often told us, the catholic liturgy of the western churches. While some congregations alter it carelessly and substantially for no better reason than to introduce variety in worship, others reject it for sectarian liturgies derived from non-sacramental churches. And all that in the name of the Gospel and evangelism! If Sasse were with us today, he would no doubt castigate us for our folly in believing that we could still retain our Lutheran substance when we had adopted revivalist, Baptist and Pentecostal forms of worship. But he would also urge us not to lose nerve, for every crisis is an opportunity for repentance and renewal. The church learns from its mistakes. Like a body it develops antibodies against spiritual sickness by suffering that sickness. Sasse may not be old-fashioned and irrelevant in his theology after all. Sasse's greatest contribution to the Lutheran Church of the third millennium may be that, stimulated by him, we rediscover the inseparable connection of the liturgy with confession and dogma and so develop a Lutheran liturgical theology, as the decline of individualism in our post-modernist society gives way to a renewed interest in ritual and ceremony.[80]

I do not, however, wish to end on that sober note but rather, as befits Sasse's own theology of worship, with a note of eschatological joy from his own pen. First, he says:

> the liturgy ... is an anticipation of the eternal worship which goes on in heaven.[81]

And then in conclusion, a somewhat longer passage:

> ... there is worship with indescribable joy in heaven and on earth. Actually it is *one* worship, for the same Sanctus resounds in heaven as on earth. ... To sing this Sanctus in the presence of God and His Christ with new tongues, to pray it with new power, that must be the goal of any renewal of Church worship, and of any liturgical work. It is the theological task of the Lutheran Church—a task which she can carry out only insofar as she has preserved the pure Gospel—to discover anew for herself and for the whole of Christendom what comfort it brings, to be able to sing and confess with the true Church of all ages: *Tu* solus sanctus (*You* alone are holy).[82]

Notes

[1] "The Lutheran Church and the Liturgical Movement" (1948), *S&C*, 33-46. See also *SS*, 131.

[2] *ISC* II:65-73; *RTR* 16.3 (1957): 65-75. See also "Lent and the Christian Life," *Lutheran Herald* (11 March 1961), 68-69.

[3] *Z*, 23.

[4] See "The Lutheran Church and the Liturgical Movement," *S&C*, 33-46.

[5] David W. Fagerberg, *What is Liturgical Theology? A Study in Methodology* (Collegeville, MN: Liturgical Press), 1992.

[6] *SS*, 133.

[7] *S&C*, 4-11.

[8] "Ecclesia Orans," *ISC* II:56-64. Ralph Gehrke's translation in *Quartalschrift* 48.2 (April 1951): 81-96 has been reprinted in *Logia* 2.2 (Eastertide 1993): 28-33.

[9] *WCS*, 113-38.

[10] *WCS*, 11-35.

[11] *S&C*, 272-317.

[12] *ISC* II:74-91.

[13] "Liturgie und Bekenntnis. Brüderliche Warnung vor 'hochkirchlichen' Gefahren," *LB* 11 (Christmas 1959): 92-104.

[14] *S&C*, 11.

[15] "Ecclesia Orans," *ISC* II:58.

[16] "The Lord's Supper in the Life of the Church," *S&C*, 11; "The Lutheran Understanding of the Consecration," *WCS*, 138.

[17] *K&H*, 23; "The Lord's Supper in the Life of the Church," *S&C*, 11.

[18] *K&H*, 16.

[19] "Ecclesia Orans," *ISC* II:64.

[20] "Die Gegenwart Christi und die Zukunft der Kirche" (1938), *ISC* II:17.

[21] *CC*, 92.

[22] "The Lutheran Church and the Liturgical Movement," *S&C*, 43.

[23] "The Lord's Supper in the New Testament" (1941), *WCS*, 88.

[24] *K&H*, 29-30.

[25] Ibid., 28-33.

[26] "Consecration and the Real Presence," *S&C*, 292f.; *TMB*, 396, 399; *CC*, 20f.; *Z*, 55.

[27] "The Lord's Supper in the Life of the Church," *S&C*, 11; *CC*, 24.

[28] "The Lutheran Church and the Liturgical Movement," *S&C*, 44f.; *Z*, 60f.; *SS*, 133.

[29] "The Lord's Supper in the Life of the Church," *S&C*, 9.

[30] *CC*, 92; my trans.

[31] "The Lutheran Church and the Liturgical Movement," *S&C*, 43; "Der Schriftgrund der lutherischen Abendmahlslehre" (1952), *ISC* I:114; "The Lutheran Understanding of the Consecration," *WCS*, 138.

[32] *K&H*, 34f.

[33] Ibid., 67.

[34] "The Lutheran Understanding of the Consecration," *WCS*, 120.

[35] "The Lutheran Church and the Liturgical Movement," *S&C*, 40.

[36] "The Lord's Supper in the Life of the Church," *S&C*, 39; "The Lutheran Understanding of the Consecration," *WCS*, 117; *TMB*, 95, 104.

[37] "Consecration and the Real Presence," *S&C*, 301f.; "Liturgie und Bekenntnis," *LB* 11 (1959): 103.

[38] "Die Gegenwart Christi und die Zukunft der Kirche" (1938), *ISC* II:14.

[39] "The Lord's Supper in the Life of the Church," *S&C*, 4.

[40] "Word and Sacrament, Preaching and the Lord's Supper," *WCS*, 24-26.

[41] "The Lord's Supper in the Life of the Church," *S&C*, 5.

[42] Ibid., 12.

[43] *K&H*, 79.

[44] "Die Gegenwart Christi und die Zukunft der Kirche," *ISC* II:17; "The Lutheran Church and the Liturgical Movement," *S&C*, 46.

[45] "The Lord's Supper in the New Testament," *WCS*, 88.

[46] "The Lutheran Understanding of the Consecration," *WCS*, 121.

[47] "The Lord's Supper in the Life of the Church," *S&C*, 4.

[48] "Word and Sacrament, Preaching and the Lord's Supper," *WCS*, 26.

[49] Ibid., 25.

[50] Ibid., 121.

[51] Ibid., 121.

[52] *K&H*, 79.

[53] *WCS*, 31, 34.

[54] *WCS*, 137; cf. *S&C*, 5.

[55] *ISC* II:58.

[56] *CC*, 23.

[57] *ISC* II:57.

[58] Ibid., 61.

[59] *S&C*, 37.

[60] *ISC* II:59.

[61] Ibid., 58.

[62] *CC*, 23.

[63] Cf. ibid., 15.

[64] Ibid., 24.

[65] *ISC* II:59f.

[66] Ibid., 61.

[67] Ibid., 60-62.

[68] Ibid., 63.

[69] *Z*, 164.

[70] *ISC* II:60; my trans.

[71] Ibid., 61.

[72] Ibid., 63; my trans.

[73] "Bekenntnis und Liturgie," *Freimund* 81:456-58; *K&H*, 34; *WCS*, 33f.; *S&C*, 291.

[74] *WCS*, 117.

[75] *Freimund* 81:457.

[76] "Bekenntnis und Liturgie"; "On the Nature of the Church's Confession," *LTJ* 2 (1968): 89; *WCS*, 117.

[77] *S&C*, 41, 279; *LB* 11 (1959): 92f.; *SS*, 131f.

[78] "Der Schriftgrund der lutherischen Abendmahlslehre," *ISC* I:101f.

[79] *S&C*, 42.

[80] *WCS*, 114.

[81] "Tradition and Confession," *Lutheran World* 4:78.

[82] Cf. *S&C*, 44.

The Confessing Church: Catholic and Apostolic

Thomas M. Winger

Sasse's Ecclesiology?

Perhaps it was foolhardy to accept the task of addressing Hermann Sasse's ecclesiology, his doctrine of the church. Yet, having a long-standing interest in the heated 19th-century debate on *Kirche und Amt* ("Church and Office of the Ministry"), I was excited by the prospect. Sasse himself was deeply interested in the German and American contexts of this battle, and was fond of citing its most significant early writing: Wilhelm Löhe's *Drei Bücher von der Kirche* ("Three Books on the Church"): "They are all talking about the Church; everybody feels that 'Church' is not merely a name." But that "the Church" could serve as a title for his **entire** life and work, this fact had escaped my attention until it was brought to mind by Dr. Ronald Feuerhahn as he introduced one essay in the recently published collection:

> If Professor Sasse was a theologian of the means of grace and particularly of the Sacrament of the Altar, he was also, and perhaps even first, a theologian of church and ministry. That means to imply that he was aware of the interrelatedness of these subjects: when the church addresses the doctrine of the sacraments, the doctrines of the church and ministry will also be discussed.[1]

In another essay in the same collection, Sasse himself comments: "The liturgical movement is therefore really a seeking and a questing for the church."[2] If all these things—the Sacrament of the Altar, the Holy Ministry, the Divine Liturgy—if all these are really about the Church, then what have I got myself into?

Of course, that's not the point. This moment of despair, this failing to isolate the doctrine of the Church within Sasse's thought, is not only the inevitable failure of category thinking, but also the moment when Sasse is truly understood. For on the basis of the Augsburg Confession (AC) VII Lutherans confess that the Church is not found apart from the

Gospel being purely preached and the sacraments administered according to the Gospel. While Calvin and his Reformed children may locate the church in the elect people without regard for their outward association with the means of grace, AC VII refuses to separate the believers from those gifts which create and sustain their faith. The Church is **believers who are gathered around those means of grace**. You can't have one without the other. Sasse often noted that this Reformed **separation** of the invisible church (the "true believers") from the visible church (the "outward institution") was at the root of the ecumenical movement's faulty ecclesiology: the desire to base union on what is invisible, on the faith of the heart, rather than on consensus in the Gospel and the sacraments according to AC VII. For Sasse would agree with Löhe's illustration: the hiddenness of the church (considered by faith) and the visibility of the church (the marks which locate her, the means of grace) are simply two sides of the same coin. The movement would fail to achieve true unity as long as it neglected the latter.

Confession Defines the Church

For Sasse, the means of grace definition of the Church always returned him to the **confession** of those means. And so it is that I too am compelled today to focus on this particular theme: the Church and her confession. In April 1993 my wife and I were visiting friends in Germany. We spent a week in a small town south of Freiburg, in the home of a young pastor in the *Badische Freikirche*. One afternoon he came home from visiting an old pastor in his parish with a gift for me: the two volumes of *In Statu Confessionis*, the classic collection of Sasse essays. Inside the dust jacket of volume one was carefully preserved the cover of *Lutherische Blätter* from August 1976, the month after Sasse's death. The journal which published his essays for over thirty years remembered him with this dedication:

Thus says the Lord:
"Whoever now confesses Me before men, him will I also confess before My Heavenly Father." Matt. 10:32

. . . Over the life and death of him who is now perfected stands the confession of the Third Article:

> I have believed in the Holy Spirit,
> One Holy Christian Church,
> the communion of saints,
> the forgiveness of sins,
> the resurrection of the body
> and the life everlasting.³

At the moment of his death, his life was remembered as **confession**.

In the author's introduction to volume one of *In Statu Confessionis*, Sasse himself recalls his "conversion" from the undogmatic, *religionsgeschichtliche* theology, which he learned at the Berlin university, to true Lutheran confessionalism. Awakened by Karl Barth's call back to orthodoxy, Sasse's generation turned to Scripture and confessions:

> What we learned about the confession of the Church in the years after the First World War, in the study of Holy Scripture, in which the first confessions of the Church stand, and of the Lutheran Confessions, whose relevance became ever clearer to us in the years of the incipient church struggle from 1929/30, in the practical work of the pastoral office in those critical years for Germany, in meeting with the American churches and then in the ecumenical movement, in lively exchange with the colleagues of our generation in conferences and study groups [*Arbeitskreisen*], from which later arose what was called the "Confessing Church," all of that was put to the test when the Hitler era began.⁴

Thus Sasse describes the period in his life from 1918 to 1933 as a quest for the confession of the Church. Perhaps we may understand his words to mean that from the war until his American visit in 1925-26 he was preoccupied with the Scriptures. This was the time when he pursued his graduate work in New Testament, producing what would later become articles in Kittel's *Wörterbuch*. The American visit then renewed his commitment to the historic Lutheran Confessions. But through it all, this stress on confession has drawn him into the doctrine of the Church. In 1930 he wrote:

> This however is clear, that from this point on the question about the confession takes on a new importance. In the instant when in place of "Christian religion" the Church steps into the center of theological thought, the confession must also experience renewed evaluation.⁵

Church and confession, inseparably together.

"Jesus is Lord": Scriptural Foundation for the Confession

One phrase in the "autobiography" cited a moment ago is of particular interest: "the study of the Holy Scripture, **in which the first confessions of the Church stand**." Has Sasse subordinated the Scriptures to the Church? Does he follow Barth in reducing Scripture to a witness of the Church at that time? No, rather the opposite. His concern is to demonstrate that the Church's eternal confession is rooted in the confession which she received from her Lord in the Holy Scriptures. In 1930, as the Lutheran Church celebrated the 400th anniversary of the Augsburg Confession, Sasse produced two major writings explaining this scriptural foundation.[6] These come to a certain maturity in his *Second Letter to Lutheran Pastors* in 1948.[7] This theological foundation would equip him to diagnose the Barthian errors which later would lead to Barmen.

Modern Protestantism, rooted in the individualism of this age, conceives of confession only as an "I believe." The Church's confession to them is simply the agglomeration of individual, subjective statements of faith. Sasse writes that "modern Protestants can think of the genesis of a creed only in such a way that a large number of individuals assemble and formulate a confession in which a minimum of creedal statements are made, namely those in which all agree."[8] The influence of this modern subjectivism is found even in the Missouri Synod's own explanation of Luther's Catechism, where the question stands concerning the Apostles' Creed: "Why do we say 'I believe,' and not 'We believe'? Everyone must believe for himself or herself; no one can be saved by another's faith."[9] Sasse confesses on the contrary that "I [can] believe" only because the confession has been **given** to me by the Holy Spirit. The interchange of "I" and "we" in the Church's liturgy and confessions is an acknowledgment that the Spirit "has called **me** by the Gospel, . . . in like manner as He calls, gathers, enlightens and sanctifies **the whole Christian Church** on earth, and keeps it with Jesus Christ in the one true faith."[10] The confession is a gift to both. "The *credo* of the baptismal confession and the *pisteuomen* of the symbols of the synods and the early liturgical creeds belong together."[11] In fact, the "I believe" is a confession by the individual of the **Church's** confession into which he has been baptized: "In it [the creed, or confession of the Church] speaks not an individual Christian, but the Church of Christ, and if/when an individual expresses it, then he does so as a member of the Church and in the name of the Church."[12]

Thus when Sasse posits the question of the origin of the Church's confession, he answers that it does not begin with the individual's faith—as if the *fides qua* could produce the *fides quae*. It does not originate in the armchair theologian's need to speculate on metaphysical truths. Nor does the Church's confession even arise out of controversy, as theologians come together to make a common statement against heresy. If this were the case, then confession would not be of the Church's essence, but only of relative use insofar as the Church is confronted with error. No, Sasse answers:

> [T]he formation of creeds did not begin because of the initiative of men, but because of the will and deed of the Lord of the church. It was Jesus Christ Himself who asked His disciples, "Who do men say that I the Son of Man am?" and who then pressed the question home with the demand for an unequivocal answer: "But who do you say that I am?" Because of this question from the sixteenth chapter of Matthew, ... it is Jesus Himself who originated the formation of creeds and who therefore, if one will have it so, is the founder of Christian dogmatics. ... Therefore the church's confession is in its innermost nature an answer to a question. It is the answer of faith to the question posed by the appearance of Jesus Christ, the question: Who is He? ... No man can escape giving an answer to this question, be that answer what it may. And the confessions of the church seek to be nothing more than an answer to that same question.[13]

Because the confession originates with Christ, because the content of the confession is the gift of the Holy Spirit's revelation, there is no necessary distinction between the "I confess" and the "we confess." Both are gifts. Peter may speak **personally** in Matthew 16, but the question was, "Who do you **(plural)** say that I am?" Not long after, Peter speaks on behalf of **all** the disciples, "**We** believe and are confident that you are the Holy One of God" (Jn 6:69). There need be no contradiction, for this confession is not his own creation or possession. Christ's response to Peter highlights this: "Blessed are you Simon, son of Jonah, for flesh and blood has not revealed this to you, but my Father in heaven" (Mt. 16:17). Here in the receiving and giving of the confession the Church is born.

The confession becomes immediately the confession of the whole circle of disciples. And it is no accident that now, after the first confession has been rendered, the Church is mentioned for the first time: "You are Peter, and upon this rock I will build my *Ecclesia.*" **Confession and church belong together.**"[14]

The earliest creeds of the Church then simply unfold the truth of this scriptural confession, "Jesus is Lord." So also do the Reformation-era confessions merely safeguard the meaning of these foundational creeds in the face of recurrent heresy—they are never a "new" confession. This "eternal unity" of the Church's confession Sasse maintains in the face of Karl Barth's relativism. He was particularly fond of quoting Barth's description of the Reformed confession:

> A Reformed confession is a setting forth of the understanding that **for the time being** has been given to the universal Christian church concerning that revelation of God in Jesus Christ which is given only in Scripture, an understanding that has been formulated spontaneously and publicly by a **locally circumscribed** communion of Christians which **until further developments** guides its doctrine and life.[15]

Sasse's analysis easily exposes the *hic et nunc* nature of Barth's confessionalism as subjectivism, founding the Church's confession on the individual's personal confession of faith in his particular situation. As experience varies, so does the confession. One need read no farther than the title of Barth's series of writings, *Theologische Existenz heute* ("theological existence today"), to confirm this evaluation.

In a typically Lutheran manner, Sasse designates this Barthian theme as *Schwärmerei* ("enthusiasm"). It rests on the notion of continual revelation, which Barth draws from John 16:13, "He [the Spirit] will guide you into all truth." Sasse responds that the fulfillment of this passage is the Day of Pentecost. To interpret it otherwise would be to deny the divinely appointed means of grace, to which the Spirit has bound himself, as the Smalcald Articles confess. When the Church's confession is firmly anchored in the revelation of Christ, it abides by the same once-and-for-all-ness as Christ himself. "Thus one can designate confession as **the response to revelation**, and that means the revelation which happened once and for all in history."[16] The Christian faith is an historical faith; the church's confession always looks back into history.

> "[*Das Wahre steht schon längst gefunden*] What is true has been already discovered long ago" stands invisibly written over everything. For this reason the baptismal symbol is back-dated to the apostles, the *Constantinopolitanum* to Nicea, and the *Quicunque* to Athanasius. Accordingly, the Augustana begins with the confirmation of the *decretum Nicaenae synodi*. For modern man this is one of the most difficult stumbling-blocks. He can only conceive of a confession which completely serves the present, and averts its eyes as much as possible from history and its "facts of salvation [*Heilstatsachen*]," a confession which expresses the religious experience of present-day man and if possible a "present-day revelation."[17]

Sasse could hardly attack Barth's notion of the "existential confession" more pointedly.

In contrast to this ephemeral, pragmatic "confessing," the universal, unchanging confession of the Church operates always in three directions. First:

> As **the Church's answer** to revelation, the confession is directed **at God**. Therefore it takes its place in the divine service of the congregation, it belongs to the liturgy. All the great, primitive confessions can be prayed.[18]

Though the great dogmatic confessions of the Reformation era have this property only in places (such as Luther's catechisms), they presume the classic creeds and their use in the liturgy. The confession of the Church is meant to be **used**. Secondly, her confession is directed at the world.

> In giving her answer to revelation, the Church delimits herself over against everything which stands outside of the Church. The great task of the confession is **the separation [*Scheidung*] of truth and error, of Church and not-church.**[19]

Already in the New Testament the confession "Jesus is Lord" separated, yes excluded, the Christians both from the synagogue and from the Hellenistic mystery religions, as well as from the emperor cult. And thirdly:

> as the confession separates the Church from foreign religions, so it separates—that is moreover its task—[it separates] within Christendom

truth from error, **pure teaching** from **heresy**, the **Church** from the **sect**. ... This boundary marking [*Grenzsetzung*] between truth and error belongs to the essence of the confession.[20]

Sasse was all too familiar with the charges of "unchristian lovelessness" constantly raised against this firm confessional stand. He heard the charges that we today must overcome the polemical era and return to the "golden age" of love and unity in the early church.[21] But, he responds, even the Apostles' Creed directs itself in every line against heresy—as does the New Testament confession "Jesus is Lord" itself. He has been keen to demonstrate that this exclusionary function of confession is by divine gift and mandate, and thus is of the Church's essence.

Confession in the Ecumenical Movement

In contrast to Barth's relativism, the scriptural confession claims eternal truth; it is given to the universal Church. In these years, this thesis was the foundation of Sasse's involvement in the ecumenical movement—and the ecumenical movement was the proving ground of his confessionalism. As we have heard, Sasse was prominent on the world stage at a remarkably young age. Already at the World Conference on Faith and Order at Lausanne (1927) Sasse was active, writing the official German report of the meeting. As Ronald Feuerhahn notes:

> He was fond of recalling the opening words of the Bishop of Bombay's address to the Lausanne conference which introduced Subject V, on the Church's Ministry:
>
> > In this address I make several assumptions. It will be unintelligible unless I state them. They are these:
> > 1. This is a Conference about truth, not about reunion ... agreement about truth would be one of the firmest foundations for unity.
>
> The emphasis on truth in three of Bishop Palmer's four assumptions prompted Sasse's abiding admiration.[22]

Faith in this "Lausanne principle" was the reason Sasse would stay active for so long. His "withdrawal" from the ecumenical stage would come as it moved away from this quest for truth—a confessional quest—in favor of a reckless drive for unity. Sasse recognized a decisive change at Lund (1952), for which reason he would often parody Bishop Palmer with his own "Lund principle": "This is a conference about reunion, not about truth."[23]

He was also fond of citing the 1920 appeal of the Eastern Orthodox through the Ecumenical Patriarchate for a federative conference of Christians, a league of churches.[24] From the very beginning of their involvement in the ecumenical movement, the Orthodox have seen their role as confessors. "Whatever concessions the Eastern Orthodox Churches have made in their membership in the World Council of Churches [WCC], they have never compromised on doctrine."[25] Their participation is "not to negotiate and to compromise on doctrine, but to testify to the truth which has been entrusted to her as the true church of Christ."[26] He has similar respect for the Roman Catholic Church's stand on the truth, which she took by not participating in the WCC. Sasse firmly held that the only possibility of union lay in the confessional route: on the basis of truth, not in its avoidance; on the basis of divine revelation, not on subjective experience and opinion.[27] That the WCC chose another route would be to Sasse's deep disappointment, and the object of his mature criticism:

> Here lies the deepest problem of the W.C.C. It does not and cannot see that within Christendom there are not only differences which may be overcome by discussions, but also heresies which never will give way to the truth voluntarily and which must be excluded from the Church.[28]

"Deutsche Christen," "Bekennende Kirche," and the Nazi Regime

The second great challenge to Sasse's "confessional ecumenism" came from the events of the Nazi era. Sasse's role in these events can only be understood on the basis of how he saw the Church's confession. Already in 1920 Hitler had published his views on the role of the Church in his Nationalist program. The famous 24th article of "The Program of the National Socialist German Workers' Party" (Munich, 24 February 1920) reads in part:

> We demand liberty for all religious confessions in the State, in so far as they do not in any way endanger its existence or do not offend the moral

sentiment and the customs of the Germanic race. The party as such represents the standpoint of "positive Christianity" without bending itself confessionally to a particular faith.[29]

Hitler proclaimed in his nationalist agenda that he hoped to stir up this "positive Christianity" to support his agenda, as a weapon against atheistic Marxism, against liberalism, and as a means of uniting the nation. This latter goal was known as *Gleichschaltung,* meaning "unification" or "co-ordination" of all national institutions—but which my German dictionary defines in this context as "elimination of opposition"! The *Gleichschaltung* came to the Church through the *Glaubensbewegung deutscher Christen* ("faith movement of German Christians"), often known simply as the *Deutsche Christen* (DC). The Nazi party would eventually use their influence to create a national union church, the *Deutsche Evangelische Kirche* (DEK, 1933), and then to place Hitler's crony, Ludwig Müller, into the position of *Reichsbischof.*

The *Kirchenkampf* ("church struggle") began as the resistance movement to this process. An informal group called the *Jungreformatorische Bewegung* ("young reformers movement")[30] organized itself in Berlin on 12 May 1933 to oppose the DC campaign to have the *Reichsbischof* chosen from their party. They petitioned the Kapler committee to allow the normal ecclesiastical bodies to make the choice. Soon they had announced that their preferred candidate was Friedrich von Bodelschwingh, from the Bethel Institution in Bielefeld. (I mention this detail simply because it is significant for the "Bethel Confession" we shall discuss below.) Though the church in its *Kirchentag* duly elected von Bodelschwingh (27 May 1933), he would resign within the month, and through political influence the Nazi choice would quickly replace him at the Wittenberg national synod (27 September 1933).

That summer the Nazis raided the young reformers' headquarters in Berlin, effectively crushing the group. But very quickly a new group arose: The *Pfarrernotbund* ("pastors emergency league"), under Martin Niemöller's leadership.[31] Niemöller's group grew by early 1934 to 4,000 pastors strong, and by then became known as the *Bekennende Kirche* ("confessing church").

The leadership of this group was decisive for its theology. Martin Niemöller called for all Protestant clergy to band together against a common foe. His stand was expressed in the slogan "Back to the Bible," suggesting that the Reformation-era confessions should not be used to determine the unity or division of the present-day German church.[32] That Karl Barth was the movement's theological adviser should be obvious already in its title: the "confessing" church. The group was bound together by the need to confess in the crisis of the moment; not consensus in doctrine but merely the action of confessing. Sasse perceived that this "Confessing Church" was a far cry from the church of the Confessions. He wrote in 1974: "[Barth] developed since 1925 a concept of the confession in which the actual act of confession was dominant and overshadowed the doctrinal content of the confessions."[33] The *Bekennende Kirche* was thus from the start a capitulation to Barthian ecclesiology.

Inherent in this rally cry to join in action against a common foe was the presupposition that theological differences between Lutheran, Reformed, and Union churches should not be divisive. This too was Barth's advice.

> Today the conflict in the Church is not over the Lord's Supper but over the First Commandment, and we have to "confess." In the face of this our need and task, that of the Fathers must recede; that is, there must still be a serious opposition between theological schools, but it must no longer be divisive and schismatic.[34]

Sasse reacted very quickly to this suggestion,[35] horrified that Barth should so belittle the fundamental disagreements of these churches over the very means of grace. To Sasse, Barth was denying the Lutheran Church its right to exist as a church, and the right to debate and set forth doctrinal positions for herself. This conviction lay behind both his participation at Bethel, and his non-participation at Barmen.

Bethel Confession

In August 1933 von Bodelschwingh—now the former *Reichsbischof*—received two requests from Berlin for a "confession" to address the present crisis. Two men were asked to produce this "Bethel Confession": Dietrich Bonhoeffer and Hermann Sasse. Von Bodelschwingh asked them to take their position on the evidence of the Lutheran Confessions. We can see that on this basis Sasse would comply with the request. The "confession" was to be an exposition of the Augsburg Confession—thus not a "new" confession—, and was to be produced from within the Lutheran Church alone. In fact, von Bodelschwingh considered it not a confession at all, but rather "the initiation of a process of inner-churchly dialog."[36] Bonhoeffer hoped to bring this *Betheler Bekenntnis* to Wittenberg in September for the national *Kirchentag*, for he felt that the DC threatened the very existence of the Christian church in Germany.[37]

Once written, the Bethel document was circulated amongst a wide circle of theologians for comment—including Barth himself. Martin Niemöller was excited by it, and wrote to von Bodelschwingh, exhorting him to give it wider circulation and use. This began a process which went beyond the original intention of the document. It was to be softened and broadened so that all parties of the future *Bekennende Kirche* could subscribe. Bonhoeffer initially complied with requests for revisions, but Sasse quickly refused. Other Lutherans raised the fear that it would become a "new Augustana,"[38] and together with Sasse they made it clear that they would not lay their signatures next to the Reformed under such a "confession." By the end of the revision process, Bonhoeffer too had dropped out. What had happened? Feuerhahn comments: "The Bethel Confession (1933) was acceptable because it was produced by one confessional group. It failed, from his point of view, when others attempted to make it reach beyond that original scope."[39] As the Bethel document went through four extensive revisions, it became a union document, and Sasse could no longer leave his name attached.[40]

Barmen Declaration

Perhaps it was this experience at Bethel which gave Sasse his keen insight into the mistakes which would happen at Barmen. Sasse became involved in preparations for the "confessing synod of Barmen" (29-31 May 1934) at the request of his Bavarian *Landesbischof*, Hans Meiser.[41] His presence was intended to preserve Lutheran confessional integrity. Sasse, we must note, was not of the opinion that there could be **no** joint political effort between Lutherans and Reformed. But he was concerned that this synod not make doctrinal pronouncements on behalf of the Lutheran Church. Having been involved in the preparatory committee work, Sasse was well aware of what would be presented at this synod, the future "Barmen Declaration." When Dr. Koch-Oeynhausen, chairman of the event, refused Sasse permission to voice his objections publicly to the delegates, he presented them in writing to the chairman,[42] and then left on the morning train in disgust.

How is it that Sasse is remembered—and often ridiculed—as the would-be spoiler in the Church's ill-fated stand against Nazism? What was wrong with the Barmen Declaration? Sasse felt first of all that the Barmen synod would have the same result as the DEK in the previous year: the merger of all confessions.[43] In fact, the declaration quoted with approval the doctrinal stance of the DEK, which gave equal authority to all Reformation-era confessions. This contradicts the confession of the Church made in AC VII, which requires unanimity in the doctrine of the Gospel and sacraments. This union synod had taken upon itself to make dogmatic pronouncements for the Lutheran Church, when it had no authority to do so. Thus, Sasse concludes his protest with fiery words:

> Thus I am compelled to protest solemnly against the conclusions of the free synod as against a rape of the Evangelical Lutheran Church. I am no longer in the position to recognize in the so-called confessional front a real and effective representation of the confession of the Lutheran and of the Reformed Church, and I regret it most deeply that the great hour of a confederation of the genuine confessional churches has slipped away, and in its place the way of a new union, which wipes out and dissolves the Reformation confession, has stepped in.[44]

Sasse's hopes for two great confessional churches standing side by side against Hitler were dashed.

His position was grossly misunderstood outside of Germany as within. He recognized that in foreign countries "one was not able to see anything else in regard to Barmen than the courageous protest against the encroachments of the State on the legal sphere of the Church" but that "one knew nothing or little of the conflict which confessional Lutheranism carried on in favor of a confessional solution of the church problem."[45] But history would quickly prove Sasse right. Nelson notes that "within two years the Confessing Church was divided . . . into two wings, the 'confessing' Barth-Niemöller group and the 'confessing' Lutheran group led by Marahrens, Wurm, and Meiser."[46] The former spoke of a "Barmen Confession," the latter of a "declaration." The former were already using the "Barmen Confession" in ordination vows, alongside the Reformation confessions. The Reformed World Conference adopted it as its confession in Scotland (1937)—to Barth's great delight. So, Sasse responds, "If they want to make the Barmen Declaration their own, then we will treat it as a Reformed confession."[47]

Barmen thus became not only a watershed in Sasse's own relationship to the ecumenical movement, but also in the life of the Lutheran Church in Germany. In his forward to *ISC* many years later he wrote: "That at Barmen and later in the foundation of the Evangelical Church in Germany [EKD, 1948] nothing less was at stake than the very existence of the Church of the Lutheran Reformation, that is the conviction of a growing number of theologians."[48] The later union of the *Landeskirchen* into the EKD was simply the result of Barmen—and once again it would declare Barmen to be a binding confession:

> Therefore the newly formed EKD actually does regard its church government as bound not only to the Holy Scriptures, but also to the Confessions of the Ancient Church and "to the decisions of the first Confessional Church [*Bekennende Kirche*?] passed at Barmen." In other words, practically speaking, the church government is bound to the doctrinal decisions of the "Theological Declaration" of Barmen, which has been taken over by many Land churches in the ordination formulas and vows of the church elders [pastors?]. Now as regards the Confessions of the Lutheran Reformation, they are still being recognized in the Lutheran territories of the EKD. But since the Reformed and United Confessions in the respective constituent churches within the EKD are regarded as having equal rights, the Lutheran Confessions are actually robbed of that binding dogmatic force whereby the unity of the Church is safeguarded. With it Lutheranism ceases to be a church.[49]

Thus, when a church's confession ceases to exclude error, when it gives up its claims to truth and uniqueness, that church ceases to be Church.[50]

Nothing New under the Sun

What Nelson called "prescience" in Sasse, his remarkable ability to read the signs, to judge the winds, was simply a well-informed historical consciousness. As he read the history of the Church Sasse was able to say, "I've seen it all before." Whereas Lutherans in the 16th and early 17th centuries had a clear confessional identity,[51] the next century turned the Church upside down. "The unions of 1817 and the following years were possible because Pietism and the Enlightenment had not only undermined the doctrinal basis of the church, but, along with that, had destroyed the understanding of confessional differences."[52] Sasse would not in any way concede that Pietism was a positive movement:

> It is no mere coincidence that the end of the 17th century, when men were no longer taking the **doctrine** of faith seriously, also witnessed the departure of the confessional from Lutheran churches and at the same time the silencing of its great hymns of praise and thanksgiving [the three meanings of "confess"]. When will men stop this idle talk about "dead Orthodoxy," a charge that is completely without historical foundation, resting only on a dogma of Pietism—for Pietism has also had its dogmas, and some very obvious ones at that.[53]

The three New Testament senses of "confession" belong together: confession of faith, confession of sins together with Holy Absolution, and doxology in the liturgy. As Pietism and the Enlightenment rejected **the** confession, they gave up at the same time the means of grace by which the Church lives.

With confessional identity thereby destroyed, the churches of the 19th century looked for unity in other places. The nationalistic movement became the next in a long line of masters for the Church, subjecting her to what Sasse calls its narrow "provincialism."[54] For the unions of the 19th century arose not out of a genuine ecumenical mind, but out of a territorial rather than confessional definition of the Church.[55] Both sides in the *Kirchenkampf* inherited this political ecclesiology, accepting the presupposition of a "German church" which was defined by national borders rather than by the faith that is given. It is no surprise that the DC movement began in Prussia:

> Thus the meaning of the DC movement can be seen in this, that it has brought to completion a century-long development of the greatest and weightiest German *Landeskirche*, and has thereby clearly shown where this development had to lead. A straight line leads from Schleiermacher's talk about religion to the views of the "German faith movement," from

Friedrich Wilhelm III and his court bishop Eylert to Ludwig Müller, from the Prussian patriotic court-, field-, and feast-preachers [?] to the Thüringen national churchmen. But the end of this development must consist in this, that the Church is utterly absorbed into the state . . . .[56]

After the war the *Bekennende Kirche* proved no better. Their creation was the EKD (1948), the union of all German *Landeskirchen* on the basis of subjective faith rather than objective confession. This too Sasse would diagnose as the extension of the Prussian Union to all Germany.[57] He laments: "No one in this age possesses any longer the outlook on centuries and continents, which the Reformers and confessional writings of the 16th century have when they speak of the catholic, the universal Church."[58] The Prussian Union bequeathed to Germany a rather different church, "*Neuprotestantismus*,"[59] the "movement" which recognizes kinsmen wherever the **act** of confessing occurs, regardless of whether these "confessors" accept or deny the historic creeds and confessions. It is the fiction that Lutherans and Reformed together comprise one "evangelical church."[60] This as much as Karl Barth's advice was the theological foundation of the *Bekennende Kirche*.

Thus it happened that the German church was entirely unprepared for the challenge of the 1930s, and could no longer mount a credible opposition to a nationalism which she had already embraced:

> The mass of synods knew as good as nothing of the churchly confession, nothing of the Church's right [*Kirchenrecht*/canon law] which flows from the confession of the Church as the true exposition of Holy Scripture, her right both as public body and her inner-churchly right. The result was the symbiosis of the evangelical church and civil nationalism, which turned out to be so unhealthy in 1933.[61]

The church had already long ago given up the Gospel as her center and capitulated to the state.

> The doctrines, the church politics of the *Deutsche Christen* and whatever else one may mention: all that is the result of a long churchly and theological development. For two hundred years the "modern world" has penetrated into the evangelical church, secularized her and undermined the doctrine of the Reformation.[62]

The *Kirchenkampf* was not just the 20th-century struggle against fascism, but was the age-old battle of the church militant for the sake of the Gospel.

Confessionalism and Missouri

Sasse's remarkable "prescience" was not limited to Germany. Welcome or not, he often gave North American Lutheranism the benefit of his judgment. In the recently published volume of translations, Sasse's pointed commentary on "Confession and Theology in the Missouri Synod"[63] for the first time reaches a wide English audience—and it deserves our deepest attention. His relationship with the LC–MS was always uneasy, for "he addressed all with the call to repentance."[64] The essay is of course not devoid of compliments. Sasse was deeply appreciative that the LC–MS was one of the few Lutheran bodies to hold on to the entire Book of Concord. She was also courageous enough to break out of the "provincialism" of German Lutheranism in order to draw all sorts and manner of people into the church by missionary zeal.[65] The two of necessity go together: "For this type of Lutheranism possessed that which, given a missionary situation, makes a church a missionary church: the consciousness of calling and a firm dogmatical conviction without which missionary preaching is not possible."[66] Thus it is of utmost importance to listen to Sasse when he considers the role which the Confessions hold in the present life of Missouri. For where the Confessions fall, there falls her mission.

Sasse believed that the great strength of Missouri lay in how she had "popularized" the Lutheran confession. Laymen debated theological papers presented at synodical conventions with vigor that would put theologians to shame in other countries. Pastor and congregation had a good relationship because both understood the Confessions in a way unmatched anywhere else in the world. For this reason Sasse was particularly vexed by the change which he perceived to be afoot.

> These facts [concerning the strength of the Missouri "organization"] raise what constitutes the real question of life and death for Missouri as it has for every other Lutheran church. It is not the question concerning the strength of the external organization, the constitution, the growth of the

congregation, or the school system. Nor is it the question with respect to the position of the Confession as the basis for the message and work of the church. Rather it is the question concerning the strength of the Lutheran faith in the sense of the genuine deep faith of the heart in the saving Gospel, which the Holy Spirit alone can give. It is the question whether, and to what extent this strongest confessional church of Lutheranism is a truly confessing church, a church in which the Lutheran Confession is not merely held in honor as the confession of the fathers and therefore in force and untouchable, it is the question whether the Confession is the confession of a living faith of the congregation, and therefore the formative life-principle of the church. It is the question which Missouri, even as every other church, must ask herself in humility and must answer before the face of God: **are we still Lutheran?**[67]

Just as a father cannot pass on his faith to his child, but the child must be given faith anew by the Holy Spirit's good pleasure, so also the confession of the fathers must be taken up anew by each generation and made its own. He perceived that Missouri had left the confession to the fathers and moved on to new things. Thus he remarks with utmost regret: "**The Lutheran Confessions no longer play the role in the life and in the theological thinking of the Missouri Synod, in fact, of all American Lutheranism by far which they played during the 19th century.**"[68]

He continues: "Even in the churches of the Synodical Conference the confessions are now the undebatable or no longer debatable presuppositions of the church rather than the expression of the great consensus of faith, from the vantage point of which the great decisions of the church must be made."[69] While no one publicly rejects the Confessions, they have become irrelevant for the life of the church, relics of theological controversies without modern significance. Thus it was that Missouri too was unprepared when her confessionalism was put to the test. When "modernism" threatened Missouri she responded with "A Brief Statement of the Doctrinal Position of the Evangelical Lutheran Synod of Missouri, Ohio and Other States" (1932). Sasse was deeply troubled by this document. He did not deny churches the right to declare how they understood the Confessions where a controversy had arisen. What he objected to was that "A Brief Statement" had achieved the practical status of a new confession in Missouri, to which pastors would be pledged and by which other Lutheran bodies would be judged.[70] It, therefore, received the same criticism as the Barmen

Declaration. Just as Barmen could not be considered a confession because it was produced by a union synod, so also "A Brief Statement" could not be binding since it did not result from the consensus of the whole Lutheran church. "According to Lutheran understanding, a synod is not able to establish a new confession. This only the church can do, the orthodox church as a whole, by receiving a definite text as her confession."[71]

"A Brief Statement," however, fails also a second crucial test: the test of confessional catholicity. It does not draw upon the confessional heritage of the church in order to address a current situation. It does not have the confessional self-understanding of the Formula, for instance, which saw itself as the explanation of the Augustana.[72] Furthermore, "it contains statements (doctrine of the Scripture, of Justification, of the Church), which go beyond the statements of the Confessions."[73] "A Brief Statement"—in Sasse's judgment—did not explain the Confessions, but narrowed them and changed them. The "Statement" of the Forty-four in '45 was no better: it too made no appeal to the Confessions.

Thus both sides in Missouri's troubles evidenced symptoms of the same disease: the "recession of the 'Lutheran Confession' in the thinking and acting of their church."[74] So what must change? First Missouri must regain the biblical unity of confession: that confession of faith is always bound to worship.

> Are we mistaken if we miss this joy with our brethren in the Missouri Synod when they speak of the Confession? Are we mistaken in believing that their understanding of the doctrine is wholly orthodox, but only in the sense of correct doctrine, while real orthodoxy includes joyous praise to God? In the case of the old Missouri of Walther it is still plainly noticeable that here even as in the classical time of Orthodoxy dogma and liturgy belong together . . . .[75]

When doctrine and liturgy are divorced, the Church's confession becomes a dead letter. Secondly, it is essential that the Confessions once again become the basis of lively theological debate, and the heart and foundation of her theological life. For her life is at stake:

> it is a matter of the very existence of the Missouri Synod that it remain also in the future the church which is loyal to the confession, rooted in the Confession, and proclaiming the evangelical truth attested by the

Confession. It is a matter of her theological, not her physical existence.[76]

Just as the Roman church was once the apostolic Church of Peter and Paul and now is the church of the antichrist, so also the Lutheran Church may remain physically strong and yet lose its claim to be the Church of Christ.

Conclusions:
The Role of the Confessions in the Apostolic and Catholic Church

Sasse's discussion of "A Brief Statement" prompts the first point to be considered in conclusion. What is the role of "new confessions" in the Church? Sasse does not always and completely reject the notion. In 1930 he wrote:

> One may choose new formulas, images, or symbols, one may make use of new categories of thought, one may recognize and set forth the meaning of the revelation for all areas of life in a completely new way; but the confession remains always the answer to the great question of Jesus: who then do you say that I am?[77]

But it is clear that he believes such a confession is not really new. There is only one confession—given by the Holy Spirit in answer to Christ's revelation. And later experiences make him very wary of the idea of a "new confession." When writing about the possible merger of the German Lutheran free churches, Sasse pleads that only the Confessions be the basis of negotiations:

> This is possible only if both sides are agreed as to the real foundation of the union: not a new doctrinal declaration, a sort of Free Church Lutheran "Barmen," according to which the old Confessions are to be interpreted, but the Scriptures and the Symbolical Books of the Lutheran Church. Paraphrasing Walther, we ought to speak where the Confessions speak and be silent where the Confessions are silent. Only in this way will the *satis est* of the Augustana be fully recognized. Failure to unite on the basis of the Confessions is an admission that they have lost their unifying power. There is danger in new doctrinal statements.[78]

Neither a cross-confessional union document, nor a narrow statement which lacks the consent of the whole orthodox church, can supplant the foundational, unalterable confession of the Church.

What then is to be the role of the Confessions in today's church? It is no less true today than in Sasse's lifetime, that a confessional church will be a lonely church:

> There is hardly a conviction today which is so widely held as this, that Christianity, if it is to have any kind of future whatsoever, must be a religion of love for God and men, an **undogmatic Christianity** in mind and deed. This conviction has penetrated deeply into the churches themselves. One may say without exaggeration, that the great majority of all Protestant churches today are in fact no longer confessional churches.[79]

Gone is the day when any other Protestant church, at least, finds its self-identity in its confession. That's a fact. Yet a church without a confession, as we have heard, ceases to be a church. The church which substitutes love and deeds for true confession has lost its strength. Thus, panning the agenda of the false ecumenical movement, Sasse posits: "Is it perhaps the fact that the real strength of the churches is not to be found in the 'religion in which we all agree,' but rather in those things in which we disagree?"[80]

Yes, he exhorts us to find our strength in our confession. When Sasse proposes that the confession is the mark of the Church, he is not thereby contradicting AC VII. For the Gospel and the sacraments are only the *notae* when the former is preached in purity and the latter are administered according to the Gospel. In those words *rein* "purely" and *recte* "rightly" the Church's confession resides. To say that the confession is the mark of the Church is nothing else than to confess the means of grace. Here is the Church's strength by divine mandate. Sasse exhorts world Lutheranism:

> [What] we must learn anew is Luther's invincible faith in the power of the means of grace. Whatever the Church still has and still does should not be minimized. But she does not live from mercy, or from political and social activity. She does not subsist on large numbers. When will the terrible superstition of the Christendom of our day cease that only there Jesus Christ is powerful where two or three millions are gathered together in His name! When will we again comprehend that the Church lives by the means of grace of the pure preaching of the Gospel and by the divinely instituted administration of the Sacraments and by nothing else.[81]

The Church's strength lies in what the Lord has given her.[82]

The lessons Sasse learned from the Nazi era were hard-wrought. But he feared that the capitulation of church to state could happen in more than one way, and that it would be repeated.

> What can be done in order to prevent a new invasion of the world into the church by an imitation of secular forms of mass organizations and methods of government? And this implies the other question: What can be done in order to preserve the offices and institutions to whom the Lord has entrusted the responsibility for His church on earth? The ministry of the Word and the Sacrament and the Christian congregation are the strong pillars of the Church. . . . [E]verything has to be done in order to protect the rights and duties of the divinely appointed offices and institutions. Otherwise the Church must decay.[83]

When the Church abandons her confession and allows this incursion of secular organization, she relinquishes any claim on God's blessing, for she has given up the only way He has provided in the means of grace and the office of the ministry by which they are administered.

Thus his appeal is that the Confessions once again be the center of our pastoral and theological lives:

> Let us again become **confessional Lutherans** for the sake of the unity of the Church. . . . that we again study the Confessions, that we again and again compare them with the Holy Scripture, and that we constantly learn to gauge their interpretation of the Scriptures and their Scripture proofs more profoundly. . . . The deepest cause for the failure of the German church conflict is none other but that everyone always spoke about the Confessions, appealed to them, but knew them too little.[84]

His cry is nothing else than that each generation make the Confessions its own.

> Nominally, of course, and most certainly *bona fide*, the present generation maintains the doctrinal standards of the confessions as they have been inherited from the fathers. But a confession cannot remain a real confession, if it is only inherited. It must be confessed. We can confess it only if we are deeply convinced that it is the true interpretation of Scripture. . . . We do so with the words of the fathers because we find in Scripture the same truth which they found. But we must do so for ourselves. If we cannot convince ourselves of the truth of their statements, then it would be hypocrisy to accept the confessions.[85]

This exhortation returns us finally to my title. How does this picture of confessing differ from the *Bekennende Kirche* which so offended Sasse? Ultimately it is that the confessing movement with its existential, for-the-moment confession severed itself from the catholic and apostolic Church.[86] The true confession of the Church, by contrast, unites one with all those who have confessed through the ages—not on the basis of a common **act**, but on the basis of the confession's Gospel **content**, and its source in the unchanging, once-and-for-all revelation. The self-understanding of the Lutheran Church as her Confessions proclaim is not that she is a sect, not a break-off from the catholic Church, but that she **is** the catholic Church: "The orthodox evangelical church is the legitimate continuation of the medieval Catholic Church, not the church of the Council of Trent and the Vatican Council which renounced evangelical truth when it rejected the Reformation."[87] It is therefore the Romanists who have left the true catholic and apostolic Church by rejecting the Gospel confession.

This self-identity thrusts the Lutheran Church onto the world scene. Sasse was compelled to be on the front lines of the Faith and Order movement because of his conviction that the Lutheran confession was not only backwards-looking:

> Lutheran confessionalism . . . does not look always into the past, but it looks into the future, not only upon itself, but upon all of Christendom. It is always catholic and always ecumenical: catholic in the sense that it holds fast to the genuine catholicity of the Church of Christ in space and time, just as the Book of Concord does when it begins with the *tria symbola catholica seu oecumenica*, and concludes with a view to the coming generations until Judgment Day. Ecumenical, not in the sense of a superficial unionism, but in the sense of the faith in the *Una sancta ecclesia perpetuo mansura*, of which the ecumenical program speaks, which inheres in the seventh article of the Augustana. The Church on which we believe and which we confess in our confessional writings is not a sect with the Book of Concord as its articles of association, but it is the *Una Sancta* in which we live. Confessional faithfulness and genuine ecumenicity belong together.[88]

Given by Christ, the Church's confession must not remain the exclusive possession of Lutheranism, but must pursue its *missio*, its "sending," until "every tongue should confess that Jesus Christ is Lord, to the glory of God the Father" (Phil. 2:11).

Thus the confession is concerned not with a "for the time being," but with the end of all things. As the Church is ultimately eschatological in meaning, the place where the earthly saints experience "a foretaste of the feast to come," where they are united with "angels and archangels and with all the company of heaven," so also is her confession eschatological, uniting her not only with those who have confessed in history before her, but also with the doxology of all eternity:

> Thus the Confession not only unites the present generation, but also the orthodox church of all times. Not only are we united in the fellowship of the church and in the consensus of the true faith with those who are living today, but also with those who before us confessed the true faith and those who will do so after us, with all the believers from the beginning of the church until the Last Day, from the confessors of the *ecclesia militans* on earth to those who in heaven are glorifying Christ in a confession that now has become purely a praising of God. That is the most profound meaning of the Lutheran confession.[89]

Notes

[1] *S&C*, 15. Sasse elsewhere admits the interrelatedness of all doctrine when he calls the Church a chapter of eschatology: "Some Remarks on the Ecumenical Movement," *RTR* 12.2 (June 1953): 30-31.

[2] Hermann Sasse, "Liturgy and Lutheranism," *S&C*, 34.

[3] *LB* 113 (August 1976); my trans.

[4] Sasse, "Geleitwort des Verfassers," *ISC* I:8; my trans.

[5] Sasse, "Das Bekenntnis der Kirche" (1930), repr. *LB* 32.120 (25 June 1980): 71; my trans.

[6] Sasse, "Das Bekenntnis der Kirche," *Christliche Woche* 6.9 (September 1930): 321-33, later repr. *LB* 32.120 (25 June 1980): 70-82; and *Jesus Christus der Herr* (1930), which was revised into *Jesus Christus der Herr, Das Urbekenntnis der Kirche* (Berlin: Furche-Verlag, o.J., 1931), English translation by Norman Nagel, "Jesus Christ is Lord," *WCJC* (St. Louis: Concordia, 1984), I:9-35.

[7] "Über das Wesen des kirchlichen Bekenntnisses," *Briefe an Lutherische Pastoren*, Nr. 2, *LB* (Dec. 1948) 9 pp.; English translation by Edmund Reim, "On the Nature of the Church's Confession," *LTJ* 2.2-3 (Aug.-Dec. 1968): 88-97.

[8] Sasse, "On the Nature of the Church's Confession," *LTJ* 2.2-3 (Aug.-Dec. 1968): 91.

[9] *Luther's Small Catechism with Explanation* (St. Louis: Concordia, 1991), 100.

[10] Sasse himself quotes Luther's explanation of the Third Article in "On the Nature of the Church's Confession," *LTJ* 2.2-3 (Aug.-Dec. 1968): 91.

[11] "On the Nature of the Church's Confession," *LTJ* 2.2-3 (Aug.-Dec. 1968): 91. See also "Das Bekenntnis der Kirche," *LB* 32.120 (25 June 1980): 78: "As soon as the confession is used not only at Baptisms but also in the divine service of the congregation, it has the tendency to take on the 'we' form" (my trans.). This, of course, uncovers the **historical** reason for the "I" of the apostolic creed: it is rooted in the baptismal liturgy, wherein it confesses the faith given to the individual.

[12] "Das Bekenntnis der Kirche," *LB* 32.120 (25 June 1980): 72; my trans. He continues soon after: "A confession, also a baptismal confession, is not to be understood as 'praying words to Jesus.' Baptism indeed stands in intimate connection to the confession, but it is not a confession, unless one understands it in the sense of the Baptists. And also 'following Christ' is something other than the confession, even though both belong together" (73); my trans.

[13] Sasse, "On the Nature of the Church's Confession," *LTJ* 2.2-3 (Aug.-Dec. 1968): 90.

[14] Sasse, "Das Bekenntnis der Kirche," *LB* 32.120 (25 June 1980): 78; my trans. Emphasis is Sasse's.

[15] Karl Barth, *Wünschbarkeit und Möglichkeit eines allgemeinen reformierten Glaubensbekenntnis*, reprinted in *Die Theologie und die Kirche*, Gesammelte Vorträge, 2. Band (1928). Emphasis is Sasse's as he quotes it in "On the Nature of the Church's Confession," *LTJ* 2.2-3 (Aug.-Dec. 1968): 94.

[16] Sasse, "Das Bekenntnis der Kirche," *LB* 32.120 (25 June 1980): 75; my trans. Emphasis is Sasse's.

[17] Ibid; my trans.

[18] Sasse, "Das Bekenntnis der Kirche," *LB* 32.120 (25 June 1980): 79; my trans. Emphasis is Sasse's. On the liturgical function of the confession, see Sasse's "Bekenntnis und Liturgie," in *Freimund: Lutherisches Wochenblatt für Kirche und Volk* 81.50 (12 Dec. 1935): 456-58.

[19] Sasse, "Das Bekenntnis der Kirche," *LB* 32.120 (25 June 1980): 80. Emphasis original. Here again Sasse indicates that the Church's confession is her essential mark: "But the confession of Jesus Christ, as the great churchly confessional formulas express it: that is the border between Church and not-church" (81); my trans.

[20] Sasse, "Das Bekenntnis der Kirche," *LB* 32.120 (25 June 1980): 81; my trans.

Emphasis is Sasse's.

[21] Sasse, "Some Remarks on the Ecumenical Movement," *RTR* 12.2 (June 1953): 39: "They try to restore the unity of the church by wiping out from the history of the church of the 16th century and by going back to the 'Ancient Undivided Church' which actually has never existed, as every historian knows, but is a dream of 17th century theologians who were tired of controversies and of 19th century Romanticism which reads its own ideals into the past."

[22] Ronald R. Feuerhahn, *EC*, 6-7. Feuerhahn quotes Bishop Palmer from H. N. Bate, ed., *Faith and Order Proceedings of the World Conference Lausanne, August 3-21, 1927* (London, 1927), 233.

[23] Sasse, "Some Remarks on the Ecumenical Movement," *RTR* 12.2 (June 1953): 33.

[24] Feuerhahn, *EC*, 196 & 283.

[25] Sasse, "The Ecumenical Movement in the Roman Catholic Church," *RTR* 23.1 (Feb. 1964): 13.

[26] Sasse, "How Has Rome Changed?" *His* [Inter-Varsity Christian Fellowship] 26.3 (Dec. 1965): 30a; qtd in Feuerhahn, *EC*, 208 n. 732.

[27] See Feuerhahn, *EC*, 263.

[28] Sasse, "Ecumenical Responsibility," *RTR* 13.1 (Feb. 1954): 15.

[29] Qtd in E. Clifford Nelson, *The Rise of World Lutheranism: An American Perspective* (Philadelphia: Fortress, 1982), 304. The following pages of Nelson provide a helpful summary of these events. Nelson, 314, notes that Sasse was the only major Protestant clergyman to attack this nationalist platform in print—even before 1933. "With hindsight today's interpreters of the 'church struggle' readily admit that Sasse's sharp words were biblically prophetic and evangelically confessional and that Sasse himself was prescient" (314-15).

[30] Though Nelson, *The Rise of World Lutheranism*, 315, lists Sasse among the members, Feuerhahn, *EC*, 17, notes: "While not a signer of the original manifesto of the 'young Reformers of Berlin' (*Jungreformatorische Bewegung*), he was involved in the movement at an early stage."

[31] Nelson, *The Rise of World Lutheranism*, 324.

[32] Feuerhahn, *EC*, 136-37.

[33] Sasse, letter to Leiv Aalen (21 June 1974), qtd in Feuerhahn, *EC*, 165. The Bethel experience did little for Sasse's judgment of Bonhoeffer. "Sasse, for his part, had come to see Bonhoeffer as an 'enthusiast' because the latter credited the living event of communal, actual confessing with so much power that antitheses dividing churches dwindled to antitheses dividing schools." Eberhard Bethge, *Dietrich Bonhoeffer, Theologian, Christian, Contemporary*, trans. E. Mosbacher, *et al.*, ed. E.

Robertson (London: Collins, 1970), 475f. Qtd in Feuerhahn, *EC*, 168.

[34] Karl Barth, *Theologische Existenz heute* 7 (26 Jan. 1934), English translation qtd in Feuerhahn, *EC*, 89.

[35] Sasse, "Union und Bekenntnis," *ISC* I:273-79.

[36] Feuerhahn, *EC*, 80.

[37] Bonhoeffer writing to his mother from Bethel (20 Aug. 1933), in *Gesammelte Schriften*, ed. E. Bethge (Munich: Chr. Kaiser, 1959), II:79.

[38] Schlatter and Merz, for instance. See the introduction in Bonhoeffer, *Gesammelte Schriften* II:87-88.

[39] Feuerhahn, *EC*, 10.

[40] Feuerhahn, *EC*, 85-86, remarks that he finds no further reference to Bethel in Sasse's correspondence—an indication perhaps of his disgust at the results.

[41] Feuerhahn, *EC*, 87.

[42] This document is published in *ISC* I:280-81.

[43] Feuerhahn, *EC*, 96.

[44] Sasse, *ISC* I:281; my trans.

[45] Sasse, "Concerning the Status of the Lutheran Churches in the World," trans. P. Peters, *CTM*, 20.8 (Aug. 1949): 617. Feuerhahn notes that Sasse was quite aware of the misconception of the German situation among people abroad: "There was quite a false picture that on the one hand there was the Confessing Church lead [sic] by Barth and Niemöller, resolute and uncompromising while the direction represented by the Lutheran bishops was halting and one of compromise" (*EC*, 107).

[46] Nelson, *The Rise of World Lutheranism*, 328-29.

[47] Sasse, "Die Barmer Erklärung—ein ökumenisches Bekenntnis?" *Lutherische Kirche* 19.6 (1 June 1937): 75. Sasse does not deny that the Barmen Declaration contains biblical truth. But in rejecting the distinction between Lutheran and Reformed, it is false in its totality as a confession. "For if that declaration is a confession, then it is a typically Reformed confession . . . , which however as a whole is for this reason already unacceptable, because it serves the concealment of differences, the evasion of the truth question, and thereby opens gate and door to enthusiasm." "Bekenntnis und Bekennen: Lehren aus fünf Jahren Kirchenkampf," *Lutherische Kirche* (15 May 1937): 55.

[48] Sasse, "Geleitwort des Verfassers," *ISC* I:9; my trans.

[49] Sasse, "Concerning the Status of the Lutheran Churches in the World," *CTM* 20.8 (Aug. 1949): 618. As often happens, the translator seems to have missed Sasse's crucial distinction between the true confessional church of the Augustana, and the

"confessing church [*Bekennende Kirche*]."

[50] Sasse does not mean thereby to deny all erring Christians the right to be called "church." He argues that until modern times **all** major church bodies were confessional, and understood each other's confessions to be mutually exclusive— whether right or wrong. Today's non-confessional unions give up the right to be "church" as they cease to exclude error. Thus he concludes: "we state the objective and historic-dogmatical facts of the case, namely that the Lutheran Churches of our time— with exceptions which we do not want to mention here—that at least the leading churches of the world are not any longer churches in the light of the Formula of Concord" ("Concerning the Status of the Lutheran Churches in the World," *CTM* 20.8 [Aug. 1949]: 621).

[51] Sasse, Review of "A History of the Ecumenical Movement 1517-1948," *RTR* 14.1 (Feb. 1955): 4:
> ... the strength of the Reformation lay in the inexorable seriousness with which the Reformers regarded their confessions. The problem of intercommunion did not exist at all. All churches of the 16th century, as the church of all ages, were convinced that intercommunion is possible only where the *consensus doctrinae* exists. ...The churches of the Reformation continued simply the usage of the Church since the beginning. There is not and cannot be a *communicatio in sacris cum haereticis aut schismaticis*.

[52] Sasse, *HWS*, 24.

[53] Sasse, "On the Nature of the Church's Confession," *LTJ* 2.2-3 (Aug.-Dec. 1968): 89.

[54] Sasse, "Konfessionelle Unbußfertigkeit? Ein Wort zum Verständnis des lutherischen Konfessionalismus," *Allgemeine Evangelisch-Lutherische Kirchenzeitung* 68.11 (15 Mar. 1935): 246.

[55] Sasse diagnosed the same error in the WCC, which chose to group churches geographically rather than confessionally.

[56] Sasse, "Bekenntnis und Bekennen," *Lutherische Kirche* (15 May 1937): 52; my trans. Feuerhahn, *EC*, 121, comments: "The struggle which arose out of the Prussian Union in the early 19th century was seen by the author [Sasse] as the basic issue for the mid-20th century struggle; the response to the Union in the Lutheran 'Awakening' gave the norm and inspiration for the current post-war efforts."

[57] Sasse, "Die deutsche Union von 1933," *ISC* I:265, makes this statement of the *DEK* (1933). He saw the *EKD* (1948) as the continuation of this earlier "federation."

[58] Sasse, "Konfessionelle Unbußfertigkeit," *Allgemeine Evangelisch-Lutherische Kirchenzeitung* 68.11 (15 Mar. 1935): 247.

[59] Sasse, "Bekenntnis und Bekennen," *Lutherische Kirche* (15 May 1937):53, (my. trans.):

New Protestantism, which today in Germany indeed possesses no identifiable theological representation, but which nevertheless as an inheritance of the 19th century is still a great force not only in the DC but also in the "Confessing Church," understands the churchly confession from the confession of the individual. Wherever an unshakable "Here I stand, I can do no other" resounds, there is genuine confession. The churchly confession arises as the pooling of individual confessions, and confessional church—or as people in these circles prefer to say: confessor-church or confessing church—[arises] through the coming together of individual confessors.

This article, whose title betrays his intention to distinguish "Confession" from the verb "to confess," grounds the *Bekennende Kirche* firmly in Pietism, which values fervor over truth, and says "just believe" apart from asking "believe what?"

[60] The necessity of distinguishing Lutheran from Reformed is the theme of the entire writing *Here We Stand* (*Was heißt lutherisch?*). Sasse rejected the term "Protestant" and even "Evangelical" as a useful designation of common theological heritage.

[61] Sasse, "Geleitwort des Verfassers," *ISC* I:8; my trans.

[62] Sasse, "Union und Bekenntnis," *ISC* I:276; my trans.

[63] Sasse, "Confession (Confessionalism) and Theology in the Missouri Synod (1951)," *S&C*, 189-220. This is a translation of his *Letter to Lutheran Pastors*, No. 20.

[64] Feuerhahn, introduction to "Confession and Theology in the Missouri Synod," *S&C*, 189.

[65] Sasse, "Confession and Theology in the Missouri Synod," *S&C*, 192: "Missouri is the church of home missions among Lutheran churches." Thus Missouri presents all men individually with the Gospel, and will not accept the premise that a man is bound by nationality to a particular church. Nevertheless, Sasse warns, "Missouri is in danger of seeing only individuals, and ignoring the blessing which lies in the state, which man has not chosen for himself."

[66] Sasse, "Confession and Theology in the Missouri Synod," *S&C*, 195.

[67] Sasse, "Confession and Theology in the Missouri Synod," *S&C*, 202. Emphasis is Sasse's.

[68] Sasse, "Confession and Theology in the Missouri Synod," *S&C*, 205. Emphasis is Sasse's.

[69] Sasse, "Confession and Theology in the Missouri Synod," *S&C*, 205-6. The first example Sasse raises concerns the liturgical movement and its attempt to introduce the epiclesis. He comments that no one bothers to ask in response what the Formula of Concord confesses about the consecration.

[70] Sasse, *S&C*, 211, asserts that the Missouri Synod in convention (1947) established "A Brief Statement" as "official doctrine," and thus the rule by which other

bodies were measured and by which fellowship was given or denied. Thus, it in fact achieved the status of a new confession.

[71] Sasse, "Confession and Theology in the Missouri Synod," *S&C*, 206.

[72] "[I]t is our purpose, neither in this nor in any other writing, to recede in the least from that oft-cited Confession [the Augustana], nor to propose another or new confession" (FC SD Preface, par. 5).

[73] Sasse, "Confession and Theology in the Missouri Synod," *S&C*, 207.

[74] Sasse, "Confession and Theology in the Missouri Synod," *S&C*, 213.

[75] Sasse, "Confession and Theology in the Missouri Synod," *S&C*, 208.

[76] Sasse, "Confession and Theology in the Missouri Synod," *S&C*, 214.

[77] Sasse, "Das Bekenntnis der Kirche," *LB* 32.120 (25 June 1980): 76. Thus each new confession arising from the consensus of the whole, orthodox Church, is an elaboration of earlier creeds to defend against new heresy:
> ... the Nicene Creed loses its original meaning if it is understood as sufficient for all times, a minimum confession containing that on which there must be agreement in the Church of Christ, and leaving open all questions not expressly mentioned therein. ... Thus the Creed must be understood as a confession of that one faith which God the Holy Ghost gives to the whole Church as to every single believer. It was, indeed, formulated at a certain time, but expresses the one great truth which was already confessed earlier by the Church of the apostles and martyrs in primitive formulas and which had to be confessed later in more elaborate form in the doctrinal statements of Ephesus and Chalcedon against the heresies of Nestorianism and Monophysitism which readily accepted, but unfortunately misinterpreted the Nicene Creed. In later centuries again the Creed had to be safeguarded against new misinterpretations. This is the meaning of all great confessions of the 16th century which, though contradicting each other, each one in its way, tried to express the real meaning of the Nicene Creed (e.g. what the words "for us men and for our salvation" actually meant) over against new errors and heresies. ("Some Remarks on the Ecumenical Movement," *RTR* 12.2 [June 1953]: 37-38.)

[78] Sasse, "Concerning the Lutheran Free Churches in Germany," *CTM* 18.1 (Jan. 1947): 43.

[79] Sasse, "Das Bekenntnis der Kirche," *LB* 32.120 (25 June 1980): 70.

[80] Sasse, Review of "A History of the Ecumenical Movement 1517-1948," *RTR* 14.1 (Feb. 1955): 8.

[81] Sasse, "Concerning the Status of the Lutheran Churches in the World," 625. See also Sasse, "Selective Fellowship," *Australian Theological Review* 28.3 (Sept. 1957): 50: "Thus the first concern of every congregation must be to see that the means of grace are kept in their purity."

[82] At the point of means of grace and liturgy, the Church's essence is most bound up with her confession. Sasse, "On the Nature of the Church's Confession" (1948), *LTJ* 2.2-3 (Aug.-Dec. 1968): 89:
> No church can really be a church without a confession which it takes seriously. The liturgy itself is an outgrowth of such a confession, and the Pope was perfectly right when in his encyclical *Mediator Dei* he reminded the liturgical movement of the Roman Catholic Church that the familiar dictum '*Lex supplicandi lex credendi*' not only can, but must be inverted. Just as surely as in the history of the Church a dogma is usually first prayed and then defined as an article of faith, just so surely at the Church's beginning the confession of faith precedes liturgy.

For further exploration of the *lex orandi* theme see: Paul De Clerck, "'Lex orandi, lex credendi': The Original Sense and Historical Avatars of an Equivocal Adage," *Studia Liturgica*, trans. Thomas Winger, 24.2 (1994): 178-200; and Thomas Winger, "Lex Orandi Revisited," *Logia* 4.1 (Epiphany/Jan. 1995): 65-66.

[83] Sasse, "Ecumenical Responsibility," *RTR* 13.1 (Feb. 1954): 17-18.

[84] Sasse, "Concerning the Status of the Lutheran Churches in the World," *CTM* 20.8 (Aug. 1949): 624.

[85] Sasse, "Selective Fellowship," *The Australian Theological Review* 28.3 (Sept. 1957): 48. Sasse, as always, call us to repentance with his words. The continuation suggests that the root of many problems lies in the ignorance of our pastors: "But we should all ask ourselves whether we have studied them properly. How many students of theology have even read the Book of Concord from cover to cover? How many of our candidates for ordination have even read the New Testament in Greek from cover to cover, to say nothing of the Old Testament? Our fathers did that. How many psalms do you know by heart in Hebrew, how many passages of the New Testament in Greek? How many articles of the Augsburg Confession do we know by heart, in Latin, of course? If we consider these questions we might understand the changes that have taken place in the Lutheran Churches, and we have to ask ourselves, every one of us: Is this not perhaps the deepest reason why 'we **find** no doctrinal differences' any longer where our fathers found them?" (49)

[86] The Barmen declaration falls short of being a confession for the Church not only because of its union character, but also because it fails the test of catholicity: "It was not born from the consensus of the true church"—Sasse, writing in 1936 about the Barmen Declaration, in *ISC* 1:283; my trans. Even if it had the agreement of the participating churches, it still lacked one thing:
> the consensus with the Fathers. For a genuine churchly confession expresses not only the consensus of "those living at the time," but it also binds the church of the present with the church of all time. Therefore all genuine confessions make direct reference to the confessions of the orthodox church which already exist. (*ISC* 1:283; my trans.)

[87] Sasse, *HWS*, 110.

[88] Sasse, *ISC* I:10; my trans. Sasse warns that the truly catholic nature of the Lutheran confession is threatened by the individualism of a crassly congregational polity:
> There is especially one function which a church body of more or less congregational type cannot fulfill. This is the maintenance of the bond with the church of the fathers which is so important for the Lutheran Church. Our confession establishes not only the bond between those who now live, but also with those who have confessed the true faith throughout the centuries. . . . The catholicity of the confession in space and time would be destroyed if the church body which confesses '*magno consensu*' were atomized and pulverized into a mere aggregation of individuals or small groups. ("Selective Fellowship," *Australian Theological Review* 28.3 [Sept. 1957]: 51.)

[89] Sasse, "On the Nature of the Church's Confession," *LTJ* 2.2-3 (Aug.-Dec. 1968): 96.

In the Forecourts of Theology: The Epistemology of Hermann Sasse and the Relationship between Philosophy and Theology and between Natural Theology and Revelation in His Works

Tom G. A. Hardt

It might seem to be a case of too great ambition to submit Hermann Sasse to scrutiny on a point which seems rather remote from his central themes. Taking his epistemology as well as the relationship between philosophy and theology in his works as the subject for a lecture may appear as a kind of myopia on the part of the dedicated disciple which makes the great man have an opinion on anything and everything. Touching as it may be, this hardly deserves the name of a strictly scholarly approach. Yet there is a defense of my choice of topic. It is not merely the *a priori* fact that any person, especially a professor of theology who has worked for decades with historical subjects, must at least unconsciously have developed or at least accepted and applied some theories on how we acquire knowledge, how we can make use of it in our work, and how it affects our treatment of sacred theology. It is rather an *a posteriori* experience of this speaker that Hermann Sasse actually had ideas on these matters, an experience that once in 1965 at an Easter Sunday dinner in my home in Stockholm involved an oral discussion on the matter. It should at once be said that there was a difference between us on this point, which still is present in my mind, and which should make my listeners aware of the possibility that I may be not only a dedicated but also a critical disciple, who thus may be suspected of mixing the scholarly task of giving an adequate picture with the selfish wish to present his own views, which are, of course, of no special importance at all at this centenary of a great spirit who was not only spirit but also flesh and blood and a lovable, fatherly friend.

It should at once be added that today's lecture will not be founded upon a mere *Tischgespräch* (table conversation), a kind of source which I have in other connections tried to prove unreliable, at least when without support in more trustworthy parts of the *Weimarana*. The reference to the 1965 discussion will merely serve as an interesting introduction to something that will later on be supported by references to Sasse's works and letters.

What Sasse said, when I directly questioned him concerning his views on the philosophical foundations for our scholarly, theological work, was that our approach to the world that we examine and penetrate in different ways will always be decided by the present, admittedly always changing, state of natural science. He exemplified his argument by pointing to what he took to be the breakdown of the principle of causality through the discoveries of Werner Heisenberg. Heisenberg showed, so was his opinion, that we cannot predict what will happen, the bond between cause and effect being broken forever, or rather, for as long as that discovery stands unquestioned. It should be emphasized that, in Sasse's epistemology, the stress on the interimistic character of such scientific insights serves the wish never to be associated with a *philosophia perennis*, being thus in itself a both understandable and laudable desire to keep Christianity undefiled by a pagan philosophy, where the damage wrought by Aristotelianism on Christian doctrine is for all times a warning sign. *Vestigia terrent*. To Sasse, the supposed impossibility of modern man's believing any more in the basic concept of causality proved that natural science has taken the place of ancient philosophy, a conclusion that he did not, however, articulate. Since I myself had raised the question which he had answered, I felt entitled to raise an objection to Sasse's argument, an objection which I will spell out in this context, asking my listeners to remember that they hear only one side of the conversation, and that it is an expression of my critical attitude, and thus is to be received with some caution. I actually said to Sasse that whatever Dr. Heisenberg saw in his scientific investigations was most certainly an observation built on a full and unlimited trust in the basic law of causality, as he must have been confident that there was an interrelationship between the moves of the infinitely small particles under his observation and the testimony of his senses, that the former was the cause and the latter the effect, and that cause and effect were knit together by the law of causality that thus forever, without any interimistic reservation about tomorrow's discoveries, was part of mankind's *philosophia perennis*.

What did Sasse answer to that? It would be wrong to state, "Ad hoc Sasse nihil," as it would imply that he would have nothing to say; but, as far as I remember, he said nothing. Maybe an outburst of toasts or a change of dish silenced him. Yet I do remember a witty limerick by another guest, a lady theologian and Anglicist, heard over the table, which added two lines to Alexander Pope's famous couplet:

> Nature and Nature's law lay hid in night.
> God said "Let Newton be!" and all was light.
> This could not last, the devil murmured "Woe!"
> God said "Let Einstein be!" and all was status quo.

It is not impossible to advance further on the point of causality and to show its background in Sasse's way of thinking. During my many years of contact with Sasse I received a great number of books from him of many different kinds, but only in one case did he send me a book that was a carefully made duplicate of his own printed copy, now in the United States. It was Heinrich Scholz's *Eros und Caritas. Die platonische Liebe und die Liebe im Sinne des Christentums*.[1] This author, professor of philosophy at the University of Münster, is referred to five times in Sasse's *Sacra Scriptura*, and Sasse expressed in one of his letters to me his great appreciation of Scholz as a philosopher: "He was one of the greatest thinkers in Germany, theologian and philosopher."[2] Scholz has as one of his points against the Aristotelian proofs of the existence of God that the idea of causality, as present in the proof of the First Unmoved Mover, is built on an outdated idea of movement, which has been superseded by natural science. Even more important to Scholz, however, is the idea that the Aristotelian Unmoved Mover and First Uncaused Cause implies His inability to hear prayers and makes Him an entirely other kind of God than the Christian God. The proof of the existence of God found in Thomas, for example, that there must be a First Mover, is accordingly described by Scholz in the following way: "Consequently this proof for the existence of God is the heaviest blow against the foundation of Christianity ever delivered by a great thinker"[3]—in this case Thomas Aquinas. Scholz even writes that the prayers directed towards God on a Christian Sunday would dissolve the First Mover.[4] In his copy of Scholz's book Sasse had marked this passage with a pencil and inserted an exclamation mark in the margin. We will show how these lines always remained in his memory.

I am sorry to say that this discussion at table did not lead to any epistolary exchange of thoughts between Sasse and me, but I remain nowadays quite convinced that not merely the question of causality but even the entire conflict experienced by Sasse between classical philosophy and Christianity might have its foundation in the impression left on Sasse's mind by Scholz's philosophy as presented in the book *Eros und Caritas*. The more I deal with the problem the more I see that book as a kind of key to many of Sasse's statements. Not seldom will a friend of Sasse's feel a déjà-vu experience when looking through *Eros und Caritas*.

With Scholz Sasse shares an admiration for Blaise Pascal. One of Sasse's favorite quotations from Pascal is the well known "Le coeur a ses raisons, que la raison ne connaît point."[5] The interpretation given to these words by Sasse is the one commonly accepted, viz., that the heart (or our feelings) fortunately overcomes the supposedly rigorous demands of our intellect, which does not cover the essential points of life. Actually, however, Sasse's and most other people's understanding of Pascal is not correct. What Pascal says here is rather to the contrary. He tells an unbeliever that his unbelief is not due to his use of reason, as he claims. It is a choice of his evil heart, which does not listen to reason. As we will see, this detail, unimportant in itself, is very much part of the problem that I will treat in the coming parts of this lecture.

I wish to point to the interesting fact that Sasse saw a similarity[6]—which certainly existed—between Scholz and the famous Swedish theologian Bishop Anders Nygren of Lund, which gives us the possibility to trace parallels—although not more than that—between Sasse and the Lundensian theology concerning the relationship between philosophy and theology, and maybe also between Scholz and Nygren, whose works, *Eros und Caritas* and *Den kristna kårlekstanken. Eros och agape*,[7] appeared in 1929 and 1930 respectively. Thus it is already quite apparent that what actually inspired Sasse in his warfare against Aristotelianism was the intention to save the Gospel and to keep undefiled by the world, to keep the distance between Jerusalem and Athens. I will make this more evident in the coming parts of my lecture, but it is important to face this fact at an early stage.

It does not, however, as I see it, imply that this legitimate aim can be used to cover any attack from Sasse's side—in the wake of Scholz—against what he regarded as a false *philosophia perennis*, a standing expression in his works used to designate the danger of canonizing a standard philosophy as Rome has done in regard to Thomism and thereby—according to Sasse—Aristotelianism. I permit myself to spell out already at this point that according to my opinion there is and always will be a kind of commonsense philosophy that is already present in the biblical material and that will be the necessary condition for entering its world as well as any world of any kind. A full trust in causality, for example, belongs to this commonsense philosophy and epistemology.

That Sasse was a foe of Aristotelianism is a well known fact, but I would like to present some material as proof texts. I will then try to analyze it more closely. To an American theologian he wrote on 2 March 1968 that the differences between himself and the recipient of the letter "seem to lie in the field of philosophy rather than in theology." This means not only that the person in question entertained certain philosophical notions but also necessarily that Sasse did too. Thus we cannot claim philosophical innocence for Sasse. From his own philosophical point of view Sasse makes clear that the addressee shares his shortcomings with "our orthodox Fathers especially in the 17th century" who had "too uncritically" accepted certain philosophical assumptions of Aristotle and Cicero, following the philosophy of Melanchthon. Among those followers of Melanchthon Sasse also counts Franz Pieper, who is not only one of his main targets but who perhaps may be regarded as the real cause for Sasse's repeated dealing with the problem at least during the later years of his life. In this conflict Sasse thinks himself entitled to find support in Luther and the Formula of Concord.

The support that Sasse claimed to find in Luther came from the famous *Heidelberg Disputation* and the *Disputation Against Scholastic Theology*. When taking cognizance through a copy—Sasse generously provided me with copies of his correspondence, thereby keeping me informed—of what he had written to the theologian in the United States, I apparently made an objection on this point, the exact content of which is no longer accessible to me, as I have only a very few copies of my letters to Sasse. It is nevertheless materially visible in

Sasse's answer of 20 April 1968. I had rejected those writings of the early Luther as not only pre-reformational but also as Platonistic. What I wrote at that time was later to become a lengthy footnote in my dissertation, where I refer to other scholars such as Link and Hunzinger who also see in this early Luther work a conscious siding with Plato against Aristotle and that generally speaking St. Augustine's Neoplatonic heritage is being revived in the early Luther's works.[8] A good summary of what can be found here is Ernst Bizer's formulation, "Verzicht auf das Sichtbare ist die Genugtuung, die wir Gott schuldig sind—To abstain from the visible is the satisfaction that we owe to God." The visible world is here Aristotle's world; the invisible, spiritual world is Plato's. It would be very wrong to say that Sasse in any way was a Platonist, which would be the very peak of paganism both to him and to the much admired Scholz, but undoubtedly the inspiration that he received from the young Luther made him open to the thought that the direction towards the external world that occupies Aristotle was in itself unbiblical and that a natural theology based on observations of nature would be in some way untenable. I do not say that these thoughts were in any way clearly developed by Sasse or that the full consequences were ever drawn. It would be wrong to say, for example, that the epistemological consequence to Sasse would have been that we receive knowledge through divine illumination and not through observation. Yet the impact of the young Luther could lead to such conclusions, and the idea hovers in an unarticulated way over some Sasse texts at least as an inward tension.

I think it important to use this occasion to make clear that Sasse always adhered to the idea that there was an early Reformation discovery, as the standard answer was in German university circles of his youth, and that thus the young Luther was to him already dogmatically a Lutheran, although Sasse constantly used the classical expression "Luther in der Periode seiner Vollendung" about the aged Luther. It did not, however, say much more than that we get wiser when we grow old, as we all know or believe. Sasse thus most expressly rejected the new insights that are the fruits of Ernst Bizer and Uuras Saarnivaara and since then have become accepted by many other scholars. It never harmed his idea of justification by faith, but I do think that it produced some unclarities on the points that are under treatment today. Sasse did not feel very much convinced when I tried to prove that to Luther Romans 1 became a reliable testimony of God's existence, making it a kind of parallel to Luther's discovery of the external Word as the way to God, which replaced the young Luther's preference for the invisible. When I even sent Sasse copies of Franz Xavier Arnold's book *Zur Frage des Naturrechts bei Martin Luther* (Munich, 1937), which carefully proves, as I think, how Luther shares all the essential convictions of classical natural theology, I apparently received no answer. It should be remembered that Arnold wrote in 1936 and that he was under the spell of Nazism, as can be seen from the preface. I will later in my lecture return to that time and to Sasse's stand on natural theology at the time of the Barmen Declaration.

Sasse referred for support not only to Luther but also to the Formula of Concord:

> Luther would never have approved what Pieper still thinks of the natural knowledge of God. Our confessions do not ascribe more to natural man than 'ein dunkles Fünklein der Erkenntnis, daß ein Gott sei.' (Sol. Decl. II,)—English: 'a dim spark of the knowledge that there is a God'— Why has Pieper not noticed that?

This reference to the Formula of Concord sometimes has another shape in Sasse's writings. In his *Sacra Scriptura* it is said that Chemnitz has a very modest view of the natural knowledge of God, calling it "either nothing or imperfect or feeble."[9] Quite correctly Sasse identifies Chemnitz's words in his *Loci* with what the Formula of Concord said about the dim spark of knowledge. When, however, Sasse puts this in contradiction to what Franz Pieper or the orthodox fathers say, it must be said, with all due reverence for Sasse as a great teacher of the church, that he is mistaken. What Chemnitz develops here is exactly what Sasse denies, and it can all nowadays be studied without any difficulties in the English translation given in the [J. A. O.] Preus edition of the *Loci*, Part I, Chapter I, "The Knowledge of God." Here, for example, Chemnitz defends the idea that the existence of God is proved by the orderly process of cause and effect and that this thought is highly necessary for the external discipline on earth that God thereby upholds. There is no difference at all between what is said, on the one hand, by Chemnitz as the coeditor of the Formula of Concord and, on the other, by Franz Pieper.

Sasse is, however, dead set against Pieper's claim that the proofs for the existence of God appeal to any reasonable man. Sasse rhetorically asks, "What has become of the dim spark of knowledge? Eventually you have finally won [*tandem vicisti*], Thomas, one might exclaim."[10] These harsh words must be regarded as a consequence of Sasse's being under the spell of Scholz, who had come to regard the very use of the biblical notion of God in the connection of natural theology as a denial of the Christian revelation. It is merely a verbal repetition of Scholz's words 41 years earlier, when Sasse writes in a letter to me of 8 December 1970: "How could Thomas identify the God of Aristotle, who would cease to be God if he heard one single prayer, with the God of the Bible?" One must consider the implications of this question fully to understand Sasse's zeal in fighting what he and Scholz thought was a blow against the foundation of Christianity. Even if we do not share his views, we are bound to understand the deep seriousness with which he treated this question. At the same time we must realize, so I think, that Sasse equally shares Scholz's conviction that on account of scientific considerations reason could not be used to work within this specific field. This rejection is thus based both on biblical and scientific grounds.

We shall now look into the way that Sasse tried to explain the background of the orthodox school of theology that he met in the United States, and which he found necessary to criticize. I will first give a few quotations. "They must get rid of the 'greulicher Heide Aristoteles'—'the awful pagan Aristotle', but they cannot and must not accept Kierkegaard. The trouble is that the American theologians (right and left) have no idea of science."[11] "Another difference in our theological thinking is to be found in the different understanding of history. Walther and his people migrated from Germany before the great historical scholarship that started with Ranke changed our way of looking at the world."[12] "When Walther migrated to America there was no historical scholarship worth speaking of in German theology." "When our fathers migrated from Germany to Missouri, the academics among them came from the German humanistic gymnasium of that time, where neither historical research nor natural science were taught."[13]

It would be much too easy to go on with quotations of that kind. It is possible that they will cause a certain feeling of irritation, especially among my American listeners, but I think that the only possible way to deal with them is to try to analyze them. What do they say? It seems to me that all of them build on the assumption that I have tried to outline from the very beginning of my lecture, viz., that our approach to knowledge is based on the discoveries of science, which is always moving, acquiring new insights, pushing the border to the unknown or rather, in this case, abandoning it as indefensible. Science in this case is not only natural science but also history as a parallel subject, also passing over thresholds. It is a consequence of this kind of argument that some periods are still in darkness, and that these periods start at different times in different places. The Western world is reached by the light of the new day later than the German universities, where the discoveries are made. In some way an older generation corresponds to the pre-logical man of Lévi-Strauss; actually Sasse on one occasion uses the expression "prähistorische Anschauung."[14] This is Sasse's firm conviction.

At the beginning of my lecture I tried to defend the presence of a *philosophia perennis* in the human mind of all times, which means that we cannot divide the world of knowledge into basically different periods, as far as concerns the general "Betrachtung der Welt" ("our way of looking at the world"), as Sasse says. We do not of course discuss individual, undeniable scholarly gains such as the discovery of America and of penicillin but something else, something more fundamental, the very approach to knowledge, at which Sasse aims. Another way of scrutinizing Sasse's evaluation is to find out if the Missourian fathers such as Walther were really so cut off from the European world of learning. It would lead us too far afield to go into details, but I want to point out one fact that to me is utterly convincing as a proof that the Missourian fathers were well acquainted with the undeniable progress of historical research of their time, this taken in the limited sense and not as creating something absolutely new in our approach to knowledge. In Walther's theological paper *Lehre und Wehre*, we find a review of "Leopold von Rankes *Sämmtliche Werke* [collected works]," which expressed the greatest admiration of von Ranke and his work, especially for his contribution towards a right understanding of the Lutheran Reformation.[15] The review commends the 32 volumes of von Ranke's *Sämmtliche Werke*, to be ordered from Siemon & Brothers in Fort Wayne for a price of $ 2.25 a volume!

Someone, apparently Walther, has added to the review a warning against some speculative theological thoughts in von Ranke's works, for example, about the relationship between Luther and Zwingli. This critical commentary, which also recognizes von Ranke's greatness and does not want to challenge the preceding review, is in itself a proof of the most detailed knowledge of Ranke's works. It seems safe to say that the Saint Louis of 1868 was as much a part of German learning as Dorpat in Russia. It must be regretted that Sasse did not know about such an article. If he had, he would undoubtedly have retracted a few of his statements, finding that he and Walther were one in their evaluation of von Ranke, and that their difference may not, after all, have been so deep as he believed.

Having come this far, it is time to turn to what some of my listeners—perhaps rightly—may have wished to hear from the very beginning as the starting point. If it is now left to the end of my lecture, it is in order to give it an appropriately happy ending. It is Hermann Sasse as the great man in church history, defending natural theology against Barthianism; Hermann Sasse as the Lutheran defender of the God-given natural orders against Karl Barth's Christocracy and theocracy; Hermann Sasse at the peak of his career in Germany. Actually we have already heard, if we have listened carefully, that Sasse did not deny natural theology. There is a dim spark of the knowledge of God also in the pagans, so he says. However dim, it is there, and there were occasions when this was made very, very clear.

In a long letter to the Council of the Confessing Church of Silesia in Breslau, Sasse writes in 1936 against Karl Barth's abuse of the first thesis of the famous or notorious Barmen Declaration a few words which not only express his adherence to natural theology but which are also a splendid example of his admirable style that caused also his enemies to recognize his literary, some said journalistic gift. For that reason I quote the entire sentence first in German and then bring an English translation:

> Soll man für den unsinnigen Satz Karl Barths von der Verwerflichkeit der von der Reformatoren beibehaltenen Elemente der sog. natürlichen Theologie zum Märtyrer werden? Wer wird denn das glauben, daß die Chinesen nicht von Natur wissen, daß man Vater und Mutter ehren soll, daß man nicht töten, ehebrechen, stehlen und lügen soll? Sie wissen das

doch nun einmal. Sollen in Deutschland Märtyrer für die eigensinnige Behauptung Barths sterben, sie wüßten es nicht?

Are we to become martyrs for Karl Barth's unreasonable opinion that the elements of natural theology retained by the Reformers must be condemned? Who will then believe that the Chinese do not know by nature that we should honor father and mother, that we should not kill, not commit adultery, steal, and lie? After all, they do know that. Are martyrs to die in Germany for Barth's self-willed statement that they do not know?[16]

In his "Vom Sinn des Staates" written four years earlier in 1932, we find similar statements in a passage that tries to explain the "relative truth" of natural theology.[17] After the same serious reservations that we have already become acquainted with, Sasse presents something that he means legitimately to correspond to natural theology. That is the orders of creation (*Schöpfungsordnungen*), through which God sustains His creation. Something has remained in the mind of fallen man, "the hunch of God's existence, which lives in all religions, and a final knowledge about eternal norms."[18] That was the conviction that made Sasse protest against Karl Barth's denial of natural theology. To this extent also on this point Sasse may rightly claim to be the great Lutheran confessor that he certainly was in so many other ways.

We may, of course, ask why "feelings" should be more exempt from the curse of sin than the "reason" which not only Franz Pieper but also Luther and the Lutheran Confessions referred to in their defense of natural theology. The answer, as I have tried to prove here, and which I now shortly summarize, is that to Sasse, as to so many others of his time and his cultural climate, trust in reason as leading us to the source of our existence, taken in the sense of a *cognitio legalis*, a knowledge of the Law, seemed impossible because of its historical connection with paganism and because natural science had made impossible the basis of metaphysical arguments. Yet Sasse saw the absolute necessity of upholding the defense of natural theology in some way, and the emergency exit left open was then the feeling, the *Ahnung*, Pascal's "heart," as Sasse thought. This statement does not diminish the theological stature of one of our century's greatest theologians, my dear, fatherly friend, Hermann Sasse.

[1] Heinrich Scholz, *Eros und Caritas. Die platonische Liebe und die Liebe im Sinne des Christentums* (Halle: M. Niemeyer, 1929).

[2] Letter of 31 May 1972.

[3] Scholz, *Eros und Caritas*, 62; my trans.

[4] Ibid., 55, n.1.

[5] Blaise Pascal, *Pensées et Opuscules* (Paris: Classiques Hachette, 1963), 458, n. 277.

[6] *SS*, 141, n. 32.

[7] Anders Nygren, *Agape and Eros*, trans. Philip S. Watson (New York and Evanston: Harper & Row, 1969).

[8] Tom G. A. Hardt, *Venerabilis et adorabilis Eucharistia. Eine Studie über die lutherische Abendmahlslehre im 16. Jahrhundert*, ed. Jürgen Diestelmann, trans. Susanne Diestelmann (Göttingen: Vandenhoeck & Ruprecht, 1988), 89, n. 44 (Swedish original, 82, n. 44).

[9] *SS*, 145; my trans.

[10] *SS*, 146; my trans.

[11] Letter to Tom Hardt of 29 August 1959.

[12] Letter to an American theologian, 19 June 1968.

[13] "Als unsere Väter aus Deutschland nach Missouri auswanderten, kamen die Akademiker unter ihnen vom damaligen deutschen humanistischen Gymnasium, auf dem weder Geschichtsforschung gelehrt wurde noch Naturwissenschaft." Letter to German church leaders, August 1971; my trans.

[14] *SS*, 93.

[15] *Lehre und Wehre* (1868): 117-121.

[16] Qtd from Martin Wittenberg, "Hermann Sasse und Barmen," in W.-D. Hausschild, W. Kretschmar, and C. Nicolaisen eds., *Die lutherischen Kirchen und die Bekenntnissynode von Barmen* (Göttingen: Vandenhoeck & Ruprecht, 1984), 103; my trans.

[17] *ISC* II:355.

[18] *ISC* II:356.

Hermann Sasse and the Mystery of Sacred Scripture

Kurt E. Marquart

The venerable doctor of the church whose hundredth birthday we celebrate this year taught us anew to see Scripture, Sacrament, and Church in light of the supreme mystery of the Incarnation, and that in turn in light of the Pauline-Lutheran theology of the cross. While the validity of this perspective is beyond dispute among confessional Lutherans, Sasse's own particular applications of it to the inspiration and inerrancy of Holy Scripture remain controversial.

The new Sasse volume edited by Kloha and Feuerhahn has raised the whole issue with an admirable clarity and urgency for English-speaking Lutherans. Especially valuable, in my view, is the painstaking essay by Jeffrey Kloha, which, for the first time, gathers together hitherto loose ends into a coherent pattern. Kloha, in my opinion, rightly identifies the nature, the occasion, and the time of the change in Sasse's understanding of biblical inerrancy.[1] Prior to 1951 Sasse had limited inerrancy to "theological" matters only. At the end of that year he gave up that limitation. The watershed event here was the adoption by the Joint Intersynodical Committees, of which Sasse was a prominent member, of the *Theses on Scripture and Inerrancy* on 13 December 1951. These statements thereby became part of the *Theses of Agreement* documenting the dogmatic consensus between the two Australian Lutheran churches, and adopted by them in 1956/1959, and in the enlarged and final form of the *Theses* in 1966.

Kloha also points out that in "the middle and late 1960's Sasse was forced to clarify his own views as the result of theological discussions in both the United States and Germany . . . ."[2] There is no doubt of Sasse's continuing global interests and involvements. My task in this paper, however, will be to shed some light on the little-known Australian Lutheran context of that time, which subjected Sasse's and the *Theses*' understanding of inerrancy to some unexpected stresses and strains, almost, one might say, to the breaking point. In other words, I propose to start where Kloha left off.

This conception of my task virtually dictates its shape as a "narrative theology" of sorts, with some conclusions of course at the end. And, to anticipate, I must say that in working through this material again after all these years, I have come to believe that here lies the key to the mysterious non-appearance of Sasse's projected book *De Scriptura*.

I. Sasse, Lutheran Union, and Inerrancy

Since the division of 1846, there had been two separate Lutheran streams in Australia. One became the Evangelical Lutheran Church of Australia (ELCA), with strong fellowship ties to the Missouri Synod, and the other, the United Evangelical Lutheran Church of Australia (UELCA), identified with the ALC of 1930, and especially with the old Iowa Synod. Both had their headquarters and seminaries (Concordia and Immanuel, respectively) in Adelaide, South Australia. Some preliminary agreements had been achieved by the time of Sasse's arrival in 1949. Without Sasse's weighty intervention, however, and precisely on the UELCA side, it is almost impossible to envisage the kind of consensus which led to the union of the two churches in 1965. He supplied the decisive ingredients: (1) the vision of CA VII as the concrete basis for dogmatic and sacramental unity and fellowship among Lutheran churches, and (2) the agreement regarding the inspiration and inerrancy of Holy Scripture. Once these two elements were in place, the final "breakthrough" became almost inevitable.

It is difficult for those who were not there to appreciate the enormous appeal of Lutheran reunion, once the idea had become feasible. The prospect of union created a gravitational attraction and momentum which were virtually irresistible. None of us who were members of the constituting convention of the Lutheran Church of Australia will ever forget that event. Ten thousand people—probably the largest concourse of Lutherans in the history of Australia— thronged the oval in Tanunda, South Australia, for the Thanksgiving Services on the morning and afternoon of Sunday 30 October 1966. Here were echoed the strains of "Now Thank We All Our God," with which the early Lutheran immigrants had celebrated the happy endings of their arduous sea-voyages of several months. And as those early settlers had—sometimes immediately upon arrival—taken the oath of loyalty to Queen Victoria, so their successors at Tanunda resolved at once to "send a letter or cable to Her Majesty the Queen, . . . informing her of events leading up to our re-union and the formation under God of the Lutheran Church of Australia, and pledging our continued allegiance and prayer both for herself as Sovereign" and for "all who hold authority under the Crown."[3]

Beneath the sentiments and the solemnities, however, lay unresolved theological tensions whose intensity would have astonished the casual observer. The very suddenness with which the *Document of Union* was thrust upon the two churches early in 1965 was odd. The 19-21 January 1965 ELCA Queensland District Pastors' Conference was informed of the *fait accompli* that the two seminary faculties had achieved a "breakthrough," and that the resultant *Document of Union* would be presented for adoption to the ELCA's triennial convention in two months' time! The stunning speed of this development may have had something to do with the rise within the ELCA itself of certain frictions between what for simplicity's sake we may call the "Adelaide theology," on the one hand, and the "Queensland theology," on the other. As one observer, Friedemann Hebart, put it in the March 1965 issue of *Lutheran Student*, published at the University of Adelaide:

> Unpleasant rumours are filtering down from the north that ELCA Queenslanders are not uniformly behind union. It is ironic that the ELCA General Synod, which started this week, is being held at Toowoomba, which has in recent years become a centre of ultra-conservative Lutheranism, and which is most likely to cause the proposed union considerable embarrassment.

The Queensland Pastors' Conference could not "in good conscience accept the proposed 'Document of Union' in its present form . . . as an adequate and God-pleasing resolution of differences," and asked the District President (F. W. Noack), to convey their concerns to the authorities in Adelaide.[4] By February a 72-page pamphlet appeared, entitled *The E.L.C.A. at the Crossroads in 1965*. Written by me and distributed by the District's Parish Education Committee (Pastor C. Priebbenow, Chairman), the tract, without mentioning the *Document of Union* by name, reviewed the outstanding issues, and put on record the neo-orthodox invasion of the Missouri Synod then in progress.[5] There was a 12-page appendix about the "Scharlemann Case." It was felt that this might be the last opportunity for some time to address such issues via official channels in Australia.

When the *Document of Union* was debated and voted on, section by section, at the General Pastors' Conference preceding the ELCA Convention in March, a block of nearly twenty pastors, mostly from Queensland, voted "No." That was because no amendments of any kind could be considered. The impending division on the Convention floor was averted when it turned out, in private sessions with the leadership, that the *Document*'s objectionable language could be changed after all by mutual agreement among the Intersynodical Committees. This ultimately produced a text which clearly settled the one unresolved doctrinal issue between the two churches: that of church fellowship. The settlement, now enshrined in the *Theses of Agreement* (V, parr. 25-29), fittingly follows the paragraphs 17-24, which set out the implications of CA VII, and are largely Sasse's work.[6] On the strength of the assurances that such necessary changes would be made, opposition to the *Document* ceased, and it was adopted with relief and unanimity.

The Queenslanders knew of course that certain historical-critical sympathies, inimical to biblical inerrancy, existed in the Adelaide seminaries. Two considerations, however, persuaded them not to treat this as an obstacle to union. One was the argument that this question had not divided the two churches historically, and that even now it was an issue within both seminary faculties and not between them. The other was the firm undertaking, offered especially by Dr. H. Koehne, the new president of the ELCA, soon to be vice-president of the LCA, that these matters would be resolutely addressed by the new church's Commission on Theology and Inter-Church Relations (CTICR), on which the Queensland concerns would be fairly represented. This undertaking was fully honored in the years that followed.

Since no one could predict how long these discussions might take, or what their outcome would be, the Queenslanders decided to place their convictions on record, so that there could be no misunderstanding about this in the future. Accordingly on 7 May 1966 a Special Convention of the Queensland District, upon the recommendation of its Pastors' Conference, unanimously adopted *A Declaration and Plea*, which set out our objections to "the twin evils of Liberalism and Ecumenicism." On the subject of biblical inerrancy, the following errors were rejected:

> . . . that "inerrancy," as applied to Scripture, might mean something other than the total absence of any errors or contradictions whatsoever; or that

inerrancy could be limited to the "theological content" or the "divine side" of Scripture, as distinguished from the entire sacred text as such; or that some things presented as facts by Scripture might be "theologically true" without being factually true; or that "inerrancy" could be defined on the basis of an examination of the text for alleged errors, rather than solely and alone on the basis of the texts in which the Bible itself explicitly teaches its own inspiration and inerrancy.

The document also rejected as an error the view "That Genesis 1-3, for example, could be taken in some figurative sense, so that 'theistic evolution' would be permitted as at least a possible explanation of the way in which the human body was formed."

It would be an understatement to say that the two seminary faculties did not respond favorably to the document. A flurry of meetings ensued, designed to assuage the Queenslanders' growing alarm. Sasse played a prominent role in these proceedings. It would serve no purpose to attempt here a blow-by-blow account of these preliminaries. Some illustrative vignettes will have to suffice. One participant, who later felt compelled to leave the LCA, remembers as the upshot of a July 1966 meeting in Adelaide:

> The Queensland pastors were told quite frankly at this meeting, that there were numerous errors and contradictions in the Scriptures, and that the Holy Spirit made use of these human weaknesses to give His Word to men. The top church officials, too, appeared to be somewhat taken aback by the forceful assertions of error in the Scriptures on the part of their seminary professors.[7]

Perhaps in the hurly-burly of the lively exchanges, "seeming errors" were not always clearly distinguished from actual errors.

Drs. Sasse and Hamann, Jr., were deputized to represent their respective faculties at the August 1966 ELCA Queensland District Pastors' Conference in Toowoomba. As the minutes make clear, both men were at pains to assert their commitment to inspiration and inerrancy, as confessed in the *Theses of Agreement*. Yet both made provocative claims about the collateral Genesis issue:

> Dr. Sasse claimed that Genesis 1-3 is not real history. . . . Augustine tried three times to interpret Genesis 1 literally without success. . . . The truth of the Exodus story remains truth even though mathematically the

numbers (600,000) may not have been correct. ... The creation story presupposes that the earth is older than the stars and the galaxies because they speak to simple people like us and Moses. "My grave concern is that the church makes the same mistake as in the time of Galileo," said Dr. Sasse.

Hamann was willing to take the details of the Fall account in some figurative sense "and questioned also whether there was a real Garden of Eden. These things are quite possibly figurative. It was maintained that all these views are permitted by the Theses of Agreement."

The minutes, kept by Concordia Seminary Professor Dr. F. Blaess, of a further special meeting in Adelaide report among Sasse's critical responses to the Queensland *Declaration and Plea*: "It was difficult to discuss the Declaration and Plea because of the underlying concept of truth as absolute correctness, a concept which he could not accept." At the conclusion of this September, 1966, meeting it was resolved:

> Since God indeed cannot lie nor lead astray, no Christian should say that the Bible endorses errors or mistaken human notions. It is in fact God's inerrant and non-deceiving Word. However, as the *Theses of Agreement* state, this inerrancy cannot and need not always be demonstrated. It remains an article of faith. So it is true teaching to insist on the inerrancy of Scripture, although one must also admit that there are many facts about Scripture which seem to run counter to this claim, where faith in the God who cannot lie must take precedence over and subdue the objections of reason.

It was further resolved: "No teaching or theological work shall be regarded as in harmony with the Theses of Agreement if it conflicts with this statement."

The concluding convention of the ELCA's Queensland District recognized that its earlier attempt to tie the property of Concordia Memorial College, Toowoomba, to the doctrinal content of the *Declaration and Plea* had failed, but thanked the UELCA Queensland District for its "unequivocal statement on the absolute inerrancy of the Holy Scriptures in the Theses of Agreement." The resolution concluded with a reaffirmation of "our joy that the amalgamation of our two Churches has become a reality."[8]

If this recital has seemed tedious and scrappy, Ladies and Gentlemen, I can only apologize. I know of no other way to put before you the concrete church situation within and against which Sasse's understanding of the *Theses* on inerrancy had to define and refine itself. Although we cannot even in the church—perhaps especially in the church—get away from what Sir Isaiah Berlin called "the crooked timber of humanity," our brief remaining narrative can now sail smoothly along polished formulations which exhibit a certain elegance in the progressive unfolding of the issues.

The new theological commission (CTICR) convened in August 1967. A list of eight questions on the inerrancy/Genesis complex, formulated by Professor C. R. Priebbenow, was submitted as a proposed basis for discussion.[9] In a quite uncharacteristic moment of anger, Dr. Sasse said: "These are not theological questions, and should not be discussed here." Nonetheless on 30 August he graciously supplied a written analysis, on ten foolscap pages, single-spaced.

Taking up Question 7 first, Sasse challenged the close connection between logic and theology: "Whatever we have to say on the following pages, it must first of all be stated that a statement can be logically correct and theologically incorrect and vice versa." He cited Luther: "To state that a theologian who is not a logician is a monstrous heretic (*Theologus non logicus est monstrosus haereticus*) is a monstrous and heretical sentence. This in opposition to common opinion."[10] Aristotle himself, said Sasse, realized that his "principle of contradiction" could not be proved but was "an axiomatic assumption that one and the same cannot be and not be at the same time, an assumption which, e.g., does not exist for Indian thought." Similarly, today, we know non-Euclidean geometries. "Why then," asked Sasse, "should the Church absolutize a logic which . . . can never be regarded as final and absolute?" Among examples of logical offenses against theology, Sasse gave this: "Since Holy Scripture can be and is being interpreted [God] must have given us, so we are told, an infallible teaching office which explains the Bible—a perfectly logical conclusion."

On Question 8, certainly provoked by recurrent themes in the Australian discussion, Sasse responded: "I cannot understand how anybody can deny that the Bible knows of 'factual propositional truth,' e.g. in statements of what God is, does, what has happened, etc. The contrary opinion has arisen out of the fact that the concept of truth in the Bible has still other aspects." Therefore: "It was a great mistake when some theologians have tried to do away with the idea of propositional truth."

To Question 5 Sasse answered: "It is this absence of a clear and direct Biblical statement that Holy Scripture does not and cannot contain errors which makes the 'a priori' way impossible and compels us to choose another way." Regarding St. John 10:35 he said that it "is quoted by the Orthodox Lutheran theologians, but never, as far as I can see, as a proof-text for the inerrancy of Holy Writ. The word itself proves not more than the absolute authority of Holy Scripture." Yet in answer to Questions 4, 6, and 7, Sasse wrote that "inerrancy must be regarded as a valid conclusion from inspiration"—a remark conceding considerable scope to logic and *a priori*.

Under Question 6 Sasse agreed that inerrancy meant the absence of error, and that this applied not only to "theological propositions found in Scripture, but to Scripture as a whole." Yet there followed what can only be described as a list of counterexamples, of which the following is representative:

> The question is: What is meant by the term "error of fact"? Would our beloved opponents [!] regard the necessary limitations of the Biblical writers as children of their time, e.g., their use of the literary methods of their age, their limited knowledge of nature and history as "errors" or producing errors? If today a historian would give in an historical book exaggerated numbers of people who took part in certain events, this would be rightly regarded as false statements, as either lies or errors. If an ancient writer did use figures more in an illustrative than in a statistical sense, he did what everyone expected him to do. That was the custom of that time. . . . Why did God the Holy Spirit allow Stephen (who spoke under inspiration according to Matth. 10:20) to narrate the history of the Fathers in a way which cannot be reconciled with the stories as we find them in the Pentateuch? . . . Who was here in error, the Hebrew Bible or the Greek Bible, or Stephen or Luke? The whole concept of "errors of fact" that underlies the questions addressed to us is not applicable to the Bible.

The disquieting implication here was that either "the whole concept of inerrancy" is not applicable to the Bible, or if it is, that it is meaningless.

Finally, Sasse held that:

> . . . the opinion that man is a product of a natural evolution from lower

forms of life contradicts the clear doctrine of the Bible. ... Nor is it possible to distinguish with the Roman doctrine between the creation of the human body and the creation of each individual soul, the first having natural causes, the second being a supernatural act of God. ... Man as a whole is God's creature.

Near the end Sasse went to the brink:

> We are bound to the doctrine of our Lord and His apostles of the creation and the fall of man. We do not know in detail what the exact picture of earth and heaven, sun, moon and stars was which Jesus had in the state of his humility. He has not left us a cosmology. As Son of God He shared the omnipotence and omniscience of God the Father. ... But only in particular and rare cases he made use of the prerogatives of his full divinity. ... But otherwise his glory remained hidden behind the humility of the obedient Servant of God.

For the next meeting of the CTICR the chairman, Dr. Koehne, reported the desire of the Queensland District pastors—now the united LCA body—to have certain questions of concern "(in respect to the implications of the Theses of Agreement on Inspiration)" addressed in detail by the Commission prior to the 1968 General Convention of the LCA. The questions put to the CTICR by Dr. Koehne were:

1. Whether the concept of inerrancy excludes also errors "of fact" or only errors of theology?
2. Is it possible to accept the Scriptures as "absolutely authoritative" without regarding them as inerrant?
3. Is there anything in the Bible concept of "truth" which conflicts with the traditional understanding of inerrancy? If so, what?
4. Whether a figurative understanding of Genesis such as would allow for some form of evolutionary origin for at least the body of man is tenable in the light of the New Testament understanding of Genesis?

The second question clearly arose out of Sasse's distinction of 30 August 1967 with reference to St. John 10:35.

At first there was some resistance in the CTICR to any clear definition of inerrancy. One of the anti-logical persuasion even opined that inerrancy could not be defined since it was a mystery. However, the church plainly expected clear answers. The upshot was that while the complexities of Genesis were left to another day, the 1968 General

Pastors' Conference and LCA Convention received and adopted *Inspiration and Inerrancy: An Explanation of Paragraphs Dealing with Inspiration and Inerrancy in the Theses of Agreement*.[11] The crucial sentence was: "The Theses of Agreement use the term 'inerrancy' in its normal sense of freedom from all error and contradiction, 'factual' as well as 'theological.'" A reminder was included that "a deliberate disregard of the Theses in teaching and preaching would appear as evidence of bad faith, and would constitute a serious threat to the unity of the Church."

Soon, however, the CTICR found itself obliged to reopen the question of the correct understanding of inerrancy. A few requests had been received for reconsideration of the 1968 language. Thereupon old divisions within the CTICR itself came to the surface again. Several essays were prepared and debated. The biggest challenge was to arrive at a clear statement of what exactly the point of difference was. Intensive debate finally succeeded in formulating the precise point at issue. It must have come as a shock to the 1970 LCA Convention to be told in the CTICR Report that there were now two conflicting understandings of the *Theses of Agreement* on inerrancy, which needed to be sorted out.[12] The conflict was over Thesis VIII,10, that the holy writers "retained the distinctive features of their personalities (language and terminology, literary methods, conditions of life, knowledge of nature and history as apart from direct revelation and prophecy)." The question was whether "as apart from direct revelation" meant to distinguish *between* Scripture and the authors' knowledge when not under inspiration, or *within* Scripture itself between revealed and not revealed matters.[13]

The essence of position one was that "the Servant Form, i.e., the limitations of human knowledge of nature and history or other distinctive features of the personalities of the writers did not find expression in any statement of God's written Word in such a way as to result in error." Position Two, by contrast, held, in its somewhat serpentine phrasing, that:

> ... the words "as apart from" also point to the possible absence in some cases of a[14] direct revelation in areas of history or science or geography and the like, so that the holy writers not only retained all their limitations of knowledge of nature and history and all other distinctive features of their personalities, but were actually permitted by the Spirit of God to

give expression to them in the human side[15] of that written Word of God. Consequently, it is held, there is evidence in God's written Word of statements which deal specifically with aspects of history or science or geography and the like, which may not be factual in the light of more certain human knowledge in such areas. Nevertheless they hold that this in no way invalidates the truth or inerrancy or authority of God's written Word or makes God a liar, but rather points to the Servant Form of the written Word of God.

I am happy to report that my subcommittee version of this wording, discussed in Dr. Sasse's presence, features my handwritten note at the top: "Sasse rejects Pos.[ition] 2."

Although the task of reconciling this deep-seated difference seemed at times hopeless, it must be regarded as a singular divine gift that genuine agreed statements could be offered by the CTICR to the LCA by 1972, when they were unanimously adopted. Key provisions were:

> ... while understanding inerrancy in the normal sense of freedom from all error and contradiction, "factual" as well as "theological," the Theses state that this inerrancy "cannot be seen with human eyes nor can it be proved to human reason; it is an article of faith, a belief in something which is hidden and not obvious."
>
> This understanding of inerrancy implies that, although error may appear to be present in the Scriptures, it is not really so. . . .
>
> Some ways of speaking or teaching in the matter of inerrancy which are contrary to the sound doctrine of the Scriptures and of the Theses of Agreement are herewith specified:
>
> 1. to speak of "errors" in the Holy Scripture;
> 2. to hold that what according to clear biblical statements "actually is or actually happened," may be regarded as what actually is not or actually did not happen; . . .
> 4. to use modern knowledge as a means to judge any biblical statement and attack the authority of Scripture; . . . .[16]

The Genesis issue was resolved at the same time and in the same sense and spirit,[17] but we can obviously say no more about it here. For good measure the LCA resolved in 1975:

It is clearly the right and the duty of the Church, in the face of current challenges, to define how it understands the Scriptures and the Confessions. Therefore, explanations and amendments of the Theses, as well as any other statements of a doctrinal nature, submitted to the entire Church after thorough theological examination and discussion and adopted by it, must be accorded the same authority in the Church as the Theses themselves.[18]

II. Personal Reflections and Conclusions

Although Doctor Sasse did not, as I recall, take a very active personal part in the final shaping of the Australian consensus statements of 1972, they bear his stamp—in what they say, in what they don't say, and in how they say it. Not that he was necessarily happy with every provision. No doubt he would have put several things differently. But the overall sense of Lutheran confessional responsibility and solidarity owed a great deal to his single-minded devotion to St. Paul's *theologia crucis*, as that had been given Luther's Reformation to recover.

Sasse's enormous influence had nothing to do with what we now call "leadership qualities," which can supposedly be acquired by means of "assertiveness training." His personal presence in those last years was, like St. Paul's, completely disarming and unintimidating. But one sensed in him at once that unaffected gentle gravity which flowed from the fact that for him theology was not a profession or a hobby, but his very life. Even if one had encountered him somewhat adversarially at first, it was as impossible to dislike him as it was not to learn from him. I recall one tense pre-union meeting in Adelaide, at which Sasse had gone on at some length bashing the "fundamentalism" of certain views of Scripture. Finally the venerable Dr. Henry Hamann, Sr., who was the ELCA's patriarchal figure as Sasse himself had become the UELCA's, asked for the floor and delivered himself of a lucid and magisterial disquisition on the subject. After that speech Dr. Sasse said with a touching meekness: "If Dr. Hamann is a fundamentalist, then I am a fundamentalist too!"

This same unfailing courtesy and consideration Sasse extended also to his young colleagues, who must sometimes have been a thundering nuisance to him. Only once do I remember Sasse really infuriated. Brash young country pastor that I was—before I became a brash old professor—I once made the mistake of blurting out in a meeting, probably in connection with "beefed up" numbers in the Old Testament: "But Dr. Sasse, this is exactly what Dr. Scharlemann is saying in Missouri!" Sasse was livid, and almost shouted: "Do not speak to us about Scharlemann! He is an American general. We are humble Australians!" No doubt the differences did not end there.

What Sasse once wrote about Barth, adapting a philosopher's *bon mot*, applies to him as well: "A great theology is not one against which nothing could be said, but one which has something to say."

Sasse was aware of the source and direction of his own biases. Of his controversial "Letter 14" he wrote in 1968: "I wrote this in 1949/50 when I was still not able to see the problem of inerrancy properly, as none of us German professors, even the most conservative, were."[19]

From his background Sasse had imbibed the standard aversion to the theologians of Lutheran Orthodoxy, which yielded only gradually to a more sympathetic view. Sasse's early critical comments, for instance, were apparently taken over at second hand from Karl Barth.[20] Of course, Sasse was never a Barthian. He understood that "Barth's doctrine of the Word of God ends in a Nestorian tearing apart of divine word and human word."[21] Or even more dramatically: "But where one ends with Barth's doctrine, that becomes clear, when now it resounds from New Guinea over to Australia: 'The Bible is full of errors. That is the Incarnation.'"[22] Yet it is not clear even in these discussions that Sasse ever broke quite free of that sweeping historical-philosophical panorama which Barth had devised as the backdrop for understanding 17th century Orthodoxy.[23]

Sasse's unrestrained enthusiasm for Jaroslav Pelikan's youthful production, *From Luther to Kierkegaard*, belongs in this context.[24] Here is the whole neo-orthodox thesis of the grand abduction of the Reformation by Luther's successors and their reversion to Aristotelian slavery. Sasse seems to overlook here the unpleasant implications of Pelikan's theory for the Formula of Concord, a Confession which Sasse usually defended against its detractors.

Much more realistic about Pelikan's book was the reaction of Dr. Henry Hamann, Sr. An oral tradition which I believe to be reliable has an appalled Hamann threatening to write a response entitled *From Pieper to Pelikan*. True, Sasse was not nearly so happy with—indeed he was quite critical of—the intrusion of Pelikan's "companion volume," *Luther the Expositor*, into the American edition of *Luther's Works*.[25] But even then he concludes by calling Pelikan "a theologian from whom we expect great things."[26] I shall give the last word on this to old Dr. Hamann, who wrote in his review of Pelikan's *Luther the Expositor*:

> Dr. Pelikan is, to say it roundly, too greatly influenced by certain modern Luther scholars to be entirely reliable. For he has adopted the literary vice of some *Lutherforscher* who manage to walk, with eyes tightly closed, past dozens and hundreds of the clearest possible pronouncements of Luther in order to pitch and pounce upon some doubtful passage, on the strength of which they attempt to foist upon the Reformer teachings quite different from, and perhaps utterly opposed to, those which he actually professed and defended.[27]

In the course of our Australian discussions we often heard about that silly Gospel-harmony which troubled poor Jairus' daughter with three separate risings from the dead. How unrepresentative that was of Lutheran Orthodoxy was pointed out to Dr. Sasse from the great Chemnitz-Leyser-Gerhard *Harmonia Quatuor Evangelistarum*, where the accounts from Mt. 9, Mk. 5, and Lk. 8 are combined without any such nonsense.[28] From the same source it was shown that St. John 10:35 had indeed been cited by the early Lutherans to prove the errorlessness of Scripture.[29] As for Luther's own position on Scripture, one can hardly improve on the massive documentation and incisive analysis by Dr. William Oesch,[30] not to overlook the careful work of Gottfried Wachler.[31] I do not know if Sasse had made references to the Large Catechism's "God's Word can neither err nor deceive" (*nec potest errare nec fallere*; LC IV:57)[32] prior to this point's being raised in the Queensland *Declaration and Plea* (May, 1967).

As an antidote to the bad press accorded the old dogmaticians, two works were especially commended to Dr. Sasse's attention: Robert Preus' *Inspiration of Scripture*, and Bengt Haegglund's *Die Heilige Schrift und ihre Deutung in der Theologie Johann Gerhards*. With Preus' work Sasse was already acquainted, and had in fact a high regard for it. Haegglund's book he intended to order and examine with care.

On 2 March 1968 Sasse wrote to me: "Our main difference seems to lie in the field of philosophy rather than theology." This was in reference to the discussion about Luther, logic, Aristotle, and Orthodoxy. On 16 August 1970 he wrote:

> A short word on the problem of evolution. I have never been able to understand why the Americans are so preoccupied with this issue, on the secularist side as well as in Christian circles. Perhaps because evolution has become a sort of Religionsersatz for many. We who have been brought up on Goethe's philosophy of nature have never been impressed by Darwin who applied the economic phenomena of the industrial revolution to nature, just as we never have been impressed by Newton.

Sasse was completely right, of course, to warn against building any part of the house of faith and of theology on the quicksands of philosophy. Luther had exorcised the demons of scholasticism, and they must never be allowed back in. Any future treatment of prolegomena will have to sort out in detail Luther's profound contributions on that score. Such an endeavor will need to be informed also by the new and quite significant developments in Luther research, particularly as spearheaded in Finland by Tuomo Mannermaa and his school. This represents a rediscovery of the mature Luther, with his sturdy ontological, or even better, incarnational realism, which now challenges certain philosophical predilections which seem to have governed the earlier fascination, in the wake of Karl Holl and the "Luther Renaissance," with the young Luther.

Luther's incarnational-sacramental realism is just the point here. Sasse above all saw with crystal clarity that there is no middle ground between Luther's *est* and Zwingli's *significat*. Clever words may disguise but can never resolve the stark dichotomy. And of course Sasse insisted on the *est* in the Sacrament, in the Incarnation, and in the divine-human Scriptures, which three he knew to be one.

Yet in the matter of inspiration and inerrancy Sasse tried persistently to find a middle course between the traditional Lutheran teaching and various modern substitutes, including the Barthian.[33] Sasse's thought was clearly behind the following critique by the joint Adelaide faculties of the Queensland District's (ELCA) position:

> Unfortunately, the statement regards all attempts to speak of the Scripture in a way which is not that of the "old, orthodox" theologians as an attack on the majesty of God, and shows no awareness of any position that is not either "old orthodoxy" or un-Christian liberal denial of the authority of

Scripture. If it is seriously held that these are the only two possible positions, we can only vigorously reject such a judgment as being an invalid opinion incapable of logical or historical proof and one which in its very nature cannot be made into an article of faith.[34]

The Queenslanders replied: "We regret that no potential third position has been actually spelt out."[35]

The scope within which a third or middle view might be located, seems to have narrowed for Sasse over time, as in his view the distance between "Luther" and "Orthodoxy" narrowed. In 1951 Sasse spoke of the Missouri Synod having taken over "the doctrine of the later Orthodoxy" without even asking "whether this doctrine is Lutheran, and whether it can be brought into harmony with the Confession." Indeed, there was "a deep chasm" between Luther and Orthodoxy.[36] In the "Footnotes to Letter 14" (1967/69) Sasse distinguished between "doctrine" and "form": "If, thus, we Lutherans have every reason to maintain and defend the doctrine of the Inerrancy of Holy Scripture, we have, on the other hand, no reason to preserve the form of this doctrine as we find it in the Orthodox Fathers, and as it has developed in all churches of Christendom" in the 16th and 17th centuries.[37] His 1967 essay, "Confessional Churches in the Ecumenical Movement," written "in grateful acknowledgement" of Sasse's Springfield doctorate, further reduced "form" to "terminology":

> It is really astonishing that even great theologians of our time rejected inspiration because the scholastic form of this doctrine in the Orthodoxy of the fathers is no longer tenable. In other questions they can distinguish a dogma of the church and the theological terminology in which it may be shrouded. Why not here?[38]

Sasse's bristling at "Aristotelian logic" always suggested that here some arbitrary human yoke was being forced on Scripture and the church. What was difficult to appreciate in the whole neo-orthodox climate—which blamed the Fall not so much on Adam as on Aristotle—was that logic actually constrains not God but our own language. Without such constraints we should be free to babble nonsense and twist God's Word at will. Without the right linguistic, logical discipline we might just as well render "In the beginning God created the heavens and the earth" as "In the beginning the cuckoo swallowed the hedge sparrow"—as Luther put it so memorably against the sacramentarians.[39] If Aristotle had invented the law of contradiction, then it would be an arbitrary convention, to be replaced by something better, as Euclidean geometry has been. Yet there is good reason to believe that, technicalities aside, Aristotle merely discovered, rather than invented, the law of contradiction. For unless it holds, no human discourse has any meaning at all. If "the Word was made flesh" does not rule out "the Word was not made flesh," and if "This is My Body" is really equivalent to "This is not My Body," not only theology but all communication is at an end. Even the notoriously slippery and counter-intuitive domain of quantum physics cannot abolish basic logic without collapsing into gibberish.[40]

Of course Sasse continued to insist on the EST in the sentence "Scripture IS the Word of God." His search for a third way, an alternative to Orthodoxy, concentrated on the "human side" of Scripture, which had allegedly been forgotten or denied by Orthodoxy. Sasse wrote for instance: "What the fathers of Missouri like Pieper should have rejected was not the 'human side of the Bible' as such, but the 'Nestorianism' of liberal theologians of the 19th century who ended with a purely human Bible and lost the Word of God . . . ."[41] Yet Pieper had never rejected the human side "as such." What he rejected was "human side" talk which functioned as code for error. He wrote:

> By the way, the modern theologians do not really mean the "human side" of Scripture when they say that the human side has been overlooked by the dogmaticians. By the human side, about which they are so concerned, they mean the alleged errors in Scripture.[42]

It turns out that it is just the analogy to the Incarnation which makes it impossible to think of a human side of the Bible wandering off by itself, as it were, into error. Sasse saw that clearly himself. He wrote in 1966, to lay to rest once more the ghost of Letter 14:

> The task of the Lutheran Church is to understand the Bible, as Luther did, as Jesus Christ's book, because it is the book of the Holy Spirit, who in the entire Bible, from first to last page, bears witness to Christ. In saying this we know well that, just as Christ's human nature has its hypostasis (personal existence) in the divine nature, even so in the Bible the human side of the Scripture also has meaning and essence (Wesen) only by virtue of the fact that in it the pure Word of God is given to us.[43]

The Christological parallel is just that, a parallel, or a paradigm of which inspiration is an analog—not an identical copy. This becomes very clear when we test the relation of earthly and heavenly realities in the Sacrament by an application of the Chalcedonian adverbs. We see at once that there is an incongruity with the anti-Nestorian ἀχωριστῶς—without separation). That is because the Personal Union of God and Man in Jesus is permanent and indissoluble, whereas the Sacramental Union is limited to the divinely instituted use: consecration, distribution, reception (FC SD VII:86).

If we now try the Chalcedonian words on the relation of human and divine in Scripture, we find an awkward fit at the anti-Eutychean end of the scale. What might it mean that we are not to confuse God's Word and man's in Scripture? Are we then to look for transcendent divine meanings floating above, behind, and beyond the plain sense of the text as given in human language (Hebrew or Greek)?

The Christological analogy, properly applied, checkmates every effort to pry loose from the singular mystery of the divine-human text a more or less autonomous "human side," which might then become a fitting object for critical operations. Whenever Sasse ran up against this boundary, he drew back. He refused to cross it, for he knew that to do so would be to sacrifice the EST of his and the church's solemn confession that Holy Scripture IS the Word of God. He also must have noticed that others who tried to run with his rhetoric often suffered derailment. After Sasse's death, for instance, his younger colleague Maurice Schild said in his tribute:

> Sasse could take up and maintain his position on Scripture, by constantly pointing to the Gospel which everywhere is the real point in Scripture ("the child in the manger"), while letting information (*Mitteilungen*) of a geographical, scientific, or other sort from the ancient world be the "swaddling clothes," wrapped in which the Child lies—for the sake of our weakness (Chrysostom). Also the doctrine of Scripture has to be *theologia crucis*.[44]

There are of course authentic touches here. But such a wholesale disjunction between "Gospel" and "geographical, scientific," and other sorts of information is impossible. Buddhism and Hinduism may not ultimately need space-time particulars—but the Incarnation involves them necessarily and inextricably.

This is why Sasse's probings for a third way, a *tertium quid*, always came to naught, and had to come to naught in the end. Here, if I am not mistaken, lies the real reason—a favorite Sasse formula—why his projected opus *De Scriptura* never materialized. I believe that he came to see the impossibility of his quest for the holy grail of a third way. At least no concrete attempt in this direction ever succeeded. This is why we are left with fragments, with an unfinished symphony on the theme. *Tertium non datur*.

The failure, however, strikes me as one of detail, of tactics, not of strategy. Certainly that is preferable to the other combination often seen in academic theology: flawless tactics, but strategic disaster!

Sasse's "strategy"—to evoke the church militant as his environment—was to see the mysteries of Scripture, Church, and Sacrament as part and parcel of the one great Mystery of Christ, God and Man, crucified and risen. There is a tantalizing reference to a lost Sasse paragraph "which dealt with the interconnection of Word, Sacrament, and Incarnation."[45] Sasse suggested in this reference that the final paragraph had been left out by the editor of *Accents in Luther's Theology*. I asked my colleague Heino Kadai about this last week, and he assured me that Sasse's essay was printed just as submitted, without omissions. Indeed the German version in *Sacra Scriptura*, published by F. W. Hopf in 1981, offers no additional concluding paragraph either. We shall have to forgo it, then, and make up for its loss as best we can.

It needs to be remembered that Sasse had come a long way—and not only geographically—from his German professorate, *extraordinarius* though it mainly was, as we heard earlier. Sasse was seventy years old at the time of the Lutheran union in Australia (1965), and nearly eighty at the time of the settlement of 1972. No one could be expected at that stage of life to re-configure fundamentally the decisive paradigms of his thought-world.

Despite the recurrent, philosophically induced, haziness on inerrancy in detail, Sasse's "trajectory," to borrow that dreadful term, aimed at a consistent integration of Incarnation, Word, and Sacrament. There can be little doubt that this objective is deeply, indeed uniquely, Lutheran, and that from its vantage point various inadequacies of conventional and often smug theologizing may and even must be criticized.[46] One cannot but be eternally grateful to Sasse for such critical challenges to one's thinking.

The burden of Sasse's theology was the theology of the Cross. What must be clear at the end of the day—or of the trajectory, if you prefer—is that Luther's mature *theologia crucis* does not debunk or discount, but on the contrary demands a high Bibliology, just as it demands a high Christology and a high doxology of the Sacramental Presence. His reflections on Baptism in the Large Catechism lead Luther to lay down a general truth: "Therefore, we constantly teach that the sacraments and all the external things ordained and instituted by God should be regarded not according to the gross, external mask (as we see the shell of a nut) but as that in which God's Word is enclosed" (LC IV:19).

The point of *theologia crucis* is to walk by faith, not by sight. And this holds also for Scripture, to which Luther adapts the 22nd Psalm: "It is a worm and no book, compared to other books"[47]—that is, as arrogant fleshly wisdom sees it. What *theologia crucis* opposes is not a high view of the external things of God, but rather any profaning of these divine treasures by grounding them in or deriving them from or painting them up in the garish, meretricious colors of the self-indulgent wisdom of the world and of the flesh. That, after all, is the essence of all theology of glory. The true grandeur and glory of Holy Scripture is that this is "where Christ teaches Christ most purely" (*ubi Christus Christum purissime docet*).[48] This favorite Luther-citation of Dr. William Oesch is a good summary of Sasse's intent as well. He cited it in Letter 14.[49]

Implied here is the specifically Lutheran, because deeply biblical, understanding that Christians are never faced with Scripture in the abstract—any more than they encounter an abstract Christ or an abstract Sacrament. The church, as Sasse always insisted, is gathered by God not round a noncommittally "open Bible," but round the Confession, that is, the rightly understood and proclaimed Bible. Sasse knew what modern Lutherans are discovering for themselves: that no recovery of Scripture is deep or genuine unless it entails also a recovery of the Confession. A second concretion implicit in Luther's and Sasse's Bibliology is that the Christian is not left "alone with his Bible," as Harold Bloom wrote of the anti-sacramental Southern Baptists.[50] Rather, the Lord has created a special channel through which the Scriptures are meant, normally, to reach us, and that is the office of preaching the Gospel and administering the holy Sacraments (CA V). The Scriptures are first of all to be preached, not merely read.

In this context Dr. Sasse clearly recognized the fundamental significance of the battle about biblical inspiration and inerrancy.[51] To President J. A. O. Preus of the Missouri Synod he wrote: "The term inerrantia cannot and should not be given up—the meaning is quite clear, the absence of real error in the Bible."[52] Sasse's reference in this connection to Nicaea's *homoousion* suggested what John Stephenson was to express later in the title of an incisive essay: "'Inerrancy'—The *homoousion* of Our Time."[53]

The Preus connection suggests a fitting way to conclude. Dr. Sasse visited the Springfield campus of Concordia Theological Seminary several times, and was given the doctor of divinity degree by that institution. Two things Dr. Sasse told me repeatedly about his special fondness for the seminary in which it is now my privilege to serve. The first is that Springfield was the only place on earth for which he felt really homesick! The second concerns his last leave-taking from that seminary. President J. A. O. Preus had driven him to the airport and said: "Dr. Sasse, I'm glad that you are an old man, so that you will not see the misery which will come upon our church." Then Sasse would become very grave and say quietly: "And now I have had to see it."

The editorial tribute composed at the time of Dr. Sasse's death by my colleague, David Scaer, for our seminary's house organ seems uncannily to anticipate the dynamic which has now issued in our happy commemoration here nearly twenty years later:

> But if one confessor of truth has been taken from us, he has left many disciples behind, intent on following in his footsteps. The tribute offered here is not a perfunctory one, but a tribute offered by one who saw that in Hermann Sasse confessional theology was still a live possibility in the Lutheran Church. We would be hard pressed to find a greater confessional hero in our time.[54]

Notes

[1] *S&C*, 419.

[2] Ibid.

[3] 1966 *LCA Report*, 34.

⁴ January 1965 *Minutes*, 4.

⁵ Missouri Synod officials got the 1965 Detroit Convention to sidestep *Crossroads* on the basis of the falsehoods that the report had been "unofficial" and that "the Evangelical Lutheran Church of Australia, in convention assembled at Toowoomba in 1965, has rejected this report" (LC–MS 1965 *Proceedings*, 97).

⁶ Par. 7 of the *Document of Union* at first said this: "We declare that wherever continued cooperation in the preaching of the Gospel, and the administration of the Sacraments, and worship exists, there we have normally a witness to the world of unity in the faith and a profession of church fellowship." That troubling word "normally" robbed the definition of its force, especially since it seemed to pave the way for the counterthrust of the immediately following par. 8: "We recognize, however, that cooperation (cooperatio in sacris) in periods of emergency, and sporadic cooperation in various aspects of the work of the Church (cooperatio circa sacra), are not necessarily a witness to a unity in faith." The final version (parr. 28 and 29 of the *Theses of Agreement*) drop the "normally" from the first sentence, and change the second to this: "There are, however, forms of cooperation between Churches not in Church fellowship that are not necessarily a witness to unity in faith."

Also, the statements about the Lutheran World Federation (in which the UELCA had to relinquish its membership as a condition of union) were put into a separate paragraph 16, so as not to give the impression that the LWF was an example of the sort of "association or federation of churches" in which membership "is in itself neither bidden nor forbidden in the Holy Scriptures" (par. 15).

⁷ Melvin John Grieger and Toni Marie Westwood, *Division in the Lutheran Church of Australia* (1994), 3. I regret that I possess only a "prepublication issue" of this book, printed especially for the occasion of my visit to Australia in 1994.

⁸ *Synodical Report*, Queensland District, ELCA, December 1966, 11.

⁹ "Defining [of] the Basic Issues Arising Out of Genesis Chapters 1-3: 1. Is human evolution a permissible opinion, which does not affect the Biblical doctrine of creation, or is it ruled out by that doctrine? 2. Does the New Testament understand the Genesis Creation and Fall account as literal historical fact, or as something else? 3. Is the Church bound to the New Testament's understanding of Genesis, or may she entertain contrary ideas? 4. Is it valid to understand Scriptural inerrancy to mean that there are no errors of theology, but that there could be errors of fact in Scripture? 5. Is it valid to define Scriptural inerrancy on the basis of a human examination of difficulties (a posteriori), or must it be defined solely on the basis of Scripture's own claims about itself (a priori)? 6. Does 'inerrancy'—as applied to Scripture—mean 'absence of errors,' or may it be taken in some other sense? 7. Is it logically and theologically consistent to say (a) that Scripture is the Word of God, and (b) that it is subject to errors of fact? 8. Is factual, propositional truth a Biblical idea, or is it foreign to the Bible?"

¹⁰ AW 1:226.14ff; AE 31:12.

[11] 1968 *Official Report*, 260-62.

[12] 1970 *Official Report*, 224-25.

[13] In an unsigned, undated document of six foolscap pages, single-spaced, entitled "On the Inerrancy of the Scriptures," Dr. Hamann, Sr., the chief author together with Dr. Sasse of the *Theses* on inspiration and inerrancy, formally put his position on record, in response to a request. The document was produced probably in 1966, in the very early stages of the discussion. Wrote Hamann: "Neither is there anything contrary to the repeated assertion of the inerrancy of Scripture in the statement, made to show that the inspired writers were men and not supermen, that their natural knowledge of natural things did not exceed the general knowledge possessed by men of that age or time. For in that sentence is included the highly important limitation: 'Apart from direct revelation and prophecy.' For when these men received revelations from God and when they uttered prophetic words, that is to say, when they were under that influence or afflatus which we call inspiration, they did know, speak, and write what was beyond the natural knowledge of men" (2). In the very first paragraph Hamann had said: "The men who framed the 'Theses of Agreement' with much prayer, thought, and labour, using the word 'inerrancy' and the adjectival form 'inerrant' some half dozen times in Art. VIII,10, surely did not play with these words nor use them in some mystic or esoteric sense, unknown heretofore." On another occasion Hamann said that the "Theses were not drawn hastily but after many months of long discussion" and "that the distinction between truth and fact by a St. Louis gentleman came much later and in no way had influenced the formulation in the Theses . . . ." *Minutes of a Special Meeting with Queensland Pastors* (18 September 1966), 1.

[14] The words "absence in some cases of a" were accidentally dropped from the text as given in the official Convention *Report*. The clause is thereby rendered pointless. The correct text appears in the CTICR Sub-Committee minutes of 26-28 May 1970, p. 4, as "Draft 4 by Dr. S. P. Hebart." The CTICR minutes of 19-20 June 1970 record "*RESOLUTION 12*: THAT Dr. Hebart's statement is a correct description of the two positions." Page 10 of these minutes notes the presence of Dr. Sasse, among others.

[15] The Sub-Committee minutes of 26-28 May 1970 do not have the words "the human side of" at that point, which were part of an earlier draft.

[16] *The Theses of Agreement and Inerrancy*, in *Doctrinal Statements and Theological Opinions of the Lutheran Church of Australia* (Adelaide: Lutheran Church of Australia, Revised third edition June 1989), B1.

[17] "Genesis 1-3: A Doctrinal Statement," *Doctrinal Statements*, B2-B5. The intertwining of the inerrancy and Genesis issues in the Australian discussions was no accident. It was after all in the Book of Genesis that the notion of "myth" had first been intruded into the Sacred Scriptures. The surrender of the "historical-factual" nature of the account had been due not to any textual considerations but to "the insight into the incompatibility of the biblical proto-history with the newly-won scientific and

historical knowledge about the initial state of the world and of mankind." Christian Hartlich and Walter Sachs, *Der Ursprung des Mythosbegriffes in der modernen Bibelwissenschaft* (Tübingen: J. C. B. Mohr [Paul Siebeck], 1952), 35; my trans. And as Norman Nagel observed some years ago, "when the Old Testament springs a leak, the water is soon seen seeping into the New." "Anglican Christology of the Upper Stream From *Lux Mundi* to *Essays Catholic and Critical*," *CTM* 26.6 (June 1955): 404. As a historian, Sasse was thoroughly aware of these links: "The problem of the 'Inerrancy' of Holy Scripture became urgent in the 19th century when the clash between what was regarded as the biblical doctrine of Creation and the views of modern science developed into a major crisis of Christianity." *S&C*, 106.

As late as 1971 this impossible proposal was floated in the CTCIR: "Since the questions of the authorship and the source hypothesis relating to the book of Genesis are matters that belong to the area known as O. T. Introduction in theology and therefore deal with the human side of the Word of God, they may be decided on the basis of human judgment and appraisal."

The 1972 *Doctrinal Statement* ruled out also any normal reading of this strange sentence: "Since the purpose of the inspired OT accounts on Creation is not to offer a cosmogony, they are not interested in preserving any one 'Weltbild' that is obsolete" ("On the Understanding of the Old Testament Teaching on Creation," by the Faculties of Concordia and Immanuel Seminaries, 19 July 1966). The *Statement*'s emphatic last sentence negates any easy disavowal of "cosmogony": "In this confused age the Church must reflect serene confidence in Genesis as the Creator's own account of what happened in the beginning."

[18] "The Status of the Theses of Agreement and Other Doctrinal Statements," *Doctrinal Statements*, A25.

[19] *S&C*, 345.

[20] See *S&C*, 349, n. 31, and 427f., n. 16.

[21] *SS*, 159; my trans.

[22] "Das Ende des konfessionellen Zeitalters?" [Letter No. 61, 1967], *ISC* II:281.

[23] See for instance *S&C*, 87.

[24] See *S&C*, 161, 184, 217-18, 430. Sasse's detailed review of Pelikan's book in the Adelaide *Lutheran Quarterly* 4.3 (July, 1951): 133-38, contains mild criticisms, to be sure, but takes the chapter attacking Lutheran Orthodoxy to be "especially illuminating and in some respects the heart of the book" (135).

[25] *S&C*, 430, n.2.

[26] *RTR* 20.2 (June 1961): 57.

[27] *Australasian Theological Review* 22.3 (September 1961): 108.

[28] *Harmonia Quatuor Evangelistarum* (1652 ed.), 1:737.

[29] Ibid. I:1787, II:1255f. Cf. *S&C*, 335.

[30] *Solus Christus*, a special issue of *Lutherischer Rundblick* in 1971, was a Festschrift in honor of Dr. Oesch's 75th birthday. Under the heading "Luthers Grundeinstellung zur Heiligen Schrift" (38-72) the booklet reprinted two of Oesch's essays from the *Rundblick* of 1964 (no. 2, 58ff.) and 1965 (no. 1, 2ff.). Also most helpful for our Australian discussions was Oesch's magisterial, "Die Lehre von der Inspiration und ihre Anwendung auf die Urgeschichte," *Fuldaer Hefte* (Berlin: Lutherisches Verlagshaus, 1960), 9-75.

[31] *Die Inspiration und Irrtumslosigkeit der Schrift. Eine dogmengeschichtliche und dogmatische Untersuchung zu H. Sasse, Sacra Scriptura, Biblicums Skriftserie* nr. 4 (Uppsala: Stiftstelen Biblicum, 1984), English translation in *Wisconsin Lutheran Quarterly* 81.4 (Fall, 1984). This information is taken from S&C, 427, n. 16.

[32] See *S&C*, 108.

[33] See, e.g., *S&C*, 330, 413, 422.

[34] *RESPONSE to "A Declaration and Plea,"* duplicated copy in author's possession, n.d., 2.

[35] Either draft proposal or actual reply by Qld. Dist. Pastors' Conference, duplicated copy in author's possession, n.d.
A certain preference for trichotomies over dichotomies led at one stage to this formulation of the *status controversiae*:
1. Some hold that, by virtue of its inspiration and authority, the Biblical text is inerrant, i.e. free from all real errors and contradictions.
2. Others believe that complete inerrancy does not necessarily follow from inspiration and authority so that peripheral inexactitudes or mistakes of various kinds may be admitted.
3. Still others are reluctant to speak of errors and contradictions and would prefer to speak in terms of the human side of Scripture, its limitations and deficiencies (CTICR Sub-Committee minutes, 17/2/70).

This of course was easily reducible to a real dichotomy by the combination of (1) and (3), as eventually happened.

[36] *S&C*, 216-17.

[37] *S&C*, 110.

[38] *LTM* 2.2 (August-December, 1968): 85. This issue of the *LTJ* was dedicated to Dr. Sasse, in honor of his twenty years' service in Australia. The article cited was reprinted from the Spring 1967 *Springfielder*.

[39] AE 37:32.

[40] See, for instance, Lawrence Sklar, *Philosophy of Physics* (Boulder, San Francisco: Westview Press, 1992), 195-200, and Sunny Y. Auyang, *How is Quantum*

Field Theory Possible? (New York, Oxford: Oxford University Press, 1995), 12-13. The applications of logic differ, to be sure, in quantum and classical physics; but that is because of differences in the entities dealt with, not because of a fundamental change in logic. This seems relevant to Sasse's favorite examples of "contradictions," like Law and Gospel. The opposition here is not logical but ontological. Mixing up questions of logic with questions of ontology, i.e., the nature of entities, seems to be an heirloom of Hegelian "dialectic."

[41] *S&C*, 412.

[42] Francis Pieper, *Christian Dogmatics*, 3 vols. (St. Louis, MO: Concordia Publishing House, 1950), I:236.

[43] *S&C*, 336.

[44] Maurice E. Schild, "Hermann Sasse in seiner Bedeutung für das australische Luthertum," *LB* 30.115 (9 August 1978): 50; my trans.

[45] *S&C*, 411.

[46] It saddened and irked Sasse that the confessional Lutheran churches of America, especially the Missouri Synod, were of such little theological help to themselves and to others in the great global crises of confession. See for instance *WCC*, 62ff. And on the eve of the 450th anniversary of the Reformation Sasse asked pointedly: "And what do our American brethren say? They say nothing. They expire from admiration for the magnificent achievements of German theology.... And what does the venerable Missouri Synod say and do, which only a lifetime ago was still considered the citadel of Lutheran theology? It says nothing, and imitates everything. Mesmerized it gazes upon the giant serpent of the Lutheran World Federation, till the latter has swallowed it." *ISC* II:268; my trans. Especially disappointing to Sasse was the capitulation in *Marburg Revisited*. He wrote, in the first number of the new *Lutheran Theological Journal*: "If we ask the great Lutheran Churches of America: 'What is the Sacrament of the Altar'? We hear confused voices which are tantamount to the answer: We do not know exactly what it is except that it is not quite what Luther believed and what our fathers have confessed it to be. We can no longer express the mystery of this sacrament in the simple words of the Catechism: 'It is the true body and blood of our Lord Jesus Christ ....' We have seen light, for we have revisited Marburg" ("What Is the Sacrament of the Altar?" [August 1967], 9).

[47] WA 48:31.4.

[48] WA 5:61.1.

[49] *S&C*, 68.

[50] Harold Bloom, *The American Religion* (New York: Simon and Schuster, 1992), 204.

[51] "The question of the inspiration and inerrancy of the Holy Scripture is in our days one of the most important problems of all churches who still know themselves

bound to the authority of the Bible." "Concerning the Bible's Inerrancy" (1966), *S&C*, 334. Already in Letter 14 Sasse had said: ". . . the theology of the Ev. Lutheran church today knows no more burning problem than the doctrine concerning the Holy Scripture." Ibid., 53.

[52] H. Sasse to J. A. O. Preus, 24 February 1970. Copy in files of Walther Memorial Library, Concordia Theological Seminary, Ft. Wayne, Indiana.

[53] *Logia* 3.4 (Reformation/October 1993): 4.

[54] *Concordia Theological Quarterly* 41.2 (April 1977): 2.

Where Rhine and Tiber Met:
Hermann Sasse and the Roman Catholic Church

Gottfried Martens

Speaking in front of such a well-educated assembly, I can certainly presuppose that you know, of course, that nowhere on earth do Rhine and Tiber meet. Both rivers are separated by the Alps and flow in two totally opposite directions. Rhine and Tiber—they therefore seem to symbolize Protestantism's view of the relationship between itself and the Roman Catholic Church: both churches are separated by the huge mountain range called Martin Luther, have different springs, and flow in two totally different directions. The Protestant Church, founded in 1517 by the courageous hammer blows of a rebellious monk at the door of Wittenberg's Castle Church, is a stronghold of religious freedom. The dogmatically encrusted Roman Catholic Church, on the other hand, is a relic of the Middle Ages. No wonder that both churches nowhere meet on earth!

This was, of course, not the view of Hermann Sasse. He was not a Protestant, but a deeply catholic theologian in the best sense of this word.[1] He knew a lot about the mystery of the church, where Rhine and Tiber and hence the Lutheran and Roman Catholic Churches indeed do meet, or, to express it more exactly, right where the Lutheran and the Roman Catholic Churches spring from the same source, have the same course, have the same history for almost 1500 years, and head for the same destination, the day of judgment and life eternal.[2] No, the Roman Catholic Church could not be insignificant for an ecumenical churchman like Hermann Sasse.[3] The longer he lived, the more intensively he struggled with and for this church, and in this struggle the outlines of his own theology, or, more exactly, the outlines of the theology of the Lutheran Confessions became distinctly perceptible from yet another perspective.

Hermann Sasse never contented himself with repeating clichés from the times of confessional polemics; it is amazing to see how fully the Roman Catholic Church gets into his field of vision and how thoroughly he tries to do her justice without succumbing to the danger of ecumenical enthusiasm. Hermann Sasse and the Roman Catholic Church—no, this is not an exotic theme, chosen to fill up the list of theological lectures at such a symposium as this, for by dealing with this topic we come up again and again against the heartbeat of Hermann Sasse's theology.

Hermann Sasse and the Roman Catholic Church—no, I will not be able to summarize the result of this lecture in just one sentence. It is a very complex relationship, full of tensions, and I want just to inquire into this relationship and begin to sketch it. I will now try to examine this topic in three steps, beginning with an historical survey.

I

Hermann Sasse's struggle with and for the Roman Catholic Church mainly took place during his Australian period. Before World War II the Roman Catholic Church was not so much a special and prominent theme in Sasse's publications. Of course, he was well informed about her and took her into consideration in his presentations, but his rare statements mirror the fact that during that time there were not enough contacts between the churches to have inspired a more thorough treatment of the Roman Catholic side. Hermann Sasse's ecumenical activities concentrated upon the World Conference on Faith and Order; he was a member of the German delegation at Lausanne in 1927 and, later on, a member of the Continuation Committee and the Executive Committee, until, by imposing travel restrictions on him, the Nazis forced him to withdraw in 1935.[4] The experiences of his educational stay in the United States and the appeal of the Patriarch of Constantinople in January 1920 for a League of Churches, for a federative conference of Christians in view of common problems and persecutions, were certainly decisive motives for his ecumenical commitment at that time.[5] As the Roman Catholic Church did not take part in that beginning ecumenical movement during those years, it is understandable that she was not the obvious thing to deal with for Sasse.

Nevertheless the Roman Catholic Church came into Sasse's field of vision more and more, as he became a professor of church history and the history of Christian dogma at Erlangen University. Here he had to deal with the common history of the Roman Catholic and Lutheran Churches, and it was a special concern of Hermann Sasse that the history of the Lutheran Church does not begin just in 1517 or 1530. "A church that is not concerned with patristics becomes a sect," he stated in 1936[6]—a remark that remains true also 60 years later! As a church historian he regularly spoke of the Catholic churches in the plural,[7] perceiving the Eastern Orthodox churches as Catholic churches as well, thus relativizing the claims of the Roman Catholic Church even from an historical perspective.

Already before World War II we find a first idea of the future importance of the Roman Catholic Church for the ecumenical movement in Sasse's sight, when he writes in 1938: "The great questions which stand between the Lutheran Church and the Reformed Church cannot be settled by ignoring them, but only by answering them. And if we do not answer them, Rome will some day do it for us."[8] It is against this background that we have to understand Hermann Sasse's choice of themes for his seminars.[9] Thus, for example, he worked with his students during World War II on the doctrine of the Eucharist in the writings of Thomas Aquinas. No, that was not just an historical delicacy for him, but a very topical, nay, truly ecumenical subject: here Rome is answering one of those controversial questions that Sasse mentioned above, and the Lutheran Church is not a neutral observer in this case, but definitely stands at Rome's side as far as the doctrine of the Real Presence is concerned. Sasse points out the ecumenical attitude of Lutheran Orthodoxy at that point, which could without any difficulty adopt the medieval *Corpus Christi* hymns as an expression of its own faith.[10] Sasse occupied himself with Thomas Aquinas especially thoroughly anyway, referring to him again and again in his publications; and in his inaugural lecture at Erlangen University as an *ordinarius* after the end of the Nazi regime he places Thomas Aquinas as a teacher of the Church side by side with Martin Luther.[11]

Already during those last German years Sasse had his ear very close to what was going on in the Roman Church. Shortly after the pioneering book of the Roman Catholic theologian Joseph Lortz on *The Reformation in Germany* was published in 1942, bringing a new Roman perspective on Martin Luther, Sasse offered a seminar on this book at Erlangen;[12] and in an address one year later he observes, "At least in German Catholicism a better, deeper understanding of Luther is awakening."[13]

Already more than ten years before the Second Vatican Council began, Hermann Sasse foresaw that the vernacular Mass would be introduced in the Roman Church in a couple of years[14]—a bold prediction during the pontificate of Pius XII! But during that time, shortly after World War II, we also find the sharpest attacks that Hermann Sasse ever launched against the Roman Church. He calls her the greatest and most dangerous heresy that has ever arisen in the history of the Church and continues to the effect that the Lutheran Church was born in the struggle against this heresy, and thus it is inherently improbable that this struggle should ever cease so long as the Gospel and Roman Catholicism exist.[15] And then he even equates the claims of the Pope with those of Adolf Hitler and Joseph Stalin, and the cult of the Pope with the Führer principle of German National Socialism, stating that the Roman Church's struggle against Communist totalitarianism in Eastern Europe is nothing other than a struggle of one totalitarian system against another.[16] Those were harsh words, but nevertheless in the same article Sasse affirms the necessity of a deep theological dialogue between Lutherans and Roman Catholics and supports all attempts to start it again[17]—and this at a time when Roman Catholics were not even allowed to hold a common table prayer with Lutherans.[18]

The essay on the Roman Church from which I have just quoted was the first one that Hermann Sasse sent from Australia to Germany;[19] from now on he observes the relationship of both churches from the other end of the world.

A few months later there came the memorable 1 November 1950 when the Pope made use of his infallibility *ex cathedra* and proclaimed the dogma of St. Mary's assumption into heaven. This proclamation moved Hermann Sasse very deeply. In an essay he states that all Christendom trembled in view of this proclamation, which Sasse calls a major sign of the last times. Here not only a human error is made, here the Antichrist reveals himself.[20] As the Pope lays claim to the whole Church, Sasse underlines the obligation of the Lutheran bishops to protest against this assumption in the twofold sense of this word.[21]

But however vehemently Sasse took his stand against the position of Pius XII, he reacted all the more passionately on the election of John XXIII and the announcement of the subsequent Council. Very quickly Sasse began to perceive what this Council would mean not only for the Roman Church but also for the Church Universal.[22] He called the Council the greatest event of church history in our time,[23] nay, a turning-point of church history.²⁴ Sasse soon connects great hopes with the Council, but over against enthusiastic expectations of a fast reunification of churches he remains a Lutheran realist.

Thus from 1959 on the Roman Church gets a fixed place in the center of Sasse's theological work, from then on it remains continuously in Sasse's field of vision. When the Council started, Sasse was well prepared as an observer; he was thoroughly acquainted with the theological discussions going on within the Roman Church at that time.²⁵ Observing the Council itself, however, was no easy task for Sasse, dependent as he was on press reports and personal correspondence.²⁶ Nevertheless his numerous documents on the Council—Sasse published over 25 articles on the Roman Church and the Council between 1959 and 1970²⁷—show that he was very well informed about what was going on during the individual sessions. With bated breath Sasse followed the discussion about the Decree on Divine Revelation during the first session, later calling it one of the most dramatic moments in the history of the Roman Church when the theological majority of the First Vatican Council, the conservatives, were stopped by the Pope himself after they had tried to continue the formulation of the new decree in the same style as their theological predecessors had done one hundred years ago.²⁸ To his astonishment Sasse finds out that the majority and minority of the First Vatican Council are now precisely reversed,²⁹ nay, that the legitimate concerns of modernism in the Roman Church, having been globally condemned for a long time, are now being taken up by the Council. Sasse joyfully observes that the Bible Movement in the Roman Catholic Church has grown in importance under the leadership of Augustin Cardinal Bea since the encyclical *Divino afflante spiritu*, so that the very theologians who were influenced by Bea and this movement were now setting the tone of the Council.³⁰

With Augustin Cardinal Bea I have just mentioned the key figure in the relationship between Sasse and the Roman Church. The "Holy Father of the non-Catholics,"³¹ as he was called, was not just some unimportant representative of the Roman Church, but overall the most influential theologian in the Vatican, nay, more or less the chief theologian for no fewer than four popes. And it was with this man that Hermann Sasse got in touch through the mediation of the publisher Dr. Herbert Renner from the former Lutheran Publishing House in Berlin.³² This contact was the beginning of a "deep friendship of old age," as Sasse later called it.[33] Beginning with the Council until Bea's death in 1968, a lively exchange of letters took place between Sasse and Bea or his secretary Stjepan Schmidt.[34] For Sasse it remained a special experience that during a journey to Europe in 1965 he was allowed to meet Cardinal Bea in Rome and to be his personal guest. Sasse later called this visit a highpoint of his life.[35] Cardinal Bea was the leader of the majority of the Council that finally succeeded in bringing about an ecumenical opening of the Roman Church which went even so far as the fateful statements on relationships to non-Christian religions. While Sasse owed a lot to Cardinal Bea, as far as his own theology of Holy Scripture was concerned, he very distinctly distanced himself from Bea's thoughts about salvation outside the church as they find expression in the decrees of the Council.[36] Both theologians knew each other sufficiently well that Sasse could utter his warnings against this neo-Roman course very frankly.[37] The importance of this contact between Sasse and Bea during the Council must not be underestimated for both sides.[38]

In the course of the Council and during the years after one can observe a slight but steady change of attitude in Sasse's writings concerning the Council. At the beginning Sasse rejoiced about the new style of the *aggiornamento* (updating), as it was introduced by Pope John XXIII. Sasse observed the respect shown by Roman theologians for their separated brethren and the pastoral language that took the place of the speedy anathemas of the past.[39] Marveling at this reformation starting in the Roman Church, he stated that Rome has finally recognized its situation and begun to react.[40]

Of course, the ecumenical churchman Sasse is especially moved by the fact that Rome now wanted to open dialogue with other churches by presenting an inviting and fascinating initiative for the reunification of the churches.[41] He perceived the challenge of this approach and worried about who on the Protestant side might be able to give an answer to the new Roman position.[42] In the following years Sasse became more and more astonished at the unexpected flexibility of the Roman Church. With deep respect he acknowledged the Roman Church's courage in starting such thoroughgoing reforms,[43] which he appraised as a sign of deep trust in the power of the Holy Spirit.[44] At first, moreover, he was sure that the good dogmatic foundation of the Roman Church would not be touched by those reforms,[45] nay, on the contrary that the Council would simultaneously seek to dispel all ecumenical fanaticism.[46] Sasse never gave up this deep respect for the Council's courage, but less and less could he rejoice at his early observation that the Roman Church would never be again what she used to be before the Council. Especially the practical results of the Council gave rise to fear and criticism in Sasse. He passionately warned the Roman brethren against repeating the mistakes of the Protestant churches and the ecumenical movement. Shaking his head, he stated that the rock of St. Peter was beginning to crumble.[47] With sadness he observed the decay of the Roman Mass, the breakdown of church discipline, and a process of secularization that did not spare the Roman Church either.[48]

In spite of this fundamental criticism and disappointment, or sometimes even resignation, Sasse continued in the post-conciliar period to commit himself to ecumenical dialogue with the Roman Church. In Australia he met with Cardinal Bea's successor, Cardinal Willebrands, and he actively took part in the dialogue with the Roman Church in Australia on the doctrine and practice of Holy Baptism and still expressed himself about the results very confidently shortly before he died.[49] Thus the Roman Church remained a focal theme of his theological work until the end.

Up to now I have deliberately not mentioned Sasse's family contacts with the Roman Catholic Church. Sasse's wife, Charlotte, had been a member of his congregation in Oranienburg back in the 1920s, when he got to know her after she had announced her desire to convert to the Roman Church and Sasse was ordered to talk her out of this step. He succeeded in doing this—and married her. Nevertheless his wife remained very fond of the Roman Church in her piety throughout her life. Sasse's son Hans was also inclined towards the Roman Church for a long time, until he actually converted to her in connection with his marriage. Of course, it was hard for his father to accept this step; nevertheless, Sasse would not have been Sasse if his theology had been influenced and changed by this fact. All manner of speculations and descriptions, as, for example, in the memoirs of the Erlangen professor Walter von Loewenich,[50] are totally untenable, as Hans-Siegfried Huß, an intimate friend of Hermann Sasse, has attested to me by letter. It was the catholic horizon of Hermann Sasse's theology that made him take such an ardent interest in the fate of the Roman Church and nothing else.

Hermann Sasse and the Roman Catholic Church—already this first historical survey has underlined how impossible it is to contain this relationship in just one sentence. Great fascination and harsh distance; far-reaching hopes and deep disappointment; a great willingness to learn from the Roman brethren and the knowledge that the doctrine of the Lutheran Church must never be sacrificed on the altar of church politics—all these aspects have to be seen together to get a real picture of Hermann Sasse's attitude towards the Roman Church. I now want to expose and detail this complex relationship first by speaking about the Roman Church as a challenge for the Lutheran Church in Sasse's view, and then about the challenge which Sasse himself directed over against the Roman Church.

II

When Hermann Sasse comes to speak of the Roman Catholic Church in his early writings and lectures, he regularly adduces quotations of Martin Luther wherein the Reformer says explicitly or implicitly that the church has not perished under the papacy, nay that in the papistic church also the Gospel and the sacraments could be found.[51] And what was true for the time of the Reformation is valid for the Roman Church today as well. Shortly after World War II Sasse wrote:

> ... the current vitality of the Roman Catholic church derives not from her international political activity, nor from the miracles of Fatima and other prodigies, nor from her achievements in speculative theology, nor from the new dogmas concerning the Blessed Virgin Mary for which, to the distress of some of the Roman church's own theologians, the Curia is making preparations. She possesses her present vitality in spite of all these things and in spite of everything un-Christian and anti-Christian that happens in her midst. The real source of her vitality in this remnant of her primitive heritage in spite of all these things and which she still retains and which she knows how to renew again and again: The profound truth of *the Real Presence of Christ in the Sacrament of the Altar*. It is one of the most noteworthy signs of the times that the Roman Catholic church seeks to make the center of her spiritual life precisely that primitive and Scriptural tenet which ... Martin Luther so doughtily defended against Zwingli and the sixteenth century Enthusiasts.[52]

Liturgy and Real Presence—these are the two points where Sasse regards the Roman Church as a challenge for his own Lutheran Church.

Concerning the liturgy Sasse stated: "As a matter of fact, there is no doctrine of the Reformation that was not already in the prayers and hymns of the medieval Church."[53] Sasse thought especially of the *sola gratia*, referring again and again in his writings to the words of the *Dies irae*—"King of majesty tremendous/Who dost free salvation send us/Fount of pity, then befriend us"[54]—and to the prayer in the Canon of the Roman Mass where God is described as "not weighing our merits, but pardoning our offenses" ("*non aestimator meriti, sed veniae largitor*").[55] Thus, in spite of all heresies, here in the liturgy the true Gospel was preserved. Looking at the Roman Church, Sasse observed the importance of the liturgy for the preservation of true dogma in the Church; thus addressing his own Church he wrote: "There is no more damning an indictment of a theologian than to say that he knows nothing about liturgy"[56]—a gentle reminder for Lutheran seminaries still today! Precisely because of the preservation of the Gospel in the liturgy Sasse could express the thought that the real unity of Christian churches is already realized in their common adoration of Christ.[57] Accordingly there is nothing more anti-ecumenical than to substitute for common Catholic liturgy do-it-yourself liturgies for worship services which more strongly resemble school instruction or an entertainment show than they do a service of the catholic and apostolic church.

In addition to the preservation of the Gospel by the liturgy in the Roman Church, Sasse again and again referred to the Sacrament of the Altar by which even more frankly and clearly the Gospel was preserved in the Roman Church:

> This conviction of the miraculous preservation of Christ's Supper in the Church before the Reformation is the necessary presupposition of Luther's criticism of the Roman Mass. Apart from this conviction we can understand neither Lutheran eucharistic doctrine nor the Communion Service of the old Lutheran Church, the Sunday celebration of the Mass purified from the notion of sacrifice.[58]

In contrast to certain strange catechetical models according to which the Lutheran Church stands somewhere in the middle between Rome and Geneva in the doctrine of the Lord's Supper, Sasse was not reluctant to take sides with Rome as far as the issue of the Real Presence is concerned. Thus he writes to Cardinal Bea in 1967 that, "We Lutherans side with the Pope, when he fights in Mysterium Fidei against the new Zwinglianism, just as Luther lauded Pope Nicholas II for his Christian procedure against Berengar."[59] Sasse criticized the dogma of transubstantiation because of its inherent rationalism,[60] surely not because it expressed the doctrine of the Real Presence too massively!

Because of this common stance with Rome Sasse censured the efforts to establish unions between Lutherans and Calvinists for ecumenical reasons because the fundamental common ground between Lutherans and Roman Catholics would thereby be destroyed.[61]

Hermann Sasse's deep conviction was that the Roman Catholic Church, as a church living on the power of the Sacraments, is truly a church of Jesus Christ. But exactly because of this fact Sasse now exhibited his inopportune view of the Pope as the Antichrist, a concern that runs throughout his writings even still at the end of his life.

Today the characterization of the Pope as the Antichrist is regarded as a nasty piece of invective, as an ecumenical no-no.[62] It strikes many theologians as a special step forward that in ecumenical documents the Protestant side now solemnly declares that the Pope is no longer the Antichrist.[63] Hermann Sasse, however, looked much more deeply into this matter. For him the doctrine of the Pope's being the Antichrist is not an insult or an intemperate outburst, but, on the contrary, presupposes the acknowledgement of the Roman Church as really being a church of Jesus Christ. Only **because** the Roman Church subsists on the Gospel can the Antichrist arise in her midst, abusing the truth in order to justify his errors.[64] In Liberal Protestantism, on the other hand, where Christ's incarnation and vicarious atonement are denied, the Antichrist could not arise, because such groups have ceased to be the church of Jesus Christ at all.

Why is the Pope the Antichrist? Not because of his way of living, not because of his personality, Sasse underlined, but because of his function and his doctrine.[65] It is man's presumption of wanting to take God's place that becomes apparent in the papacy. The papacy and the cult of St. Mary therefore belong closely together and come to coincide in the pronouncement of the dogma of the Assumption in 1950,[66] where for Sasse the apocalyptic reality of the Pope as the Antichrist has been revealed once more. Sasse did not deny that there may be other manifestations of the Antichrist as well. Thus he referred repeatedly to the three forms of the Antichrist that Martin Luther knew: the Pope, Mohammed, and the fanatics.[67] Yet in Rome the Antichrist has arisen in his most beautiful and seductive form, in a power that does not fade away as other powers do.[68] It is remarkable to see how vigorously Sasse stood up for the doctrine of the Antichrist. For him this doctrine is not a minor affair. On the contrary, Sasse stated, if she "did not know about the mystery of the Antichrist, the church would not be able to exist,"[69] nay, "the seriousness with which a church and a theology confront the mystery of the Antichrist will decide whether they themselves can be taken seriously."[70] In this respect the doctrine of the Antichrist was for Sasse a very serious topic for ecumenical dialogue, although he did concede that, "Our ecumenicity has not yet advanced so far that we can already think together about Luther's profound doctrine of the Antichrist."[71] This judgment of Sasse is certainly also still valid 25 years later.

Sasse's view of the Roman Church as a real Catholic church, though, of course, not as **the** Catholic Church, must now finally be developed once more in two respects.

First of all, the dogma of the *ecclesia perpetuo mansura* is an important keynote in Sasse's perception of the Roman Church; here Sasse spoke as a church historian and as a dogmatician at the same time. Sasse especially admired the patience of the Roman Church: "Patience is one of the things that distinguish the Church from the sect," he writes. "The sect must have everything at once. It cannot wait, because it has no future. The Church can wait, for it has a future."[72] Rome thinks in terms of decades and centuries, whereas Protestant ecumenical theologians try immediately to achieve everything by writing one formula of compromise after another that mostly are not worth the paper they are written on.[73] For Sasse the way Rome handles theology has not only proved to be qualitatively better in the past, but all the more important for the future. Whereas the profile of most Protestant churches is fading away, Rome's importance for the whole of Christendom is growing more and more; thus the Protestant churches are now affected by what is going on in Rome as well. This means, on the other hand, that "a grave responsibility rests on the shoulders of our Roman brothers," nay, Sasse continues in view of the growing self-disintegration of Protestantism, "the future fate of Christendom will be decided in Rome, I suppose."[74]

This quotation already leads over to another aspect of Sasse's perception of the Roman Church: the idea and the experience of a commonality of fate among the churches, as it was suggested already by the letter of the Patriarch of Constantinople in 1920.[75] Especially towards the end of his life Sasse refers to this "community of fate." Thus he writes to Cardinal Bea one year before the latter's death:

> I have especially learned from you one thing, namely that we are all together in the same boat, that we are all together the disciples crying, "Lord, help us, we are perishing," and that we all have the one Lord with us who can rule over storm and waves.[76]

Already before the Council began Sasse had written that "there is a solidarity of sin and guilt, of divine judgment and human suffering which still binds together those who confess Christ as Lord and Saviour, even if other bonds have been broken."[77] But this solidarity, Sasse realized, also relates to the fact that the devil is active in the Lutheran as well as in the Roman Church, that in both churches there are the same church-destroying developments, nay, that a possible breakdown of the Roman Church would be a catastrophe for the whole of Christendom.[78] But just because of this community of fate a **mutual** service of love between the churches is so important, consisting of warning, admonition, and prayer for each other.[79] Sasse therefore deplored, on the other hand, that, "The churches are, in our opinion, sisters that have to help each other. Why don't we hear a word of warning against the destruction of the sacraments in so many of our Protestant churches? Why don't they tell us what a sin we commit, when we ordain women to the ministry of the church?"[80] No, these words are not a tactical skirmish, not a hunt for possible allies; no, these words express a deep spiritual view of the *Una Sancta* which made Sasse willing to call on the service of his Roman brothers, to listen to what the Roman Church also had to tell him, nay, to have himself called to repentance by this church. Here once more Sasse proved to be a truly catholic churchman.

We have now beheld Hermann Sasse's deep conviction that the Roman Church and her theology cannot be left out of account by Lutheran theology, but remain a constant query and challenge. The Roman Church and her theology cannot be disregarded, because the history of the Roman Church is our history as well, because the way the Roman Church sees herself as **the** Catholic Church permanently forces Lutherans to answer and to take their stand over against the Pope's claims. The Roman Church and her theology cannot be disregarded, moreover, because the function of the liturgy and the importance of the sacraments in the Roman Church massively challenge the present practice of the Lutheran Church, and because Rome's self-assurance and her corresponding composure are certainly a shining example for the Lutheran Church as well. Finally Rome cannot be disregarded by the Lutheran Church either, of course, because both churches are too closely connected in their common fate to ignore each other in the long run.

To all of this Sasse's lifelong struggle for the doctrine of Holy Scripture must finally be added.[81] In this quest the Roman Catholic Bible Movement was again and again a special reference point. Sasse received crucial impulses in his endeavor from Rome, without ever failing to notice the clear dividing line in the doctrine of Scripture in spite of all mutuality in the acceptance of the Bible as the inspired Word of God.

That Rome is, like the Lutheran Church, a deliberately dogmatic church and that precisely this strong founding on the dogma of the early church firmly links Rome and Wittenberg to each other, nay, has them stand closer together than Luther and the modern Protestants—this insight was for Sasse self-evident and important from the beginning.[82] Sasse trusted in the indestructibility of this foundation in the Roman Church for a long time and was all the more shocked when he had to observe at the end of his life what had always seemed to him impossible, namely that this dogmatic foundation was bursting asunder in the Roman Church as had previously happened in the Protestant churches.

The commonality of a foundation upon early church dogma was self-evident for Sasse; but it was not all self-evident for him from the beginning, and rather became very exciting for him to perceive the rediscovery of the Bible in the Roman Church, not only in the practice of the congregations, but also especially in the theological pervasion and application of the dogma of the inspiration of Holy Scripture at a time when the Protestants had long since given up this dogma.[83]

On the one hand, Sasse found very critical words to speak over against the handling of the modernist problem in the Roman Church at the beginning of this century. Without especially sympathizing with the modernists, Sasse did object to the attempt to react to the questions of the modernists by an authoritarian prescription of the results of Biblical research instead of taking these questions seriously and answering them.[84]

On the other hand, Sasse was all the more delighted about the papal encyclical *Divino afflante spiritu*, composed by Cardinal Bea and issued by Pius XII in 1943. In this encyclical the First Vatican Council's worthy statements on the inspiration and inerrancy of Holy Scripture are integrated, taken seriously, and deepened, but simultaneously in the encyclical an opening towards historical research of the Bible is carried out, using the same methods as Protestant scholarship.[85] Sasse hoped for a long time that this basic approach of *Divino afflante spiritu* could be a real alternative over against the modern Protestant understanding of the Bible on the one side, which had long since given up the doctrine of the inspiration and inerrancy of the Bible and thereby tossed Protestant theology into an existential crisis, and over against Protestant fundamentalism on the other side.[86]

Sasse's hopes seemed to have come true at the beginning as the importance of Holy Scripture in the everyday practice of the church was rediscovered in Rome. With an amused smile Sasse observed that the Roman Church had now begun to grant indulgences for reading the Bible,[87] whereas the Protestant churches were in a fair way to losing Holy Scripture in their practice. Roman Catholic exegetes had very rapidly made up their lag in research and begun to produce qualitatively better exegetical material than the Protestants. At the same time the Bible Movement was giving important fresh impetus to the ecumenical movement in the Roman Church.[88]

But in the 1960s disappointment soon followed for Sasse. On the one hand, he had to experience that the Second Vatican Council's dogmatic constitution *Dei Verbum* did not take up the deep view of Holy Scripture that he had found in *Divino afflante spiritu*. The Council's statements on Holy Scripture, particularly on the Old Testament, were much more superficial than he had expected and than he had hoped for after the preliminary theological studies of Cardinal Bea.[89] Moreover, the *sola Scriptura* principle was expressly rejected in *Dei Verbum*.[90] On the other hand, moreover, Sasse was disappointed at the uncritical acceptance of the results of Protestant exegesis by Roman Catholic scholars, which meant that radical criticism of the Bible marched into the Roman Church as well, with the upshot that

Rome was now setting out to lose the Holy Scriptures again in the same way that the Protestants had already lost them.[91]

Nevertheless Sasse remained grateful all his life for the stimuli he had received from Roman Catholic scholars such as Lagrange, Bea, and others regarding his examination of the doctrine of Holy Scripture. In a letter to Cardinal Bea Sasse writes:

> In this sense we Lutherans are today seeking to establish afresh the doctrine of the inspiration and inerrancy of Holy Scripture. We must attest with gratitude that we have received the deepest impulses in this regard from the Catholic side. . . . We have learned a lot from you and shall continue to do so.[92]

Thus the issue of Holy Scripture gripped Sasse until the end of his life. The question in what respect the Roman doctrine of the inspiration and inerrancy of Scripture can be made fruitful for us as well continues to burn also 25 years after Sasse's death. Especially in his view of the doctrine of Scripture Sasse has made clear what a permanent challenge the Roman Church is once more for us today. It is certainly advisable for us to have our ecumenical horizon widened again by Hermann Sasse where this decisive question is concerned.

III

The Lutheran Church has a lot to learn from the Roman Church concerning the doctrine of Holy Scripture—this is strictly speaking an incredible assertion of Hermann Sasse mirroring the radical change that made the Roman Church such a challenge for Protestants, nay, even for the Lutheran Church. What the Protestants had carelessly given up on the one side has been rediscovered by Rome on the other. This is certainly one side of the coin, but for Hermann Sasse this observation is by no means a motive for Romanizing or ecumenical enthusiasm. On the contrary, the understanding of Scripture is for Sasse at the same time also **the** decisive point separating Rome from the Lutheran Church; after all, or more exactly, this separating point is the question of the relationship between Holy Scripture and Holy Church.[93]

With as great intensity as Sasse portrayed the Roman Church as a challenge for the Lutheran Church, does he also challenge the Roman

Church herself, working out the different basic decisions of both churches in depth and criticizing the Roman Church clearly and sharply precisely out of ecumenical solidarity, no, never from a position of arrogance, but rather from sorrow over the Roman Church's failure to offer a real alternative to the devastations of Protestantism, an alternative which Sasse deemed so urgently necessary. In fact, even in his criticism Sasse was and remains a true Catholic, one who knows that he stands infinitely closer to the Roman Church than to Liberal Protestantism and who therefore takes such passionate issue with Rome.

Already at a very early date Sasse recognized the importance of the relationship between Holy Scripture and Holy Church as the decisive question for the unification of the churches. In 1934 he said in a lecture before the Continuation Committee of the World Conference on Faith and Order:

> If we were at one with one another about what the Church is and what the Word of God is and in what relation they stand to each other, then nothing, absolutely nothing, could stop the unification of our churches. ... For here we are dealing not just with one of the many theological issues that have always existed in the Church and always will, but with **the** question against which the unity of the Western Church once shattered when it was posed to Christendom by the Reformation.[94]

Exactly this question became relevant again to Sasse at the proclamation of the Marian dogmas and at the Second Vatican Council; again and again Sasse referred to this question in this context. For Sasse an eschatological conflict of authorities is at stake here,[95] for where divine and human authority are put on the same level all doors are thrown open to "enthusiasm." Again and again Sasse therefore quoted from a favorite passage of his from the Smalcald Articles:

> In these matters, which concern the external, spoken Word, we must hold firmly to the conviction that God gives no one his Spirit or grace except through or with the external Word which comes before. Thus we shall be protected from the enthusiasts ... who boast that they possess the Spirit without and before the Word. ... The papacy, too, is nothing but enthusiasm, for the pope boasts that "all laws are in the shrine of his heart." ... In short, enthusiasm clings to Adam and his descendants from the beginning to the end of the world. It is a poison implanted and

inoculated in man by the old dragon, and it is the source, strength, and power of all heresy, including that of the papacy and Mohammedanism.[96]

For Sasse it is pure enthusiasm when the Pope or a council or the pious mind of the Church becomes a source of revelation. For Sasse the reaction of one of the opponents of the dogma of papal infallibility at the First Vatican Council, Bishop Riccio, is typical of this enthusiasm. Having voted against the dogma, he proceeded to fall down on his knees before the Pope after the majority vote of the Council and say, "Now I believe, Holy Father."[97]

Against this enthusiasm Sasse very severely set the Lutheran *sola Scriptura*, thereby turning against the self-super-elevation of man that he recognized in this Roman form of enthusiasm.[98] He thus turned also against an a-historical understanding of Christian dogma such as was unsurpassedly expressed in the last century by Henry Manning, cardinal archbishop of Westminster, who opined that "One has to overcome history by dogma!"[99] Against this Sasse always underlined the historical foundation of faith, emphasizing the importance of the *sola Scriptura* especially also because of the historicity of revelation.

Of course, Sasse also observed the subtle attempts on the Roman side to overcome the strict alternative of Scripture and Church by the concept of Tradition. According to the so-called one-source theory, Scripture is the only source of revelation that is explained and expanded by the Church. Thus Scripture and Tradition are not two separate sources, but Scripture **is** tradition, having its effects in the further history of the church.[100]

Even though the concept sounds fascinating, it is strictly rejected by Sasse mainly for two reasons. First of all, this theory is historically untenable, for the *sensus litteralis* of the Council of Trent is turned upside down when it is interpreted within the meaning of this theory;[101] and Hermann Sasse always underwent a strong allergic reaction when theology perverted history in favor of a special theory. Secondly, the whole discussion on the one-source theory was mere window dressing to Sasse, since this theory also represents something totally different from the *sola Scriptura* principle. In the last analysis this theory even posits three sources rather than two, because the pious mind of the church—that is to say, the magisterial office of the church—is added to the two other sources.[102] For Sasse the 1950 dogma of the Assumption was already a definite verification of this view, for the content of the dogma is obviously not taken from Holy Scripture.[103] And he then saw his suspicions confirmed all the more by the document *Dei Verbum* of the Second Vatican Council, in which the one-source theory is not accepted, but rather the teaching authority of the church is strengthened and thus *sola Scriptura* is definitely rejected.[104]

For Sasse all ecumenical enthusiasm in this question has been stopped by the Council, and it has once again become evident that where Christ alone is not the infallible *magister*, there the basis of the Reformation has been abandoned.[105]

In conjunction with the question of Scripture and Church, the Roman Catholic doctrine of the church as a whole was critically observed by Sasse.

With Rome's entry into the Ecumenical Movement a fascinating new ecumenical program was laid out on the table, with Rome inviting the separated brethren to return to a church that is ready for reformation and flexibility, if this helps to restore the visible unity of the church.[106]

Whereas the early Sasse still looked on the concept of a visible unity of the church with a certain sympathy, he soon realized that the expectation of such a visible unity was a kind of millennial enthusiasm incompatible with the true Lutheran doctrine of the church, a church hidden under the means of grace and only to be defined by the presence of the risen Lord[107]: *ubi Christus, ibi ecclesia.*[108]

From this standpoint Sasse severely criticized a conception of the church proceeding from the understanding of the church as the Body of Christ. This concept was used especially in the 19th century in the Roman Church in order to substantiate the visibility of the church. Sasse showed that in the course of church history and in liturgical texts this concept had never before played a decisive role, but that the church was rather seen mainly as the people of God.[109] Thus Sasse was pleased to see that the Second Vatican Council once again returns to this concept of the church as the people of God.[110]

From his ecclesiological viewpoint, Sasse likewise showed, however, a great reserve over against the frequent use of the term *fratres sejuncti* (separated brethren) in Roman ecumenical statements since John XXIII.[111] For Sasse this term was a programmatic expression of Rome's new ecumenical approach. In a certain way he very willingly accepted this term and regularly spoke after 1960 of the separated brethren in Rome.[112]

On the other hand, this expression too was a kind of window dressing to Sasse. He showed from the viewpoint of a church historian that this term can only embrace the phenomenon of schism, not that of heresy. Luther and the Lutheran Church were, however, condemned not as schismatics but as heretics, and it would not be honest to blur this fact.[113] At the same time, the use of this term for all non-Roman churches means a playing down of real heresies according to Sasse, who asks whether it is really legitimate to call all members of the World Council of Churches separated brethren.[114] Thus Sasse saw the danger of minimizing existing differences and of being taken in by illusions when this expression "separated brethren" is used too generously by Rome, nay, he saw this danger all the more when the boundaries of the church are totally dissolved and even the pagans are pocketed for the Roman Church, as Sasse found to be the case in the documents of the Second Vatican Council.[115] Even though Sasse takes joyful notice of the spirit of charity expressed by the Council,[116] he remained sober enough to perceive and to name the decisive obstacles still standing between the churches. What dissolves the basic distinction between the church, on the one hand, and Christ and His Word, on the other, is above all the church's attempt to make herself independent in her "visibility" and in her practical function as a source of revelation. This dissolution remained in Sasse's view a fundamental difference between Rome and Wittenberg.[117]

The relationship between Scripture and Church, the question of the visibility of the Church and her function as a source of revelation—we have noticed that Sasse went other ways in his critique of the Roman Church, that he went much deeper than conventional Protestant confessional polemics.

Compared with this, other topics of confessional controversy indeed recede into the background, for example, the problems of the ministry, the sacrifice of the Mass, and Mariolatry. Nevertheless, when Sasse spoke of these topics, he recognized the real problems exactly and did not put up with a superficial diagnosis.

Concerning the issue of the ministry it is especially the historical romanticism, nay, the perversion of the ministry that upset him. Sasse called the founding of the doctrine of the primacy of the Pope upon historical forgery a bad, unrepented sin of the Roman Church,[118] but he became enraged as well at the naiveté with which even Lutherans are fascinated by lists of apostolic successions and clerical pedigrees without noticing that they are thereby taken in by historical soap bubbles and by dogmatically most dubious constructions.[119] Sasse was, however, attentive enough to observe that the Roman Church does argue in this respect, in spite of her questionable understanding of succession, in a much more well-founded way than the Anglicans or certain high church Lutherans.[120]

Naturally Sasse also criticized the sacrifice of the Mass, but here too he did not confine himself to a criticism of the classical Roman doctrine, but also went into more recent theories of sacrificial representation developed by Roman and Lutheran theologians. As Sasse saw it, the historical uniqueness of the sacrifice of Calvary is severely endangered by these theories as well;[121] aside from that, they are simply not tenable from an exegetical point of view.[122]

In the last analysis, Sasse recognized in the sacrifice of the Mass as well as in both the perversions of Mariolatry[123] and the cult of the pope always the same fundamental evil: the self-super-elevation of pagan, natural man who puts himself in God's place and wants at least to cooperate in his own salvation. In this respect there is a deep inner nexus between all these degenerations.[124]

But it was not this classical agenda of controversial issues that moved Sasse the most in his view of Rome at the end of his life, but rather the development in the Roman Church at and after the Second Vatican Council, a development which Sasse himself had considered totally impossible only a short time before and which made him feel more and more sympathy for the conservative critics of this Council.[125] Whereas it was possible to discuss the classical points of controversy between the churches on a common dogmatic foundation now, during and after the Council Rome began to give up a lot of those things on which Rome and the Lutheran Church had hitherto agreed and which strictly speaking make the church to be the church.

There are above all three massive points of criticism that Sasse uttered over against the conciliar and post-conciliar process.

First, Sasse criticized the total concealment of the phenomenon of heresy in the conciliar documents. Even though their pastoral style was certainly justified, the disregarding of this basic phenomenon was for Sasse a symptom of a terrible disease, the disease of the decay of doctrinal substance in the Roman Church also.[126] Again and again Sasse used this term "disease"[127] in order to describe what he observed in Rome. With this term he likewise hinted at the infection which came from the sphere of Protestantism, as well as at the aftereffects of this development which threaten the very existence of the Roman Church. Sasse just shook his head in view of the downplaying of all doctrinal differences in Rome, as if even the boundaries between the different world religions could be dissolved just by means of dialogues. For Sasse this was simply an infinite naiveté that leaves no room for the call for repentance and instead declares discussions to be a new means of grace.[128]

But this for Sasse was not even the most important critical point. For him it was even more dreadful to observe the universalism of salvation as proclaimed by *Lumen Gentium*, which promises salvation also outside the church, also without Baptism and repentance, and declares that even pagans can enter heaven, if they have led an orderly life.[129] Sasse stated that thereby Trent's doctrine of sin and Baptism, the old principle *extra ecclesiam nulla salus*, nay, even the First Commandment, are practically abrogated, that the doctrine of salvation is unhinged at its very foundations.[130] Sasse sarcastically declared that from the Second Vatican Council onwards it is almost impossible even for a decent atheist to go to hell.[131] Here a basic preexisting consensus among the churches is carelessly dissolved. Sasse observed with great sadness that along with such indulgence towards pagan religions the enthusiastic ecumenical conceptions of the World Council of Churches celebrate their resurrection in the Roman Church as well.[132]

But in Sasse's last writings one finally finds a third massive point of criticism, especially in view of the post-conciliar development, and this criticism refers mainly to the reform of the liturgy in the Roman Church. In a retrospective view Sasse found very harsh words for this reform. The liturgical renewal in the Roman Church has done great harm to this church in the last years, he stated[133] and, even more dramatically, wrote in a letter to Gottfried Klapper five years before his death:

> The end of the Roman Church began with the destruction of the Mass. The translation into the vernacular is not to blame for this, but rather what went hand in hand with it. The greatest liturgy of the Occident has been willfully destroyed. For what now is celebrated as the Mass is no longer the Sacrament of the Altar. The place of the Mass, as it had developed through the centuries, is now taken by a production of liturgical arts and

crafts which are the very curse for every modern church.[134]

Well, we are no Roman Catholics and can only witness open-mouthed how St. Zwingli is being canonized in the Roman Church.[135]

What once made up the strength of the Roman Church and was so appreciatively perceived by Sasse, exactly that has now been willfully destroyed in the upshot of Vatican II. This represents the bitter end of Sasse's argument with the Roman Church.

Hermann Sasse and the Roman Catholic Church—we have now just at the end seen once more how Sasse broke open the usual clichés of the differences between the Roman and the Lutheran Churches and how he does not content himself with knocking down silhouette targets.

The passion with which he described the dogmatic decay of the Roman Church shows clearly in this connection that Sasse always pursued the argument with Rome with a firm look at his own church, and that it caused him pain to see that his own Lutheran Church could not reply to Rome's inquiries and could not hold back Rome's decay because her own dogmatic substance had also vanished in the fog of general Protestantism long ago. No, Hermann Sasse never criticized the Roman Church without looking at the failure of his own church. Already in 1959 he wrote in a letter:

> It seems as if all the earthly denominations which like to confuse themselves with the *Una Sancta*, need a myth in order to be able to live and justify their own existence. Rome needs the myth of the primacy of jurisdiction for Peter and his successors, a myth that was neither known to the New Testament nor to the church of the first centuries. ... The Anglicans ... need the myth of the "apostolic succession". ... Do we Lutherans perhaps have our own myth, too? Is our myth perhaps the presumption that we are still the church of the Reformation, the church of the *sola fide*, of the *sola Scriptura*, the Church of the real presence? What has been left from the great doctrines of the Reformation aside from the time-honored Book of Concord that so many pastors ... have never read completely, and a bunch of "open questions"?[136]

At a time when awareness of the importance of the Lutheran Confessions is fading away in favor of a general baptistification and an ecumenical enthusiasm, we do well to learn from Hermann Sasse's comments on the Roman Church for the benefit of our own dear Lutheran Church.

Notes

[1] See "'Petrus und Paulus.' Über die Frühgeschichte des Römischen Primats" (1964), *ISC* I: 232.

[2] See "Ist der Papst eigentlich noch der Antichrist? Bemerkungen zum evangelisch-katholischen Gespräch," *LB* 2.10 (1950): 8.

[3] Sasse "was a most deeply ecumenical thinker, and this not only synchronistically, but also diachronistically." Armin Wenz, "Hermann Sasses Beitrag zur Lehre von der Heiligen Schrift," in *Wort des lebendigen Gottes. Festgabe für Prof. Dr. Reinhard Slenczka zum 60. Geburtstag*, 2nd ed. (Erlangen: Institut für Systematische Theologie, 1993), 103; my trans.

[4] See Huß, 74; *EC*, 15ff.

[5] See Huß, 74; *EC*, 127ff.

[6] "Credo apostolicam ecclesiam" (1936), *ISC* II:110; my trans.

[7] "Das Bekenntnis der Kirche" (1930), *LB* 32.120 (1980): 79. "Das große Schisma und seine Lehren" (1954), *ISC* I:183. "Word and Sacrament, Preaching and the Lord's Supper" (1956), *WCS*, 11. "Das Ende des konfessionellen Zeitalters? Gedanken zur 450-Jahr-Feier der Reformation" (1967), *ISC* II:283. "Das unvollendete Konzil. Gedanken zum 10. Jahrestag des Vaticanum II," *LB* 29.114 (1977): 17.

[8] *HWS*, 178.

[9] See Klaus Petzoldt, "Erinnerungen an Professor D. Hermann Sasse. Aus der Sicht eines Schülers," *LB* 31.116 (1979): 29, n. 8.

[10] *K&H*, 25, n. 11.

[11] "Das Amt des Lehrers in der alten Kirche" (1946), *LB* 35.125 (1983): 179-81.

[12] See Petzoldt, "Erinnerungen," *LB* 31.116 (1979): 29, n.8.

[13] "Luthers Glaube an die Eine Heilige Kirche" (1943), *Z*, 228; my trans.

[14] "Liturgy and Lutheranism" (1948), *S&C*, 37. See also "Word and Sacrament, Preaching and Lord's Supper," *WCS*, 12.

[15] "Ist der Papst?" *LB* 2.10 (1950): 2.

[16] Ibid., 4-6.

[17] Ibid., 13f.

[18] "Nach dem Konzil" (1965/66), *ISC* I:237f.

[19] "Ist der Papst?" *LB* 2.10 (1950): 14.

[20] "Maria und der Papst. Bemerkungen zum Dogma von der Himmelfahrt Mariae" (1951), *ISC* I:205f.

[21] *ISC* I:216.

[22] "Das Konzil als Frage an die Lutherische Kirche," *LB* 11.61 (1959): 32.

[23] "Die Frage nach dem Wesen der Kirche" (1962), *LB* 14.74 (1962): 69.

[24] "The Ecumenical Movement in the Roman Catholic Church" (1964), *RTR* 23 (1964): 6; "Das unvollendete Konzil," *LB* 29.114 (1977): 1.

[25] "Die Frage der Autorität der Hl. Schrift," *LB* 11.63 (1959): 111.

[26] "The Sources of Revelation," *RTR* 22 (1963): 1, n. 1.

[27] *EC*, 123.

[28] "Heilige Kirche oder Heilige Schrift? Die Bedeutung des Sola Scriptura der Reformation" (1967), *ISC* II:291.

[29] "Das Zweite Vatikanische Konzil als Frage an das Luthertum," *LB* 17.85 (1965): 116; "Nach dem Konzil" (1965/66), *ISC* I:239f.

[30] "Rome and the Inspiration of Scripture," *RTR* 22 (1963): 41-44.

[31] "Heil außerhalb der Kirche. In piam memoriam Augustin Kardinal Bea" (1969), *ISC* II:325.

[32] Friedrich Wilhelm Hopf, "Hermann Sasse und sein Ringen um die Lehre von der Heiligen Schrift," *LB* 32.119 (1980): 44.

[33] Ibid.; my trans.

[34] *EC*, 123.

[35] "Being permitted to meet you was a high point of my life." Qtd in Friedrich Wilhelm Hopf, "Hermann Sasse und sein Ringen um die Lehre von der heiligen Schrift," *LB* 32.119 (1980): 40; my trans.

[36] "Heil außerhalb der Kirche" (1969), *ISC* II:315; *CC*, 79.

[37] See Sasse's letter to Dr. Renner, qtd Hopf, "Hermann Sasse und sein Ringen," *LB* 32.119 (1980): 45.

[38] See Huß, 88.

[39] "Nach dem Konzil", *ISC* I:238f.

[40] "Das unvollendete Konzil," *LB* 29.114 (1977): 2.

[41] "Von New Delhi nach Helsinki: Das Luthertum im Chaos der Oekumene" (1962), *LB* 14.74 (1962): 124.

[42] "Das Konzil als Frage an die Lutherische Kirche," *LB* 11.61 (1959): 51f.; "Abendmahlskonsensus mit Rom? Offener Brief an eine australische Kirchenzeitung," *LB* 22.100 (1970): 57.

[43] "Heilige Kirche oder Heilige Schrift?" *ISC* II:303.

[44] "Nach dem Konzil," *ISC* I:235.

[45] "Rom und die Ökumenische Bewegung" (1963), *LB* 15.78 (1963): 91.

[46] Ibid., 90.

[47] "Die Konfessionskirchen in der Ökumenischen Bewegung" (1969), *LB* 21.97 (1969): 64f.

[48] "Das Ende des konfessionellen Zeitalters," *ISC* II:283; "Heilige Kirche oder Heilige Schrift?" *ISC* II:293; "Heil außerhalb der Kirche," *ISC* II:316.

[49] Maurice E. Schild, "Hermann Sasse in seiner Bedeutung für das australische Luthertum," *LB* 30.115 (1978): 50.

[50] Against Walter von Loewenich, *Erlebte Theologie* (Munich: Claudius, 1979), 136; see Huß, 90, n. 52.

[51] *HWS*, 136; "Das Abendmahl in der katholischen Messe," *VSA*, 80; "Luthers Glaube an die Eine Heilige Kirche," *Z*, 238f.

[52] "Liturgy and Lutheranism," *S&C*, 35.

[53] "Liturgy and Lutheranism," *S&C*, 41.

[54] *The Lutheran Hymnal* #607, st. 8. See "Das Konzil als Frage an die Lutherische Kirche," *LB* 11.61 (1959): 33; "Luthers Vermächtnis an die Christenheit" (1946), *ISC* II:148f.

[55] See "Das Abendmahl in der katholischen Messe" (1941), *VSA*, 86, n.6; "Last Things: Church and Antichrist" (1952), *WCC*, 125; "Das große Schisma und seine Lehren," *ISC* I:183; *SS*, 331.

[56] "Liturgy and Lutheranism," *S&C*, 41.

[57] See a letter from Sasse to Cardinal Bea, qtd Hopf, "Hermann Sasse und sein Ringen," *LB* 32.119 (1980): 40.

[58] "Das Abendmahl in der katholischen Messe," *VSA*, 80; my trans.

[59] Qtd Hopf, "Hermann Sasse und sein Ringen," *LB* 32.119 (1980): 42; my trans.

[60] See "Das Abendmahl in der katholischen Messe," *VSA*, 92f.; "Zum lutherischen Verständnis der Konsekration" (1952), *CC*, 132.

[61] *CC*, 147f.

[62] Against this view, see "Last Things: Church and Antichrist," *WCC*, 124. Concerning the problem of a personalized understanding of doctrinal condemnations, see Gottfried Martens, *Die Rechtfertigung des Sünders—Rettungshandeln Gottes oder historisches Interpretament?* (Göttingen: Vandenhoeck & Ruprecht, 1992), 278f.

[63] See the latest declaration in the ecumenical document, *Die Lehrverurteilungen des 16. Jahrhunderts und die ökumenische Situation der Gegenwart*, eds. Heinrich Fries and Otto Herman Pesch (Munich, 1987), 167, 29. Professor Reinhard Slenczka broke a taboo when he contradicted this statement that the Pope is not the Antichrist in the discussion about this document and when he therefore even retracted his signature under the whole document. See *Lehrverurteilungen*, 171, and also Reinhard Slenczka, "Gerecht vor Gott durch den Glauben an Jesus Christus. Das Verständnis der Rechtfertigung in der evangelischen Kirche und die Verständigung über die Rechtfertigung mit der römisch-katholischen Kirche," *NZSTh* 29 (1987): 314f.

[64] *HWS*, 86; "Maria und der Papst. Bemerkungen zum Dogma von der Himmelfahrt Mariae" (1951), *ISC* I:211; "Das Konzil als Frage an die Lutherische Kirche," *LB* 11.61 (1959): 32.

[65] See "Last Things: Church and Antichrist," *WCC*, 116f.

[66] Ibid., 120. See also "Successio Apostolica," *ISC* I:88-90.

[67] "Successio Apostolica," *ISC* I:88; "Variata semper varianda," *LB* 22.101 (1970): 87.

[68] "Ist der Papst?," *LB* 2.10 (1950): 14; "Ökumenische Fragen," *LB* 8.40 (1956): 10.

[69] "Last Things," *WCC*, 113.

[70] "Ist der Papst?" *LB* 2.10 (1950): 14; my trans.

[71] "Die Konfessionskirchen in der Ökumenischen Bewegung, *LB* 21.97 (1969): 66f.; my trans.

[72] "The Ecumenical Movement in the Roman Catholic Church," *RTR* 23 (1964): 7.

[73] Ibid.

[74] "Das unvollendete Konzil," *LB* 29.114 (1977): 21; my trans.

[75] "Rom und die Ökumenische Bewegung," *LB* 15.78 (1963): 81; "Das unvollendete Konzil," *LB* 29.114 (1977): 4; "Nach dem Konzil" (1965), *ISC* I:237.

[76] Qtd Hopf, "Hermann Sasse und sein Ringen," *LB* 32.119 (1980): 42; my trans.

[77] "The Second Vatican Council," *RTR* 20 (1961): 40.

[78] "Heilige Kirche oder Heilige Schrift" (1967), *ISC* II:293. See also Sasse's remark, in a letter to Dr. Renner: "in America, where the devil is on the loose in the Lutheran Churches just as in the Roman Church." Qtd Hopf, "Hermann Sasse und sein Ringen," *LB* 32.119 (1980): 44; my trans.

[79] "Das unvollendete Konzil," *LB* 29.114 (1977): 18.

[80] Ibid., 22f.; my trans.

[81] See Hopf, "Hermann Sasse und sein Ringen," *LB* 32.119 (1980).

[82] "Konfessionskirchen," *LB* 21.97 (1969): 34.

[83] "Die Frage der Autorität der Hl. Schrift," *LB* 11.63 (1959): 127.

[84] "Rome and the Inspiration of Scripture," *RTR* 22 (1963): 38f.; "Das Ende des konfessionellen Zeitalters" (1967), *ISC* II:283.

[85] "Nach dem Konzil," *ISC* I:236f.; "Heil außerhalb der Kirche," *ISC* II:316.

[86] "Rome and the Inspiration of Holy Scripture," *RTR* 22 (1963):41-43. Cf. Wenz, "Hermann Sasses Beitrag," in *Wort des lebendigen Gottes*, 106, n. 49: "Sasse took a very positive approach toward Rome's opening up to modern exegesis while at the same time holding fast to the doctrine of inspiration"; my trans.

[87] "Die Frage der Autorität der Hl. Schrift," *LB* 11.63 (1959): 136.

[88] "Nach dem Konzil," *ISC* I:237.

[89] "Das unvollendete Konzil," *LB* 29.114 (1977): 9, 16f.; see also *SS*, 335f., with n. 24.

[90] "Nach dem Konzil," *ISC* I:243.

[91] "Brief an einen deutschen lutherischen Bischof," *LB* 21.98 (1969): 105.

[92] Qtd Hopf, "Sasse und sein Ringen," *LB* 32.119 (1980): 39 & 38; my trans.

[93] "Die Frage der Autorität der Hl. Schrift," *LB* 11.63 (1959): 120; "The Sources of Revelation," *RTR* 22 (1963): 12.

[94] "Die Kirche und das Wort Gottes. Zur Lehre vom Worte Gottes," repr. *LB* 33.123-24 (1981): 3; my trans.

[95] See the basic treatment of this view by Armin Wenz, *Das Wort Gottes—Gericht und Rettung. Untersuchungen zur Autorität der Heiligen Schrift in Bekenntnis und Lehre der Kirche* (Göttingen: Vandenhoeck & Ruprecht, 1995).

[96] SA III, 8; Tappert 312f. See also "Apostolic Succession" (1956), *WCC*, 90f.; "Das Zweite Vatikanische Konzil als Frage an das Luthertum," *LB* 17.85 (1965): 123; "Nach dem Konzil," *ISC* I:246; *SS*, 342.

[97] "Die Frage der Autorität der Hl. Schrift," *LB* 11.63 (1959): 126.

[98] "Heilige Kirche oder Heilige Schrift," *ISC* II:311.

[99] See ibid., 298, and also "Variata semper varianda," *LB* 22.101 (1970): 81.

[100] "The Sources of Revelation," *RTR* 22 (1963):3f.

[101] Cf. ibid., 5ff.

[102] "Das unvollendete Konzil," *LB* 29.114 (1977): 17.

[103] "The Sources of Revelation," *RTR* 22 (1963): 9ff.

[104] See a letter of 1966 qtd Hopf, "Hermann Sasse und sein Ringen," *LB* 32.119 (1980): 47.

[105] "The Sources of Revelation," *RTR* 22 (1963): 12; "Apostolic Succession," *WCC*, 88.

[106] "Das Zweite Vatikanische Konzil als Frage an das Luthertum," *LB* 17.85 (1965): 120, 123; "Heil außerhalb der Kirche," *ISC* II: 318.

[107] See Hopf's editorial comment in *ISC* I:167; "Das Konzil als Frage an die lutherische Kirche," *LB* 11.61 (1959): 38; "Nach dem Konzil," *ISC* I:245f.

[108] "Ubi Christus, ibi ecclesia" (1929), repr. *LB* 16.81 (1964): 39; *K&H*, 11; "Die Kirche an die Jahreswende" (1938), repr. *LB* 22.99 (1970): 3; *Z*, 235.

[109] "The Second Vatican Council (II)," *RTR* 20 (1961): 68f; "Die Frage nach dem Wesen der Kirche," *LB* 14.74 (1962): 73f.

[110] "Das unvollendete Konzil," *LB* 29.114 (1977): 7.

[111] Sasse traces the official use of this expression back to Cardinal Bea. See "Heil außerhalb der Kirche," *ISC* II:317, and "Das Zweite Vatikanische Konzil als Frage an das Luthertum," *LB* 17.85 (1965): 116. He was aware, however, that the expression had been used privately already around 1930. See "Rom und die Ökumenische Bewegung," *LB* 14.81 (1962): 86; "Die Frage nach dem Wesen der Kirche," *LB* 14.74 (1962): 81, and even already "Ist der Papst?" *LB* 2.10 (1950): 8. Evidence exists that this expression was used in the Roman Church already from the 17th century onwards! See Gottfried Maron, *Kirche und Rechtfertigung. Eine kontroverstheologische Untersuchung ausgehend von den Texten des Zweiten Vatikanischen Konzils* (Göttingen: Vandenhoeck & Ruprecht, 1969), 118f.

[112] "Heilige Kirche oder Heilige Schrift?" ISC II:295; "Das unvollendete Konzil," *LB* 29.114 (1977): 21.

[113] "The Second Vatican Council (II)," *RTR* 20 (1961):74-76; "Die Frage nach dem Wesen der Kirche," *LB* 14.74 (1962): 82f.

[114] "Das unvollendete Konzil," *LB* 29.114 (1977): 20.

[115] "Nach dem Konzil," *ISC* I:245-47.

[116] "Rom und die Ökumenische Bewegung," *LB* 15.81 (1963): 87.

[117] "Die Frage nach dem Wesen der Kirche," *LB* 14.74 (1962): 74-83.

[118] *SS*, 328; "Peter und Paul. Über die Frühgeschichte des Römischen Primats" (1964), *ISC* I:222f.

[119] "Apostolic Succession," *WCC*, 104.

[120] Ibid., 102f.; "Das Zweite Vatikanische Konzil als Frage an das Luthertum," *LB* 17.85 (1965): 121.

[121] *TMB*, 309.

[122] "Das Abendmahl in der katholischen Messe," *VSA*, 91.

[123] "Maria und der Papst" (1951), *ISC* I:208f.; "Zur Lehre vom Heiligen Geist," *LB* 12.66 (1960): 103.

[124] "Das Abendmahl in der katholischen Messe," *VSA*, 92; "Maria und der Papst," *ISC* I:206, 213f.; "Last Things," *WCC*, 123f.; "Zum lutherischen Verständnis der Konsekration" (1952), *CC*, 135.

[125] "Nach dem Konzil," *ISC* I:240f.

[126] "Brief an einen deutschen lutherischen Bischof," *LB* 21.98 (1969): 100; "Das unvollendete Konzil," *LB* 29.114 (1977): 20.

[127] "Die Konfessionskirchen in der Ökumenischen Bewegung," *LB* 21.97 (1969): 39, 64; "Brief an einen deutschen lutherischen Bischof," *LB* 21.98 (1969): 100.

[128] "Offener Brief an Herrn Landesbischof D. theol. Hermann Dietzfelbinger, München," *LB* 20.94 (1968): 83; "Die Konfessionskirchen in der Ökumenischen Bewegung," *LB* 21.97 (1969): 66; "Brief an einen deutschen lutherischen Bischof," *LB* 21.98 (1969): 101.

[129] "Heil außerhalb der Kirche," *ISC* II:320ff.

[130] "Das Zweite Vatikanische Konzil als Frage an das Luthertum," *LB* 17.85 (1965): 118; "Nach dem Konzil," *ISC* I:246-48.

[131] "Offener Brief," *LB* 20.94 (1968): 83.

[132] "Rome and the Inspiration of Scripture," *RTR* 22 (1963): 44; "Rom und die Ökumenische Bewegung," *LB* 15.81 (1963): 82; "Brief an einen deutschen lutherischen Bischof," *LB* 21.90 (1969): 104; "Das unvollendete Konzil," *LB* 29.114 (1977): 21.

[133] *SS*, 132.

[134] Letter to Gottfried Klapper of 2 September 1971; qtd *CC*, 105, n. 16; my trans.

[135] Letter to Peter Brunner of 4 December 1974; qtd *CC*, 106, n. 16; my trans.

[136] "Lambeth 1958," *LB* 11.60 (1959): 22; my trans.

Holy Supper, Holy Church

John R. Stephenson

Within a year of his ostensibly Lutheran ordination in 1900, Albert Schweitzer (1875-1965) averred in print that, "To Zwingli belongs the credit for being the first to treat the problem of the Lord's Supper in a scholarly way."[1] Schweitzer's Strasbourg alma mater moved within the same theological parameters as did the University of Berlin where, a year before the outbreak of the First World War, the young Hermann Sasse came to bask in the rays of such luminaries of the firmament of learning as Karl Holl, Adolf von Harnack, and Adolf Deissmann. Despite his later immersion in J. S. Bach, Schweitzer never tested his uncritical assumption that the earthly Jesus in the upper room could not have meant what Luther, along with the whole catholic tradition of East and West, had heard Him to say. But the shock waves from the trenches shattered Sasse's confidence in the school of Albrecht Ritschl (1822-1887) to which Schweitzer retained a paradoxical yet touching loyalty throughout his long exile in Lambarene. While Sasse would broadly appreciate the new direction given to European theology by Karl Barth[2] and would remain an albeit idiosyncratic ecumenist until his last breath,[3] he declined to pledge his unreserved allegiance to either Barthianism or the Ecumenical Movement. Instead, Sasse's theological identity would be determined by his discovery of and commitment to the Lutheran tradition in general and the Book of Concord in particular. Ironically enough, he first touched base with the neo-Lutheran giant Wilhelm Löhe not in a German library but during a study year at a Reformed seminary in Hartford, Connecticut (1925-1926). He would thereby step outside the respectable mainstream to believe, teach, and confess a dogma which Prussian jackboot and Enlightenment scholarship had almost erased from the church of his homeland. Schweitzer's conclusions concerning the earthly Jesus made it pointless for him to continue as a teacher of theology; so this holder of four doctorates fingered another string of his bow by practicing medicine in Africa. Sasse's unfashionable convictions about the Sacrament of the Altar made him an insufferable odd man out among university theologians in the decades dominated by Karl Barth.[4] When informed conscience forbade his acquiescence in the all-German Protestant union of 1948 and St. Louis didn't want him, Sasse was out of place in the land of his birth and betook himself much further away than Lambarene.

The writer of a modern spiritual classic insists that Christ's Gospel call can be fitly answered only by those prepared to undergo unconditional change. According to Dietrich von Hildebrand, the true Christian "*wills* to lose the firm ground of unredeemed nature under his feet and to tumble, so to speak, into the arms of Christ."[5] Like Sasse a foe of Hitler, from whose *Anschluß* of Austria he fled, the lay teacher von Hildebrand urges that "we should be like soft wax, ready to receive the imprint of the features of Christ."[6] Would it be fanciful to attribute to the Holy Spirit the rearrangement of the young Pastor Hermann Sasse's mental furniture and the transformation of his spiritual values system which took place with increasing momentum from the late 1920s onwards? After all, generic Brandenburg Protestants and Ritschlian Berlin theologians would sooner turn Buddhist than claim ownership of the sort of statements that flowed in torrents from the untenured Erlangen professor's pen in the second half of the third decade of this century. For:

> When in 1937 ([under] Asmussen['s influence]!) the Confessing Church in Halle proclaimed general eucharistic fellowship, I began the battle for the Real Presence.[7]

While Baptism is necessary for salvation, wrote Sasse in 1938, the Eucharist is necessary for the life of the church. At the Blessed Sacrament, apart from which she would be simply swallowed up by the world,[8] the church is uniquely manifested as what she is divinely intended to be.[9] Charles Porterfield Krauth's insight that the Real Presence is "among the most fundamental of fundamental" articles[10] found an echo in Sasse's bold thesis that:

> . . . ever since that hour when, in the celebration of the first Supper on the night that He was betrayed, Jesus Christ the incarnate Word of the Father, as at once the high priest and the Lamb of God who takes away the sin of the world, distributed His true body and blood to His circle of disciples under bread and wine, thereby making them members of His Body and bestowing on them forgiveness of sins along with life and salvation, the heart of the church has been beating in the Lord's Supper. Even when we

do not know it, the heart of the church is still beating today in the Lord's Supper. If the celebration of the Supper should cease, then the preaching of the Word would be struck dumb, with the result that faith would be quenched, love would grow cold, and hope would die. Where the heart dies, the body dies also. The church dies with the Supper.[11]

Expounding the doctrinal decision of Article VII of the Formula of Concord (FC) in an essay of 1941, Sasse referred approvingly to Luther's conviction that denial of the Real Presence in the sense in which he taught it has as its upshot the destruction of the church.[12]

Sasse lived and moved in the element of eucharistic theology from sometime in the 1930s until his death, but, unless I am much mistaken, the pinnacle of this major focus of his pastoral and academic career was attained in the white-hot eloquence of his publications on the Blessed Sacrament between 1938 and 1941. If permitted to take but one of Sasse's writings to exile on a desert island, I should pick *Church and Lord's Supper* of 1938; and if one further work of his could be slipped past my captors, I should add the volume *On the Sacrament of the Altar* which he edited and co-wrote in 1941. In our epoch of unavoidable yet constricting specialization we can only marvel how in these and other essays Sasse showed himself equally at home in all four theological disciplines. *On the Sacrament of the Altar* turned out to be as it were a last blast of the trumpet from the threatened species of German confessional Lutherans.[13] Its editor intended to furnish this book with only its foreword and an historical-cum-systematic article on the dogma set forth in FC VII. But some contributors failed to meet their deadlines, while others had been summoned to military service; so Sasse crafted this century's liveliest, deepest, and most convincing exegetical defense of the Real Presence, proving to all but the most radical higher critics that the earthly Jesus was the sole author of the ongoing feast of His body and blood.[14] Working in an environment where biblical authority could not be taken for granted, Sasse here practiced New Testament scholarship as a form of winsome Christian apologetic, winning an accolade from the Leipzig professor Julius Schniewind who informed his colleague Ernst Sommerlath that, "The exegetical remarks by Sasse, which he has made on the Supper in the symposium volume *On the Sacrament of the Altar*, are the best that I have ever read on the subject."[15] Moreover, prefiguring one of his major professional emphases in later life, Sasse the irrepressible ecumenist here wrote charitably, concisely, and constructively on "The Supper in the Catholic Mass."[16]

Now German divinity suffers from a justly deserved bad reputation in the area of pastoral theology. A highflying German ministerial student taking practical courses at his university once reacted with disdain to a foreigner's question whether in that semester he would be doing such things as hospital visits and helping in a parish. "No," came the shocked reply, "I'm studying the *theory* of practical theology!" All the more remarkable, then, was Professor Sasse's refusal to barricade himself behind his books from the rigors of the parochial front line. The renewal of sacramental life engaged Sasse as much in the pulpit and in addresses delivered to church groups as in his study and lecture room. Thus a wartime sermon on Acts 2:42-47 contained a hortatory reminder of what Lutheran eucharistic practice had once been and might by the grace of God be again:

> And nothing is more needful for the church of the present, even for our Lutheran church, than that she consider with total seriousness whether the breakdown of fellowship [*Gemeinschaft*] in her midst and also the breakdown of her fellowship-forming power is not simply a product of the fact that she has scarcely a shred of understanding of the Supper left, that she has shoved it into the background, indeed that she has rent from her Divine Service the celebration that was the centerpiece of Christian worship up till the Reformation and remained so in the first two centuries of the Evangelical Lutheran Church. The whole congregation certainly neither can nor should commune every Sunday, but the Sacrament ought to be celebrated in her midst.[17]

In his 42nd *Letter to Lutheran Pastors* (1956), Sasse would admonish his brethren in office that, instead of taking up "a few hurried hours" at its end, the sacraments "should really determine the whole content of confirmation instruction."[18] For:

> The proclamation of this "eternal Gospel" (Rev. 14:6) is always to be accompanied by the celebration of the Sacrament that our Lord instituted, by which His death is proclaimed until He comes. Without the celebration of this Sacrament the proclamation of the Gospel could be understood as just one of the many religious messages in the world. This does indeed happen where people are ignorant of the Sacrament.[19]

Preaching's constant accompaniment by sacramental celebration here emerges as a pastoral corollary of the distinction between Law and Gospel, as a heeding of the Lord's voice to ensure the primacy of gift over demand. And the deepest reason why the full Gospel entails both proclamation and Lord's Supper is rooted in the Incarnation itself, which is a whole that cannot be fitly mirrored and conveyed through an incomplete part. At a conference held in Nuremberg in early 1939 Sasse expressed a profound insight later widely popularized by Oscar Cullmann[20]:

> As the church's preaching of the Word, if it be the preaching of the pure simple Gospel, is nothing else but the continuation of Jesus' preaching, so his saving activity also continues in the right administration of the sacraments.[21]

Among the many remarkable features of Sasse's work were his sober realism and courageous refusal to take refuge in illusions. He was given to paint an accurate picture of Nazism's horrid face before a single concentration camp was opened,[22] and he grasped with unflinching clarity how mounting secularism is ravaging all churches without exception. North American Christendom will one day learn from bitter experience the truth of these words written in 1938:

> An increasing number of typewriters clattering away in the ecclesiastical office-buildings of the world and automobile-equipped general superintendents holding ever more conferences cannot justify intoning a *Vexilla regis prodeunt*! For such increased productivity has not yet done anything to alter the fact that the western people, in "Catholic" and "Protestant" lands alike, are drifting more and more away from the sphere of influence of the Christian message, and that church attendance and participation in Holy Communion are almost everywhere on the decline. For the process of secularization—this avalanche which threatens to bury alive all remaining elements of ancient, inherited churchly life—is accelerating as rapidly among professedly Christian people as it is among the rest of society. If the actual percentage of those still confessing the basic dogmas of Christianity could be ascertained by polling the "Christian" population of the West, what religious nihilism would be shown to underlie the thin veneer of Christian culture! Then there would no longer be anything mysterious about the volcanic eruptions of atheism and hatred of Christ that have for the past two centuries continually threatened the existence of the church. Then we would understand that

these phenomena reveal not just the will of individual men but rather a mighty inner fate of Western culture, which stood for so many centuries under the sign of the Crucified.[23]

Nor did Sasse's instinct for reality desert him in the case of his aspirations for Lutheran sacramental renewal. Back in 1580 the Spartan rite occasionally observed in the minster church of Zurich and in St. Peter's, Geneva, was manifestly not in the same ballpark as the Masses regularly and reverently celebrated in the cathedrals of Magdeburg and Upsala;[24] but much water had run under the bridge in the meantime to blur the differences between the confessions. A monumental uphill struggle would therefore be involved in the process of taking out of cold storage article 24 of the Augsburg Confession and its Apology. "We have to face the fact that a heritage that has been lost for over 250 years cannot be restored quickly."[25] This harsh truth is apt to daunt not only Sasse writing in 1956 but also ourselves at this time when the most recent conventions of Lutheran Church–Canada's Central District and of the Lutheran Church–Missouri Synod have passed resolutions encouraging a general return to the weekly celebration of the Blessed Sacrament. Since majority decisions do not of themselves convince hearts, these convention resolutions can only be implemented in the long run after a generation of unremitting effort. Sasse's studies on the Lord's Supper will not have been in vain if they encourage us to return an affirmative answer to the questions whether such Herculean labors are worthwhile, whether it makes sense to swim against the North American cultural current, and whether there is any point in rocking our already leaking ecclesiastical boats.

If any ambiguity lurks in the words of institution, then the earthly Jesus is forever wrapped in a cloud of unknowing. Sasse appositely quoted his Erlangen colleague Werner Elert's remark that the Pauline report of the Lord's Supper is "the oldest document of Christianity that bears witness to Christ's words in direct speech."[26] In company with the confessors of 1577 (Formula of Concord, Solid Declaration [FC SD] VII, 44), Sasse was keenly mindful that Jesus spoke the *verba* at the most solemn juncture of His earthly life, so that "[w]ith the Words of Institution the prophetic office of Christ is fulfilled, and His high priestly work begins."[27] Our Lord's whole ministry was a preparation for the moment in which He placed all His eggs in the sacramental basket: "all that Jesus Christ is and all that He brought, His whole person and His whole work, is indissolubly connected with the Lord's Supper."[28] The Church's teaching is nothing more and nothing less than a faithful echo of her Bridegroom's words. Of "the fact that bread and wine become the body and blood of Christ" the aged Sasse wrote that, "This and nothing else is the church's dogma of the Lord's Supper."[29]

"There is no Gospel without the Real Presence"[30] is a paraphrase of Luther[31] on the part of one convinced that the Blessed Sacrament prevents Jesus being locked up in the past[32] and His Atonement from turning into an abstract theory.[33] Sasse betrayed his familiarity with some hymn verses attributed to Wilhelm Löhe[34] when he argued that:

> ... in the Lord's Supper the boundaries of space and time are overcome: Heaven and earth become one, the inseparable interval that separates the present moment of the church from the future kingdom of God is bridged.[35]

> That heaven and earth become one, as it were, in the Eucharist is one of the fundamental thoughts in the great liturgical chapter, Rev. 4 .... Thus the Sanctus belongs to the temporal as well as to the heavenly divine service.[36]

From his construct of "consistent eschatology" Albert Schweitzer drew the dismal conclusion that the earthly Jesus went to the Cross for the sake of a tragic error. While conceding that the delay of the Parousia, which "is possibly the severest disappointment ever experienced on earth," represents "one of the most plausible arguments for unbelief," Sasse had a reply to the question:

> How is it possible for [the church] to avoid plunging into despair over the delay of the Parousia, for her not to lose her faith on its account? How is it possible for her to wait with unspeakable patience as if the measurements and laws of earthly time did not exist for her, and yet with every moment to grow in joyful assurance of her cause?[37]

For all his ingenuity, Schweitzer had left the Eucharist out of the equation and so was unaware that, "Because the church possesses this sacrament, she can wait for centuries and millennia on end. The Supper bridges the space of time between Jesus' days on earth and His return."[38] This understanding of the anticipation of the heavenly future in the earthly present prompted Sasse to exult in how all three rites recognized by the Apology of the Augsburg Confession (AP) XIII as sacraments in the strict sense:

> ... have one thing in common: they have an eschatological significance. In them the future redemption is already present. They denote not only a divine, heavenly reality, but they give us a share in it already now. The forgiveness of sins that we receive in Baptism and absolution is the anticipation of the acquittal of the Last Judgment. Our death and our resurrection to eternal life have already begun in our baptism (Rom. 6:3ff.). In Holy Communion Christ comes already now and gives us a share in the "messianic" banquet in heaven.[39]

In company with Luther in the Large Catechism, Sasse gladly celebrated the threefold festival of benefits given through our Lord's really present body and blood (Large Catechism [LC] V,21-22; 23-27; 68). Thus the Holy Supper is no illustration of the mere possibility of the forgiveness of sins, but rather "the actual forgiveness itself."[40] Taking as his cue St. Paul's indication in I Cor. 10 that the manna in the wilderness is a type of the Eucharist, in a few short sentences Sasse unfolded the biblical basis for the confessional description of the Sacrament as "the food of the soul" which "nourishes and strengthens the new man" (LC V, 23): the *pneuma* food of Christ's body and blood miraculously preserves "Israel according to the spirit on its journey through the comfortless wilderness of this world to the heavenly Canaan of the kingdom of God."[41] And he diligently demonstrated that St. Ignatius of Antioch's acknowledgment of the Eucharist as "the medicine of immortality, the remedy against our having to die" is a genuinely Scriptural perception.[42] No barrier may be put in the way of the Christology of the Formula whose rubber hits our road at the altar rail.

By now Sasse has superabundantly made good his claim that the restoration of the Blessed Sacrament to its proper place in the Divine Service "dare not be an interest only of a liturgical reform movement. It is a matter of life and death for the Lutheran Church."[43] Sasse was, by the way, no uncritical ally of liturgically-minded Lutherans. Arthur Carl Piepkorn translated a paper of his only to become the target of his polemic within a decade.[44] On the one hand, Sasse's researches in the New Testament and the Early Church convinced him that, "The Divine

Service of the first century already displayed more similarity with the Mass of one of the Eastern Churches than with a Methodist fellowship gathering."[45] Moreover, he was unsparing in his charge that, "There is no more damning . . . indictment of a theologian than to say that he knows nothing about liturgy."[46] And when a virus infection caused him to miss church on the Festival of Pentecost 1971, the housebound Sasse wrote a letter to a Queensland pastor in which, among other things, he voiced his fears about the negative effects of the destruction of the liturgy: "Since the liturgy shapes the inner life of those who live in it, such a process must have tremendous psychological and spiritual consequences."[47] When liturgy goes down the tubes, confession and dogma go with it.[48] On the other hand, though, Sasse was careful to insist that the sacramental horse pull the liturgical cart, and not vice versa: "It is out of the Lord's Supper that the *liturgy* grew."[49] And the Real Presence is "the one thing that gives the Christian liturgy life."[50]

Along with Piepkorn, Sasse began to break the Melanchthonian stranglehold on Lutheran eucharistic theology that set in when John Gerhard displaced Luther's and Chemnitz's teaching on the Consecration which is still to be found in FC SD VII, 73-87. As late as 1941 Sasse was still gingerly exploring an area which has become for some a minefield.[51] After a couple of years in Australia, he was disquieted by the state of Confessional scholarship in North America. Among the wealth of contributions by theologians in the United States to the question of the epiclesis, he noted, "I have yet to find an author who adduced the teaching of the Formula of Concord concerning the consecration."[52] Further study emboldened him, and in two essays of the 1950s Sasse firmly ditched Gerhard for Luther: "The consecrated bread is the body of Christ also when it lies on the altar or when the pastor holds it in his hand. This is the Lutheran view."[53] In his last years Sasse would welcome the results of Tom Hardt's research in this area.

Who knows what comfort Albert Schweitzer was vouchsafed on his deathbed from his much-touted pantheizing philosophy of "reverence for life"? In the vertical dimension Hermann Sasse had an upward-bearing full Gospel to die into, but like his hero Vilmar in 1868 Sasse in 1976 was overwhelmed on the horizontal plane by evidence of wholesale apostasy and by intimations of general collapse in Christendom. He had no confidence that the Lutheran clergy would rise as a body to reclaim and reenforce the confession of their church. In, with, and under the deepest pessimism, Sasse ventured to hope that some laypeople might yet keep the faith.[54] For there is nothing uniquely clerical about the Lutheran catechesis, Lutheran liturgy, and Lutheran hymnody that stand in the service of the Blessed Sacrament. In the great sacramental writing of his early 40s, Sasse had contended that the Lord's Supper is mission's friend, not its foe:

> Where the custom of churchgoing has lapsed with the consequence that the Christian congregation is dead or a-dying, there is but one single means for getting people back to church. Hunger and thirst for the Lord's Supper must be aroused in them. Whenever this hunger and this thirst awake—and it obviously does not lie within our power to awaken them—people go to church again. For hunger and thirst for God's Word can in an emergency be satisfied in one's chamber, at any rate according to that pietistic theory with which the Protestantism of the last two centuries has preached its own churches empty. Except in case of grave illness, however, the Sacrament of the Altar can only be received in the house of God. The renewal of the Christian congregation and her Divine Service therefore begins, in a way that most theologians today still find incomprehensible, when we once again seriously learn and teach what the New Testament and the Catechism say on Baptism and the Supper.[55]

Should these words be true, there is cause for regret that *Lutheran Worship* (#239) and *Lutheran Book of Worship* (#224) have dropped stanza 4 from *The Lutheran Hymnal* #305's version of "Soul, Adorn Yourself With Gladness":

> Ah, how hungers all my spirit
> For the love I do not merit!
> Oft have I, with sighs fast thronging,
> Thought upon this food with longing,
> In the battle well-nigh worsted,
> For this cup of life have thirsted,
> For the friend who here invites us
> And to God Himself unites us.

So neither Johann Franck nor Hermann Sasse will permit us to hide unrepentant behind the *fides quae*, the objective deposit of faith. Whatever criticism must be made of the existentialist vein in Barth's understanding of confession, we may not deride the act of confessing.

Reserve towards Pietism does not exempt us from the call to piety, which is the fitting lively expression of the *fides qua*, the heart's inner appropriation of our Lord's *iustitia aliena* located outside ourselves in the means of grace. Sasse's own sin-laden finitude is reflected in the fact that in certain respects his lifelong work on the Holy Supper remained uncompleted. *Corpus Christi*, his fourth and final *Ave verum*, was posthumously edited and published by Friedrich Wilhelm Hopf, and in his many writings on the theology and practice of Holy Communion Sasse raised some questions to which he gave no detailed answer. So the young Tom Hardt sprinted with the ball which Sasse diffidently put into play.[56] Dr. Sasse's many writings on the Holy Supper are to be plumbed and pondered; they are not intrinsically exempt from scrutiny; they are properly to be used as springboards for further study. There is a grain of truth in every heresy, even in individualism: Sasse cannot do our theology for us. He is, though, a spiritual father given for our nurture. His impassioned testimony to the Lord's Supper, its essence, and its benefits, poses to each of us the urgent question: can we do without the rite once instituted in the upper room, which bridges the gap between the yesterday of the earthly Jesus and the tomorrow of our Lord's glorious return, the mystery which lavishes on us everything that our divine-human Savior is and has?

Notes

[1] Albert Schweitzer, *The Lord's Supper in Relationship to the Life of Jesus and the History of the Early Church*, trans. A. J. Mattill, Jr., ed. John Reumann (Macon, GA: Mercer University Press, 1982), 63.

[2] See the chapter on "Lutheran Theology and the Modern Reformed Theology of Karl Barth," *HWS*, 161-178. "While thanking him for the revival which he has brought about" (178), Sasse found plenty to criticize in Barth. At the end of his life, Sasse would award Barth a backhanded compliment with the stinging observation that, "Through his complete denial of the sacrament of Baptism, the former renewer of the Evangelical Church became the church's gravedigger. God prevented his drawing the consequences for the Supper by taking the pen from his hand." *CC*, 79; my trans.

[3] In his January 1974 Foreword to his "last modest *Ave Verum*," Sasse regretted that 20th-century ecumenism had followed the paradigm of the Chicago-Lambeth Quadrilateral of 1920 rather than that of a "League of Churches" suggested in the same year by the encyclical of the Oecumenical Patriarchate of Constantinople "To all the

Churches of Christ wheresoever they may be." The 1948 World Council of Churches struck Sasse as so to say a "United Churches" organization which overstepped the bounds of ecumenical propriety. Sasse longed for ecumenism to embrace the model proposed by the Oecumenical Patriarchate, and hoped that post-Vatican II Rome would join in "such a genuine federation" of churches. *CC*, 10-12.

[4] "At that time [the early 1940s] anyone who advocated Luther's doctrine of the Supper was impossible in good theological company." Letter of 25 May 1957 to the future Bishop Jobst Schöne, then a student at St. Louis, qtd in *CC*, 99; my trans.

[5] Dietrich von Hildebrand, *Transformation in Christ* (repr. Manchester, New Hampshire: Sophia Institute Press, 1990), 7.

[6] Ibid., 9.

[7] Letter of 25 May 1957 to Jobst Schöne, qtd in *CC*, 99; my trans.

[8] "So far as we men can judge, a church bereft of this sacrament would be swallowed up by the world and cease to be church, just as it has in fact transpired that wherever the Lord's Supper has been permitted to decay, the boundary lines between church and world have universally disappeared and the church has been absorbed into the world. The Supper is thus the sacrament in which the church's 'foreignness from the world' and hence her essence as church of God find visible expression." *K&H*, 16; my trans.

[9] "The Supper is necessary for the life of the church, for in the celebration of this sacrament the church keeps on becoming what according to God's will she is meant to be. She here becomes visible as church in a completely special way." *K&H*, 14; my trans. Cf. also "The Lord's Supper in the New Testament" (1941), *WCS*, 93f.: "Finally, there is yet one more sense in which the Lord's Supper is an actualization of the redemption achieved by Christ. F. Kattenbusch . . . once raised the questions, whether, when, and how Jesus actually fulfills His promise in Matt. 16:18 that He would build His church, and he answered in this way: "The Lord's Supper was the act by which He founded His church (*ekkleesia*), His congregation." . . . Then the Last Supper, which Jesus celebrated with them [the apostles] as the Passover of the new covenant, is really the *organization of the new people of God*." In 1948 Sasse approvingly paraphrased the contemporary Roman Catholic liturgical movement's answer to the question, "What is the church?" "The church is there where the congregation of Christian believers gather as *ecclesia orans* (the praying church) around the altar; where the Body of the Word is received with the mouth in the Holy Communion, there is the church as the Body of Christ." "Liturgy and Lutheranism," *S&C*, 34f.

[10] Charles Porterfield Krauth, *The Conservative Reformation and its Theology* (repr. Philadelphia, Pennsylvania: The United Lutheran Publication House, 1913), 655.

[11] *K&H*, 65; my trans. See also "*Sanctorum Communio*" (1974), *WCS*, 151: "One must let oneself be influenced by the stirring prayers of the earthly church, the doxologies in which the church on earth becomes one with the church in heaven, and

the awe-inspiring songs in so many languages in order to understand that in this Sacrament beats the heart of the church."

[12] "Die Lehrentscheidung der Konkordienformel in der Frage des hl. Abendmahls," *VSA*, 189.

[13] Although *Vom Sakrament des Altars* was sold out within a year, it was not reprinted after the war. In his letter of 25 May 1957 to Jobst Schöne, Sasse charged Karl Barth with prevailing on the Munich publishing firm Christian Kaiser (which had published the first volumes of his *Church Dogmatics*) not to issue a second edition of *K&H*; see *CC*, 99. Sasse's sometime assistant, the 95 year-old Pr. Hans-Siegfried Huß, has recently told the story of the "Schwabacher Konvent" of confessional pastors, including Sasse, which planned for a Lutheran Church free of State control in the postwar period. Huß speculates that the Lutheran Church of Bavaria's accession to the "Evangelical Church in Germany" might have been prevented but for the tragic deaths in an automobile accident of *Oberkirchenräte* Christian Stoll and Wilhelm Bogner on St. Nicholas' Day 1946. See Huß, 83.

[14] "The Lord's Supper in the New Testament," *WCS*, 49-97 (*Vom Sakrament des Altars*, 26-78). See also *K&H*, 39-58.

[15] Letter of Dr. Ernst Sommerlath, 18 October 1978, qtd in *CC*, 103; my trans.

[16] "Das Abendmahl in der katholischen Messe," *VSA*, 79-94. In 1948, thus a good decade before his dialogue with Rome began in earnest, Sasse perceived that "the current vitality of the Roman Catholic church derives not from her international political activity, nor from the miracles of Fatima and other prodigies, nor from her achievements in speculative theology, nor from the new dogmas concerning the Blessed Virgin Mary for which, to the distress of some of the Roman church's own theologians, the Curia is making preparations. She possesses her present vitality in spite of all these things and in spite of everything un-Christian and anti-Christian that happens in her midst. The real source of her vitality in this remnant of her primitive heritage in spite of all these things and which she still retains and which she knows how to renew again and again: The profound truth of *the Real Presence of Christ in the Sacrament of the Altar*. It is one of the most noteworthy signs of the times that the Roman Catholic church seeks to make the center of her spiritual life precisely that primitive and Scriptural tenet which ... Martin Luther so doughtily defended against Zwingli and the sixteenth century Enthusiasts." "Liturgy and Lutheranism," *S&C*, 35.

[17] *Z*, 113; my trans.

[18] "Word and Sacrament, Preaching and the Lord's Supper," *WCS*, 23.

[19] "Word and Sacrament: Preaching and the Lord's Supper," *WCS*, 26.

[20] Oscar Cullmann, *Early Christian Worship*, trans. A. Stewart Todd & James B. Torrance (London: SCM Press, 1953).

[21] "The Lord's Supper in the Life of the Church," *S&C*, 5. Cf. also "The Lutheran Understanding of the Consecration" (1952), *WCS*, 137: "As the preaching of the Lord was accompanied by His signs and wonders, so the proclamation of His church is accompanied by the sacraments. And as the deeds of Jesus were the dawn of the coming redemption (Luke 4:18ff.; Matt. 11:4ff.), so in Baptism and the Lord's Supper we are already given what belongs to the coming world. As often as the church gathers around the table of the Lord it is already the 'day of the Lord,' i.e., the day of the Messiah (cf. Amos 5:18), the day of His return. This is the original meaning of Sunday as the 'day of the Lord,' on which John (Rev. 1:9ff.) in the Spirit could participate in the heavenly divine service while the churches of Asia were gathered for the Lord's Supper (cf. 3:20). Sunday is an anticipation of the parousia. It is this because on that day the Lord comes to His church in the Word and in the Sacrament of the Altar."

[22] "Die Kirche und die politischen Mächte der Zeit," *ISC* I:251-264, esp. 262f.!

[23] *K&H*, 9f.; my trans.

[24] "Die Lehrentscheidung der Konkordienformel in der Frage des hl. Abendmahls," *VSA*, 187f.

[25] "Word and Sacrament: Preaching and the Lord's Supper," *WCS*, 34.

[26] "The Lord's Supper in the New Testament," *WCS*, 49.

[27] Ibid., 88.

[28] Ibid., 88.

[29] "*Sanctorum Communio*," *WCS*, 149. Cf. also 155, where Sasse closes a catena of quotations from ancient liturgies with: "That is therefore the dogma of the early church concerning the Lord's Supper: Bread and wine in the Lord's Supper after the consecration are the body and blood of the Lord. Nothing more? No, nothing more."

[30] "The Lutheran Understanding of the Consecration" (1952), *WCS*, 121.

[31] ". . . for this sacrament is the gospel." AE 36:289; cf. WA 11,442.22-23.

[32] "For the Crucified One becomes a figure of the past if His true body and His true blood, what He sacrificed for our sins on Golgotha, are not present in the Sacrament of the Altar and given to us." "The Lutheran Understanding of the Consecration," *WCS*, 121. Cf. also "The Lord's Supper in the New Testament," *WCS*, 91: "Where has a historical event been more faithfully remembered than is the death of Christ in the Lord's Supper of His church? There is no other event in the history of antiquity that is so imprinted in the memory of people and lives on throughout the world today. The Lord's Supper has kept this memory so deeply alive precisely because it is even more than a memorial meal. It is not only a celebration of reminiscence like the Passover, in which the human spirit recalled the past for itself, but it is a genuine, actual *bringing into the present* of God's redeeming act through the gift of the body and blood of Christ."

[33] "But that the Lord's Supper is the re-presentation of Christ's sacrifice and the real bestowal of what is gained through this sacrifice is the clear teaching of the New Testament. . . . Understood as a sacrificial meal, it forms a bulwark against the view, widespread also in modern Christendom, that the death of Christ is to be thought of only figuratively as a sacrifice, something like the heroic death of a soldier for his country or the sacrifice of a mother for her child." "The Lord's Supper in the New Testament," *WCS*, 89.

[34] ". . . auf ewig ist verschwunden / Was Erd und Himmel trennt / Denn Gott hat sie verbunden / Im heiligen Sakrament." *Lutherisches Kirchengesangbuch* Ausgabe für die Evangelisch-Lutherische Freikirche in der DDR; Herausgegeben von der liturgischen Kommission der Evangelisch-Lutherischen Freikirche (Berlin: Evangelische Verlagsanstalt GmbH, 1980) #43, st. 3.

[35] "The Lord's Supper in the New Testament," *WCS*, 93. Cf. also "The Lord's Supper in the Life of the Church" (1939), *S&C*, 8: "With the institution of Holy Communion he gave his church something which should span and bridge over the centuries and millennia between his earthly days and his coming again in glory."

[36] "Sanctorum Communio," WCS, 149.

[37] *K&H*, 29; my trans.

[38] Ibid., 29; my trans.

[39] "Sanctorum Communio," WCS, 146.

[40] "Word and Sacrament: Preaching and the Lord's Supper," *WCS*, 26.

[41] *K&H*, 48f.; my trans.

[42] For well nigh 40 years Sasse tirelessly hammered home the eucharistic implications of Jn. 6. See *K&H*, 50-52, 63 n. 1; "The Lord's Supper in the New Testament," *WCS*, 77-81; *TMB*, 288; and *CC*, 87f.

[43] "The Lutheran Understanding of the Consecration," *WCS*, 120.

[44] See *S&C*, 32.

[45] *K&H*, 28, n.17; my trans.

[46] "Liturgy and Lutheranism," *S&C*, 41.

[47] Letter of 30 May 1971 to Pr. H. P. V. Renner.

[48] "Confession and liturgy belong inseparably together if the church is to be healthy. Liturgy is prayed dogma; dogma is the doctrinal content of the liturgy." "The Lutheran Understanding of the Consecration," *WCS*, 117.

[49] "The Lord's Supper in the Life of the Church," *S&C*, 11.

[50] "Liturgy and Lutheranism," *S&C*, 39.

[51] "Die Lehrentscheidung der Konkordienformel in der Frage des hl. Abendmahls," *VSA*, 183f. Even at this early stage Sasse refuses to limit the Real Presence to the moment of reception (184).

[52] "Confession and Theology in the Missouri Synod" (1951), *S&C*, 206.

[53] "The Lutheran Understanding of the Consecration," *WCS*, 136. "Consecration and Real Presence" (1957), *S&C*, 311: "The '*usus*' of the Sacrament to which the Real Presence is attached is by the Formula of Concord not identified with the '*sumptio*' or '*manducatio, Quae ore fit*.' It rather comprises '*totam externam visibilem actionem Coenae Dominicae a Christo institutum*,' and this is described as '*consecratio*,' '*distributio*,' and '*sumptio*.' Thus it is impossible to limit the Real Presence to the 'moment' when the elements are orally received. How this error could arise and even be accepted by F. Pieper . . . from some dogmaticians of the seventeenth century (N. Hunnius, Quenstedt) is not quite clear. For the Formula distinguishes clearly between '*sumptio*' and '*usus*' or '*actio*,' as the passage quoted above shows. That Christ is present not only in the moment of the '*sumptio*,' but in the '*usus*' was the understanding of the authors of the Formula, as also is proved by the Latin text in Sol. Dec. VII, 126 . . . : '*qui in coena sua, in legitimo nimirum eius usu, vere et substantialiter praesens est*' . . ."

[54] *CC*, 95f.

[55] *K&H*, 32; my trans.

[56] Tom G. A. Hardt, *Venerabilis et adorabilis Eucharistia; Eine Studie über die lutherische Abendmahlslehre im 16. Jahrhundert*, trans. Susanne Diestelmann, ed. Jürgen Diestelmann (Göttingen: Vandenhoeck & Ruprecht, 1988).

Consubstantiation

Norman E. Nagel

There never was such a word until the sixteenth century. It was conceived and born in darkness and survives only as it battles against the light. It may be likened unto anaerobic bacteria. Its dubious genesis, early cancer, and links are what this paper will attempt to inquire into. We may note its remarkable recrudescence in the 20th century, but that is more than we can pursue today.

Consubstantiation is identified as "Lutheran" in *The Harper Collins Encyclopedia of Catholicism* of 1995. There it is defined as the theory that the substance of bread and wine remain together with the body and blood of Christ in the eucharistic sacrament.[1] A loaded statement indeed, in which we may, for what we are pursuing today, notice particularly that the statement depends on the term substance, and observe that it is here used of bread and wine, and not of the body and blood of Christ.

Should it then surprise us that a recent identification of what Lutherans confess of the Lord's Supper as consubstantiation should come from Princeton?[2] At Princeton one may expect that they know what theology may be called Reformed, if not what may be called Lutheran. Is there something in the Reformed way of theology which virtually commits it to so misunderstanding what Lutherans confess of the Lord's Supper as to label it consubstantiation? Such was indeed the case when the word was first used by a Reformed theologian to depict the Lutheran doctrine as absurd, or what's even worse as not yet free of Rome. He does not mention the body and the blood. Have you ever heard some catechumen say, "Rome has only body and blood; the Reformed have only bread and wine; the Lutherans have all four. This is the Lutheran doctrine of the Lord's Supper." Is that what we might call consubstantiation?

What is at stake here is not whether some theologian has done his homework or not. Sasse leaves us in no doubt what is at stake, and who has ever caught him not having done his homework? He is then able to draw in illuminating instances from at times the apparently unlikeliest places. These then serve to show that we are not the first to face this issue, and how sectarian it is to think and speak (perhaps only speak) as if we were. Thus he draws to us the resources of the church *perpetuo mansura* showing how the Lord has brought her through even to such a day as ours, by way of days far worse than ours, and so calling us to live our days in the confidence of such a Lord who gathers His people to His table, and so on to the final messianic feast. In this centenary year of Herman Sasse's birth, when we give thanks for all that our Lord had use of him for, we may surely include not only his immense learning (apostolic, catholic, Lutheran), but then also his astonishing ability to gather it to a specific focus, thereby illuminating and deepening something that is Christianly crucial. This is nowhere so clear as in the Lord's Supper. This paper will attempt then something of a footnote prompted by his confession of "the true body and blood of our Lord Jesus Christ under the bread and wine, instituted by Christ Himself for us Christians to eat and to drink." This is what is at stake when Lutherans are told that they confess consubstantiation.

The closest that the documented evidence so far brings us to a smoking pen is reported by Hilgenfeld.[3] The Reformed theologian Hospinian in his *Historia sacramentaria*, published in Zurich in 1598, writes under the heading *De origine consubstantiationis seu impanationis et coexistentiae corporis Christi in pane*. Here he attempts to show that what Occam taught is what the Lutherans teach, and that may be termed consubstantiation, impanation or coexistence, or run with three prepositions, and with a fourth one thrown in for extra mockery:

> William of Occam who lived around 1300 would most gladly have embraced this view [consubstantiation] ahead of the others, if (as he acknowledges in Book 4 of the *Sentences*, q.5 [6]) there had not been put in its way the determination of the Church, and the assertion shared by other doctors, the view that no substance of the bread remains. In their estimation this statement of Christ, "This is My body," could not possibly be true unless the bread were converted and transmuted into the body of Christ. If you remove the view *transsubstantiatio*, then what remains, however, is *consubstantiatio*, or as Occam says *coexistentia*, and others *impanatio*. If this is accepted, then the words of Christ will have to be interpreted as follows: "This is My body," that is to say, "With this or in this or under this or according to this (*iuxta hoc*) is My body."[4]

Quite clearly he is mocking what he takes to be the Lutheran doctrine. What is not quite so clear is whether he has understood Occam, let alone the Lutheran doctrine. Hospinian's understanding of Occam, however, may not delay our questioning Luther's. Primary evidence for our present inquiry is the Occam that came to Luther by way of Peter d'Ailly, Cardinal of Cambrai. In 1520 Luther wrote in the *Babylonian Captivity*:

> Some years ago, when I was drinking in scholastic theology, the learned Cardinal of Cambrai gave me food for thought in his comments on the fourth book of the *Sentences*. He argues with great acumen that to hold that true bread and true wine (*verus panis verumque vinum*), and not merely their accidents, are present on the altar, would be much more probable and require fewer superfluous miracles if only the church had not decreed otherwise. When I learned later what church it was that had decreed this, namely the Thomistic, that is, the Aristotelian church, I grew bolder, and after floating in a sea of doubt, I at last found rest for my conscience in the above view, namely, that it is true bread and true wine, in which Christ's true flesh and true blood are present in no other way, and that to no less a degree than the others assert them to be under their accidents. I reached this conclusion because I saw that the opinions of the Thomists, whether approved by pope or by council, remain only opinions, and would not become articles of faith even if an angel from heaven were to decree otherwise [Gal. 1:8]. For what is asserted without the Scriptures or proven revelation may be held as an opinion, but need not be believed. But this opinion of Thomas hangs so completely in the air without support of Scripture or reason that it seems to me he knows neither his philosophy nor his logic. For Aristotle speaks of subject and accidents so very differently from St. Thomas that it seems to me this great man is to be pitied not only for attempting to draw his opinions in matters of faith from Aristotle, but also for attempting to base them upon a man whom he did not understand, thus building an unfortunate super-structure upon an unfortunate foundation.[5]

What is at first most striking here is that there is no mention of substance, let alone consubstantiation, which is only possible if there are two things called substance (according to some theory of substance) put together, or made into one without loss of either. If the substance theory is that of Aristotle, then transubstantiation is a nonsense since the accidents of a substance cannot be there without the substance. If the substance of the bread is no longer there, then neither can the accidents be there. Since the accidents are there so then also the substance, "the ultimate subject of predication."[6]

Luther derives no positive consequence from any definition of what is a substance. He is discussing transubstantiation and that depends on Aristotle's definition of a substance and so is called Thomistic. Thomistic transubstantiation was far from persuasive with every one, and certainly not with one indebted to Occam as was Peter d'Ailly. The use of the razor identifies the view which needs the least number of miracles, and, what is more, that view is cogent which is best sustained by Scripture, or proven revelation. In the passage referred to by Luther, Peter d'Ailly, who was always careful to be doctrinally above reproach, puts the reason for his view this way:

> Because it is altogether possible that the substance of the bread coexists (*coexistere*) with the substance of the body. This mode is possible; it is not repugnant to reason nor to the authority of the Bible, and it is far easier to understand and more reasonable.[7]

He does not say "consubstantiation"; he has the verb "coexists." What coexists is the substance of the bread and the substance of the body. This is not how Luther says it when he acknowledges his debt to Peter d'Ailly. Luther, even more unspeculative than Peter d'Ailly, speaks of the true body and the true blood upon the altar. Going on from Peter d'Ailly he was no less sure that the true body and the true blood are there, than are those who assert the accidents in the absence of the substance of the bread. A way forward from less sure, to more sure, to unshakably sure, is indicated by the christological analogy with which Luther concludes this section. "As with Christ so also with the Sacrament":

> In order for Him as God to inhabit a body, it was not necessary for His human nature to be transubstantiated in order for His divinity to be going on there then under the accidents of His human nature.[8]

Christologically then transubstantiation would produce some sort of Apollinarianism, while consubstantiation would come under suspicion of Nestorianism.[9] Quite un-Eutychian, or better, utterly Chalcedonian is Luther's confession which continues:

> Because each nature is there in its integrity (*integra utraque natura*) it is true to say "This man is God, this God is man." Although this is too much

for philosophy to grasp, it is not too much for faith, for which God's words count for more than anything we could figure out. Thus in the Sacrament there are the true body and the true blood, and for this to be so the bread and the wine do not have to be transubstantiated (as above Christ under the accidents), but both remain there simultaneously, so the words are true: "This bread is My body, this wine is My blood," and vice versa.[10]

For this a preposition is inadequate.

> Clinging simply to his words, firmly believe not only that the body of Christ is in the bread, but that the bread is the body of Christ.[11]

Similarly inadequate may also be the prefixes trans- and con-, and the more so when combined with an Aristotelian substance as put by Thomas. Thomas was aware of the problem that Aristotle held that accidents could not be there without the substance.[12] That he nevertheless persists in asserting this is by recourse to God as *causa prima*, and Aristotle did teach that "the subject and predicate in an affirmation must each denote a single thing," which brings the matter under Aristotle's principle of identity and contradiction. "This" therefore is identical with "body" and thus the bread is excluded. Such logical necessity laid upon our Lord is not operative in Peter d'Ailly, nor in Luther.[13]

Luther began his discussion of the first captivity of the Mass using substance and integrity as synonymous.[14] All of it as Christ gave it, with no diminution or addition, is the insistence of both these terms used here in defense against the deprivation of the cup.[15] We may then test Luther's subsequent talk of substance as equivalent to "in its integrity," unless, of course, he is being drawn into discussion of an Aristotelian and Thomistic substance, and in the passage before us, as Grane has shown, with an Occamistic understanding of Aristotle as was operative in Peter d'Ailly.[16] When Luther engages the rational problems inherent in transubstantiation he does so persuaded that the *via moderna* with its Occamist understanding of Aristotle is superior to that of Thomas. This engagement is, however perceptively he does it, not basic.[17] Not by settling what is a substance and what an accident, and whether quantity is such as to sustain accidents (pinch hitting for the absent substance), nor by replacing trans- with con- does Luther arrive at what he confesses. There is doctrine and there is opinion. For

Luther transubstantiation as opinion is here no great problem.[18] That is doctrine here which says the same as the Lord says, and this may not be brought under our measurements, definitions or control, but confessed in its integrity and substance.

There is need therefore to distinguish between Luther's use of "substance" as "in its integrity," from when he engages "substance" Aristotelianly, and from when he engages it Thomistically. Thus when he engages substance Aristotelianly (and this he does Nominalistically, as does Peter d'Ailly), then he can assert that Thomas (who is not at all Nominalistic) does not understand Aristotle.

"Which Aristotle?" may also be asked of Lateran IV, which was ten years before Thomas was born. Lateran IV made transubstantiation a doctrine, but without the whole apparatus of Aristotle. That was thoroughly worked through the doctrine by Thomas (and so on to consummation at Trent).[19] Hence Luther's dating in the *Babylonian Captivity* is not with reference to Lateran IV but to Thomas' pseudo-Aristotle. Luther's dating that the church was without transubstantiation "for more than twelve hundred years" is helped to greater precision by Sasse's:

> Berengar seems to have been the first to apply the term "substance" and "accidents" in this connection (though he did not understand them in the sense of the strict Aristotelianism, which did not enter the church until the turn of the 12th and 13th centuries). ... Berengar forced his critics to develop a theory which finally became the doctrine of transubstantiation.[20]

"Finally" we may then understand as Trent and not Lateran IV. That this is not quite the case is shown by the way Peter d'Ailly puts the case for his view of two substances coexisting, and then reluctantly bowing to Lateran IV.

If Thomas were given the chance to respond to Luther, he might well be expected to point out that Luther's understanding of Aristotle was skewed by its coming to him by way of the Occamist tradition. We would then be set for the debate as to who (or what tradition) was the more faithful to Aristotle. For this Luther is neither so reluctant nor incompetent as one might expect. Yet this is not the heart of the matter for Luther. He acknowledges transubstantiation as an opinion which does not need to be repudiated unless it is insisted on as article of faith.

Nonetheless I would not stand in the way of those who follow the other opinion which is laid down in the decretal *Firmiter*, if only they do not force us to accept their opinions (as I have said) as articles of faith.[21]

Nothing seems to be further from his mind than crossing out trans- and writing in con-. Nothing is controlled by a definition of substance. Discussion of such definitions has only negative results. There may be no diminution of what our Lord says and gives by putting this under the control of some definition of ours. This is to be confessed in its substance and integrity—*substantialiter/realiter, integriter, vere*.

Even as an opinion consubstantiation is not asserted. "Coexist" is there in Occam, Peter D'Ailly, and in Luther. "Coexist" is excluded without any hesitation by Trent. Prior to Trent there was Lateran IV which made transubstantiation an article of faith, but without all the Aristotelian apparatus later supplied to it by Thomas. This is what we have heard Luther rejecting, and only if it is insisted on as an article of faith. This would not be so clearly the case with transubstantiation as taught by Lateran IV, that is, prior to Thomas' contributions. Peter D'Ailly saw more clearly than Luther that Lateran IV's transubstantiation excludes his view of "coexist." There may be a clue here to the difference between Occamist Peter D'Ailly and Luther.

Peter D'Ailly regrets that Lateran IV's transubstantiation excludes his "coexists." Lateran IV's transubstantiation is not such a threat to what Luther is confessing: "verum panem verumque vinum in quibus Christi vera caro verusque sanguis non aliter nec minus sit quam illi sub accidentibus suis ponant." The *sub accidentibus* line of argument came, as Sasse pointed out, in the reaction against Berengar. It was not Thomistically exploited by Lateran IV as it was by Trent. Peter D'Ailly's and Occam's line of argument depends on their understanding of "substance," as does Thomas' and Trent's. These exclude each other. Whether this is so or not really makes no difference to Luther. He repeats the *verba Christi* which may not be infringed, that is in their integrity, that is *substantialiter*. That fact of the matter is simply given by our Lord. Various opinions may be more or less useful but no opinion is an article of faith. Luther has no great problem with Lateran IV's transubstantiation if understanding it as again confessing what had always been confessed of the bread and wine of which our Lord says that it is His body and His blood, "for us Christians to eat and to drink, instituted by Christ Himself."

In the liturgy there never was any doubt of what our Lord says of the bread and wine, that what He is giving to be eaten and drunk is His body and blood. In the liturgy a number of words were used to confess that after our Lord has spoken of the bread and wine what is now there and is given "to us Christians to eat and to drink" is His true body and His true blood. In the East there is μεταβολη; Sasse takes us through to the Solid Declaration:

> The Greek word *metaballein* is here [Ap 10:2f.] translated *mutare*. It is interesting that in a quotation from Chrysostom in the *Formula of Concord* (*Sol. Decl. VII, 76*, Trig. 998) the corresponding *metarythmizein* was translated *consecrare*. The Greek terminology is very rich. Besides *metaballein* and *metarythmizein*, we find *metapoiein*, *methistanai*, *metaskeuazein*, *metastoicheioun*. This variety indicates the freedom of the Eastern theologians, as well as what Western theology would call a lack of precision.[22]

We may observe the Aristotelianizing precisionists inventing the term consubstantiation. We may observe Luther coming into the freedom of the East with similar usage of terms, rejoicing in their confession of "the true body and blood of our Lord Jesus Christ." Sasse has pointed to *mutare* in the Apology and *consecrare* in the Solid Declaration as gifts from the East. Running together with these are *vere in carnem mutari, secundum carnem* (not *secundum panem*), *mystica benedictio, die Kraft des göttlichen Segens, vere et substantialiter, pane et vino* (ablative). Thus also in Luther the number of terms which ring in harmony with one another. In 1521 he confesses of Christ:

> He takes bread and with the words which He speaks, "This is my body," He changes (*mutat*) it into His body and gives it to be eaten to the disciples.[23]

In 1522: made, blessed, consecrated, and in 1523 in the *Formula missae*: blessed and consecrated.[24] In 1526 in the *Deutsche Messe*: "das ampt und dermunge," the Office and Consecration.[25] In 1533: "consecrirt odder (wie mans nennet) wandelt; vermag und schafft; wandelt odder gibt."[26]

Consubstantiation cannot survive the play of all these ringing together. They could only be picked off one at a time, to make room for something else, something other than "the true body and blood of our Lord Jesus Christ under the bread and wine instituted by Christ Himself for us Christians to eat and to drink"[27]

In Luther, in liturgy, in the Catechisms, in the Confessions, what matters most, and, as in the Small Catechism, what comes first, is "the true body and blood of our Lord Jesus Christ." These are located "under the bread and wine." Unlocated body and blood of Christ would leave us to hunt for them, and so in doubt of their being given us "to eat and to drink," exposed then to spiritualizing which makes of eating and drinking some unmouthly heavenly thing referenced to something in ourselves: mind, heart or even "faith" (as inwardly, anthropocentrically referenced), "something we do."[28]

Luther has little concern to defend the bread and the wine. That they are there is clearly what Scripture says, 1 Cor. 11:26. Bread and wine, however, never saved anybody; it is the body and blood of Christ which do that. Let the Lord worry about what He does with the bread and wine. In the thanksgiving prayers after communion there is no mention of bread and wine.[29]

Hardt has pointed out that when Luther writes theology in Latin he is held by 1 Cor. 11:26,[30] but even so he does not see that confessing this is a departure from the way the liturgy has spoken from early days. As a pastor he does not trouble people who confess the true body and blood in the way of the ancient liturgies.

Nothing then could be more un-Lutheran and un-catholic than to speak of consubstantiation, which, at the very least, would come under the same assessment as transubstantiation, "an unnecessary philosophical theory . . . a wrong attempt to explain the miracle of the Real Presence."[31]

Nevertheless there are those (and some of them within the Lutheran tradition) who find not only Luther confessing consubstantiation but also the Confessions.[32] As we observed at the outset consubstantiation is only possible if there are two substances, and the Solid Declaration does speak of two substances. Sasse quotes the offending English translation from the *Triglotta*.

> Even as many eminent ancient teachers, Justin, Cyprian, Augustine, Leo, Gelasius, Chrysostom and others, use this **simile** concerning the words of the sacrament: "This is my body", that just as in Christ two distinct, unchanged natures are inseparably united, so in the Holy Supper the **two substances**, the natural bread and the true natural body of Christ, are

present together here upon earth in the appointed administration of the Sacrament.[33]

The Latin does have *duas diversas substantias*, the German *zwei Wesen*. The *Triglotta* follows the Latin; Tappert the German, and the best he can do in English is "two essences."[34] Does the Latin prevail over the German, or the German over the Latin? In the Formula naturally the German prevails, and *Wesen* is innocent of Aristotle. That there can be no consubstantiation spooking about here is clinched for Sasse by Selneccer, "one of the authors of the Formula of Concord."

> "Although our churches use the old expressions 'in the bread,' 'with the bread,' or 'under the bread' ... they do not teach an *inclusio, consubstantiatio,* or *delitescentia* [i.e. being locally hidden]." The meaning is rather that Christ, "when giving the bread, gives us simultaneously His body to eat . . ."[35]

Even less can Bugenhagen be found guilty.[36] Chemnitz leaves us in no doubt. To the Council of Trent he calls Pope Gelasius as his witness:

> This is how Gelasius interprets the way in which the ancient church understood that the bread and wine in the Eucharist are changed or converted into the body and blood of Christ.[37]

He concludes with Chrysostom:

> "You receive the body of Christ not from the hand of man but from the seraphim." As with these words Chrysostom does not want to cast off the external ministry, so also not the elements from the action of the Lord's Supper; rather, he wants us to cling neither to the hand of the minister nor to the elements of bread and wine, but to lift up our minds to those things of which the Word speaks.[38]

Gerhard is quite explicit in rejecting consubstantiation, and Hollaz also.[39] No Lutheran then can be blamed for inventing "consubstantiation." Lohse agrees with Hilgenfeld that it was invented to rout the Gnesio-Lutherans.[40] The fact that no Lutheran espoused consubstantiation pushes us earlier than Hospinian, to the earliest known occurrence of the term in a Lutheran rejection of it. In his *De praesentia corporis Christi in coena domini contra Sacramentarios* of

1560 Heshusius wrote:

> We entertain no such notion as consubstantiation or μετουσια when we speak of the body and blood being there and given out (*exhiberi*) with the bread and with the wine. Nor do we speak of a union here as personal, natural or formal. For two things are present in diverse ways: the bread in a natural and visible way, the body is present in an extraordinary way, possible only for God and incomprehensible to us. Nor is the body of Christ united with the bread in the way the Logos assumed human nature, but the means which the Son of God uses here is that by which He brings to us and gives to us His body to be eaten and His blood to be drunk. From this it is clear how frivolous is the quibble of those who by it would overthrow the fact that the body is present. They say, "If the body is in the bread then it follows that the bread must be adored." In the same way if you concluded that since God is said to be present by way of the mercy seat (*propitiatorio*) therefore the mercy seat made of gold is to be invoked. . . . Similarly, if it were not for the hypostatic union with God, and you could think of Christ's human nature as created by itself, then in no way should it be invoked. . . . In Elijah dwelt the entire divinity, and he was present in his heart. Nevertheless Elisha did not invoke Elijah as God. So also the bread is not to be invoked, even if we cannot but confess that in the bread the substance of the body of Christ is truly present and given.[41]

Heshusius is here under pressure to refute Melanchthon's accusation of bread worship, αρτολατρεια, which is the term Melanchthon uses to describe what Heshusius confesses.[42] He is not much helped by recourse to analogy or the term "substance," into which he has been seduced by his opponents. He is Gnesio-Lutheran. His opponents are the Philippists. He responds to Melanchthon's charge of bread worship. Melanchthon does not use the term consubstantiation. He resists saying more of the bread than bread can bear. What the bread can bear then imposes a limitation on what may be confessed of it, thus making it a little more comprehensible. What is beyond that limit is bread worship, αρτολατρεια. This is understandable if it is the bread which is decisive and not the body of Christ: *iuxta panem*, "from the aspect of the element."[43]

Hilgenfeld's research takes us as far as the suggestion that the origin of the term *consubstantiatio* was its invention by Phillipists, Crypto-Calvinists, with prime suspects being Hardenberg in Bremen or Klebitz in Heidelberg. So far we have no finger prints. It was invented in refutation of what we have heard Heshusius confess. Heshusius makes this confession in a situation in which he sees it threatened by Calvin, and by his opponents in Bremen and Heidelberg who claimed to be disciples of Melanchthon.

Hospinian's line of argument runs with what he takes to be Occam's view of substance. His argument may hold only as long as the view of substance holds with which he is working. His argument cannot work without some definition of substance. If transubstantiation is rejected then the consequence of that is consubstantiation. *Tertium non datur*. It is only because everything is held within the definitions of this line of argument that we can find there as interchangeable: *coexistentia, consubstantiatio, impanatio*, as well as "with this or in this or under this or very close to this." This is to draw conclusions from a line of argument for others who are not committed to that line of argument, and, if they do use it, it is only because they would thereby show that even if that line of argument were tenable, the conclusions of its devotees might be shown to be false by use of the very argument they espouse. This produces only negative conclusions. We saw Luther attempting to do this with Thomas' Aristotle. A rejoinder from Thomas disproving the Occamist Aristotle would yet remain in the field of Aristotle. On the other hand it would cause Luther no loss to lose Aristotle of whatsoever kind whether Occam's, Thomas', Peter D'Ailly's or Hospinian's.

We may not yet, however, be clear of Aristotle. The data have shown a connection between consubstantiation and αρτολατρεια. They both come from the same or a related source, and they are both applied in rejection of the same doctrine, as confessed by the Gnesio-Lutherans. I suspect that Aristotle as diagnostic probe would prove illuminating. What I shall, however, attempt, in the few minutes remaining to me, is a diagnostic probe with the christological analogy. We have heard this enunciated by Dr. Luther in the Babylonian Captivity in 1520. We have heard it disavowed by him and by the Confessions, and by classical dogmaticians. Clearly the christological analogy is not decisive for the doctrine of the Lord's Supper. One cannot, however, say that it is irrelevant, and it may indeed prove to be diagnostically most illuminating.

Consider Gerhard's definition of consubstantiation according to which "the bread coalesces with the body of Christ and the wine with his blood into one physical mass." Forgive the bald translation. One should first translate Gerhard's Latin into Greek, as he himself leads us into doing. One φυσις evokes Monophysitism. The last attempt to embrace what was good in Monophysitism (which by hypertrophy became heretical) was at the Fifth Ecumenical Council in 553. It was rejected by the Monophysites, and some years later was gratefully quoted by the Solid Declaration confessing the doctrine confessed by the Fifth Ecumenical Council which is summed up in *enhypostasia*.[44] Thus what was wrong in Monophysitism was excluded even more clearly than Chalcedon had done.

There never was a man Jesus other than the one God was born as (θεοτόκος). Thus Chalcedon's Two Natures were confessed in a way which gave priority to the divine nature. To some this has seemed to be a threat to the human nature.[45] By the Fifth Ecumenical Council in 553 the Nestorians were thoroughly taken care of. The two versus the one was then not the problem, but how the two were related to each other, or with (*con-*) each other. Gerhard seems to understand consubstantiation monophysically, against which stands Chalcedon's ασυγχυτως (without confusion) and ατρεπτως (without change). These were Leontius of Byzantium's best weapons against his Monophysite opponents.[46] Solid Declaration 7:37 has both ατρεπτως (without change) and αδιαιρετως (without division) in the context of the christological analogy illuminating bread and body, and wine and blood, and then 38 disavows the personal union of Christ as determinative, and speaks of a sacramental union as a unique (*inusitata*) way of speaking. And Gerhard would wish to be understood as in harmony with the Solid Declaration.

In the light of Gerhard's understanding of consubstantiation the foregoing data seem to suggest that Melanchthon could only have been accusing the Gnesio-Lutherans of αρτολατρεια if he were thinking along monophysical lines, pushing his opponents' position to a rejectable conclusion, and thereby betraying his own christological leaning. Bulwark against this is the quotation of the Fifth Ecumenical Council in Solid Declaration 8:62, where we also confess:

> In no way shall any conversion, mixture or equalizing [*exaequatio*] of the natures in Christ, or of their essential properties, be held or permitted.[47]

To confess *exaequatio* would leave the way open to speak of *consubstantiatio* and ἀρτολατρεία. Equations were rejected for the sake of the Gospel when Luther at Marburg cried out against mathematics. We can only do equations if we can control the terms. Not by control of the terms, not by putting the limitations of our definitions of a what a man is and what bread and wine are; faith rejoices to hear what the Lord says and does and gives. The Lord does with His human nature what He does with His human nature, and He does with the bread what His body does with the bread. It is His body and blood that save us. Before His body and blood, before Him whose body and blood they are, we kneel, we worship, we worship "with one adoration."[48]

Una adoratione from the Fifth Ecumenical Council. "One worship," from Kleinig, from Sasse, from the ancient liturgy. One worship, same *sanctus*, to the same Lord. We are drawn in along with all those who cry, on this the day of All Saints, *"Tu solus es sanctus,* Lord Christ. Amen."

Notes

[1] *The Harper Collins Encyclopedia of Catholicism*, ed. R. McBrien (San Francisco: Harper, 1995), 363. Trent, Sessio 13, cap. 4; Heinrich Denzinger, *Enchiridion Symbolorum definitionum et declarationum de rebus fidei et morum. Quod emendavit, auxit, in linguam germanicam transtulit et adiuvante Helmuto Hoping edidit Petrus Hünermann*, Editio XXXVII (Freiburg: Herder, 1991), #1642 (530). *Decrees of the Ecumenical Councils*, ed. N. Tanner (Georgetown University Press, 1990), II:695. H. Sasse, *TMB*, 33.

[2] D. Migliore, *Faith Seeking Understanding: An Introduction to Christian Theology* (Grand Rapids: Eerdmans, 1991), 222. R. Muller does not make the same mistake: *Dictionary of Latin and Greek Theological Terms* (Grand Rapids: Baker, 1985), 80: "frequently confused with the Lutheran doctrine." Some Anglican insights may be found in E. Pusey, *The Real Presence of the Body and Blood of our Lord Jesus Christ, The Doctrine of the English Church* (London: Smith, 1885).

[3] H. Hilgenfeld, "Zur Herkunft des Wortes consubstantiatio," *Mittelalterlich-traditionelle Elemente in Luthers Abendmahlsschriften* (Zurich: Theologischer Verlag, 1971), 467-70. Hard data gathered here as nowhere else.

[4] Latin text Hilgenfeld, *Mittelalterlich-traditionelle Elemente*, 468; my trans. Sasse, *TMB*, 80, n. 49. W. Elert, *Structure of Lutheranism* (St. Louis: CPH, 1962), 302, n. 4. Pusey on Hospinian, *The Real Presence*, 338-41.

[5] WA 6:508.7-26; AE 36:28f. The ET's "At last I found rest for my conscience"

may be a little too heavy. This might be translated, "At last my thinking it over settled on the above view." Cf. Hamlet, Act 3, Scene 1, line 83. *WA* 6:508.7: "occasionem cogitandi." That bread and wine remain is here his *sententia*, which is also no article of faith. Cf. Melanchthon's similar *sententia* of mid-February, 1520. *CR* I:145, quoted by T. Hardt, *Venerabilis et adorabilis Eucharistia* (Göttingen: Vandenhoeck & Ruprecht, 1988), 133. Throughout his career Luther spoke of the bread and the wine being changed, as in the prayers of the ancient liturgy.

[6] Aristotle, *Metaphysics: books gamma, delta and epsilon* 4, 4, 1007b, ed. Christopher Kirwan, (Oxford: Clarendon Press, 1971), 12; cf. 208. J. Owens, *The Doctrine of Being in the Aristotelian Metaphysics* (Toronto: Pontifical Institute of Medieval Studies, 1978), 143.

[7] *Quaestiones supra libros Sententiarum* IV, q 6, art. 2; my trans. Leif Grane, "Luthers Kritik an Thomas von Aquin in de captivitate Babylonica," *ZKG* 80 (1969): 3, n.7. R. Seeberg, *Textbook of the History of Doctrine* (Grand Rapids: Baker, 1952), II:204. Latin text in *Lehrbuch der Dogmengeschichte* (Leipzig: Deichert, 1913), III:664.

Seeberg quotes Occam in demonstration of how closely he is followed by Peter D'Ailly. *Quodlibeta septem una cum tractatu de sacramento altaris*, IV:35. Cf. *Centiloquium* 39C. Occam's discussion of *Quaestio* VI *Utrum corpus Christi realiter sub speciebus panis contineatur* may be found in *Quaestiones in librum quartum sententiarum in Opera Theologica* VII (New York, St. Bonaventure, 1984): 62-109. E. Iserloh, *Gnade und Eucharistie in der philosophischen Theologie des Wilhelm von Ockham* (Steiner, Wiesbaden: 1956), 155-57. In this work Iserloh gets no nearer to Luther than *Schriftprinzip* and ubiquity (155, 202, 277f.). Hilgenfeld, *Mittelalterlich-traditionelle Elemente*, 393-401.

Melanchthon observed that Luther had the commentaries of Biel and Peter D'Ailly almost by heart. *CR* VI:159.

P. Tschackert, *Peter von Ailli (Petrus de Alliaco). Zur Geschichte des grossen abendländischen Schisma und der Reformconciilien von Pisa und Constanz* (Gotha: Perthes, 1877), 321. For his influences on Christopher Columbus, 334f.

[8] *WA* 6:511.34-36; my trans. Cf. *AE* 36:35.

[9] K. Beyschlag, *Grundriss der Dogmengeschichte* (Darmstadt: Wissenschaftliche Buchgesellschaft, 1991) II.1:20, *Integrität*. Cf. J. Gerhard, *Loci Theologici*, ed. E. Preuss (Berlin: Schlawitz, 1863) II:500; Locus 4, #119: "Non est unio proprie integralis." Cf. n. 14.

[10] WA 6:511.37-512.2; my trans. Cf. AE 36:35. AE's ET introduces "substance"! WA 26:445.1-15. Cf. AE 37:303.

[11] WA 6:511.19-21. Qtd from AE 36:34. Cf. WA 26:341.13-20; 447.18. AE 37:230 & 306. Hardt, *Venerabilis et adorabilis Eucharistia*, 145. Helmut Gollwitzer, *Coena Domini* (Munich: Kaiser, 1937), 39: "denn das Corpus-Sein sollte ja nicht von der dem Brote koexistierenden Substanz, sondern vom Brot selbst ausgesagt werden."

[12] *Summa Theologica* 3, q 75, art. 5, obj. 1. Cf. *Studienausgabe* [hereafter *SA*] ed. Hans-Ulrich Delius (Berlin:Evangelische Verlagsanstalt, 1982), II:186, n. 97. Biel, *Sent.* 4, dist. 12, q 1. Grane, "Luthers Kritik an Thomas von Aquin," *ZKG* 80 (1969): 8: "accidentis esse est inesse."

[13] SA II:187, n. 97. For *praedicatio identica* see Hardt, *Venerabilis et adorabilis Eucharistia*, 150. AE 36:33, n. 71. WA 26:441.36-445.15; AE 37:299-303. L. Kennedy, *Peter of Ailly and the Harvest of Fourteenth-Century Philosophy* (Queenston: Mellen, 1986), 213. Martin Chemnitz, *The Lord's Supper*, trans. J. A. O. Preus (St. Louis: CPH, 1979), 50f. Gollwitzer, *Coena Domini*, 40, n. 5: "Merkwürdigerweise hält P. Althaus die praedicatio identica für eine typisch lutherische Angelegenheit." Sasse, *TMB*, 45.

[14] WA 6:507.6; AE 36:27. WA 6:515.17; AE 36:40. WA 6:511.37: "integra utraque natura"; AE 36:35.

[15] Cf. *Verus, satis*, pure, closed.

[16] Grane, "Luthers Kritik an Thomas von Aquin," *ZKG* 80 (1969): 11f.

[17] Grane, 8: "Das Entscheidende bei Thomas ist aber die Bestimmung der Begriffe." Grane shows Luther arguing with Aristotle against Thomas.

[18] E. Sommerlath, "Das Abendmahl bei Luther," *VSA*, 117: "Er hat darum auch inhaltlich nicht gegen die römische Transubstantiationslehre gekämpft. Er nahm es als ihren großen Vorzug, daß sie realiter und substantialiter die Gegenwart des Leibes und Blutes bejahte. Sie ging ihm nur zuweit in der Beschreibung der Weise, wie es zugehe. Auch entsprach der Verwandlungsgedanke so gar nicht dem, was die Betrachtung der Person Christi in der Verbindung des Göttlichen und Menschlichen ergab. Immerhin konnte er es aussprechen: 'Ehe ich mit den Schwärmern wollte eitel Wein haben, so wollte ich eher mit dem Papst eitel Blut halten.'" WA 26:462.4. "It is of no importance to me, as I have often enough confessed, and nothing to have an argument about: Whether there is wine remaining there or not? It is enough for me that Christ's blood is there. What happens with the wine, that is however God wishes. And sooner than having nothing but wine with the enthusiasts, I would rather have nothing but blood in agreement with the pope" (my trans.) Cf. AE 37:317.

[19] Hilgenfeld, *Mittelalterlich-traditionelle Elemente*, 387: "Die Transubstantiationslehre wird fides ecclesiae, während den Theologen übrigbleibt, eine stichhaltige Begründung für diese Lehre zu finden. Diesen Versuch hat neben Alexander von Hales und Bonaventura besonders Thomas von Aquin unternommen." Cf. ibid., 402. Similarly Michael Schmaus quoted by Grane, "Luthers Kritik an Thomas von Aquin," *ZKG* 80 (1969): 7. Sasse, *TMB*, 33.

[20] Sasse, *TMB*, 28. Grane, "Luthers Kritik an Thomas von Aquin," *ZKG* 80 (1969): 6.

[21] WA 6:512.4-6; my trans. Cf. AE 36:35. Denzinger, *Enchiridion*, #800. Tanner,

Decrees of the Ecumenical Councils, 1, 230, 35: "His body and blood are truly contained in the sacrament of the altar under the forms of bread and wine, the bread and wine having been changed in substance (*transubstantiatis*), by God's power, into his body and blood, so that in order to achieve this mystery of unity we receive from God what he received from us." Sasse, *TMB*, 33: "The dogma speaks of 'substance' and 'species.' It avoids the term 'accidents,' as does also the Council of Trent."

[22] Sasse, *TMB*, 29, n. 20.

[23] *De abroganda missa privata*, WA 8:435.1; my trans. Cf. 438.3; 509.38. AE 36:341, bottom.

[24] WA 10^2:19.28; *Von beider Gestalt*. AE 36:244. WA 12:211.23; 212.27; 214.6 & 16. AE 53:26 & 28 & 30f: "modo benedictionis sinant integra et fide agant."

[25] WA 19:97.12; 99.6. AE 53:80f. WA 19:97, n. 4. *Dermunge* from *terminare, herstellen, schaffen, conficere*. WA 18:27; AE 36:317.

[26] *Von der Winkelmesse*. WA 38:210.28; 240.8; 248.28. AE 38:64 & 199 & 209. WA 30^1:53.23. LC V:9 & 14. SD VII:77.

[27] Sasse's defense of Consecration in *WCS*, 113-38. Not to be pulled apart or against each other, as Gerhard observes christologically: "Haec omnia cum sint parallela, ideo in explicatione unionis perpetuo conjungenda." Locus 4, #115; Preuss ed., 498. Sasse, *TMB*, 337.

[28] LC V:7: "als ein Ding das wir thuen."

[29] *Vom Greuel der Stillmesse* WA 18:25.8: "Ist das nicht Christus blut gelestert da yhm brod un weyn gleich geacht wird." 27.33: "Das soll noch alles das brod und weyn ausrichten." AE 36:318. WA 2:750.3: "wie und wo lass yhm befallen seyn." AE 35:61. WA 18:206.20; AE 40:216. H. Kulp, "Das Gebet post communionem, Der Gottesdienst an Sonn-und Feiertagen," J. Beckmann, H. Kulp, P. Brunner, W. Reindell (Gütersloh: Bertelsmann, 1949), 428-39.

[30] Hardt, *Venerabilis et adorabilis Eucharistia*, 136. Smalcald Articles 6:5.

[31] Sasse, *TMB*, 82. WA 6:509.20. AE 36:31.

[32] Sasse points to Seeberg *Lehrbuch der Dogmengeschichte* (Leipzig: Deichert, 1913), III:663-66; IV^1 (1917): 325; (1933): 399; trans. C. E. Hay (Grand Rapids: Baker, 1952), II:203, 287. ET does not have the term here. Sasse also points to E. Peschke, *Die Theologie der Böhmischen Brüder in ihrer Frühzeit* (Stuttgart: Kohlhammer, 1935), IV^1:288, 354-60. Seeberg concludes of Luther's doctrine of the Lord's Supper: "The most profound impulses of his religious consciousness contributed to its formulation." ET II:288. This puts him in Ritschlian relationship with Kattenbusch, the stout protagonist of consubstantiation as Luther's doctrine. For Kattenbusch what Luther was confessing is to be found in Luther's inner intuition, and this is better served by consubstantiation, better than by transubstantiation. The

question Kattenbusch strove to answer was, as he put it, "Why was the 'con' more persuasive for Luther, more clear, for his inner intuition?" "Luthers Idee der Konsubstantiation im Abendmahl," in *Forschungen zur Kirchengeschichte und zur christlichen Kunst*, J. Fisher's *Festgabe*, ed. W. Elliger (Leipzig: Dieterich, 1931), 64, 82: "Zum Schluß eine kleine Überraschung: Luther bietet nie den Ausdruck consubstantiatio. Und es ist doch der richtige, an sich klarste für seine Theorie."

Schmidt-Lauber acclaims Luther's doctrine of consubstantiation, and only regrets that he failed its consequences. *Die Eucharistie als Entfaltung der Verba Testamenti* (Kassel: Staada, 1957), 146, 111: "Sie (consubstantiatis) bezeugt das Zusammengehen von göttlicher und menschlicher Handlung in der Eucharistie." Gollwitzer is adduced in support of this. "Luthers Abendmahlslehre," in *Abendmahlsgemeinschaft?* eds. H. Asmussen, H. Gollwitzer, F. W. Hopf, E. Käsemann, W. Niesel, E. Wolf (Munich: Kaiser, 1937), 99.

More recent is Gollwitzer's approval of Kattenbusch's application of the term to Luther, although in Gollwitzer's judgment Kattenbusch did not give sufficient precision to the concept of consubstantiation, nor in Gollwitzer's view did Luther. Gollwitzer, *Coena Domini*, 48. Gollwitzer is quoted only with approval by V. Vajta; *Die Theologie des Gottesdienstes bei Luther* (Stockholm: Svenska Kyrkans Diakonistyrelses Bokførlag, 1952), ET *Luther on Worship*, trans. U. Leupold (Philadelphia: Muhlenberg, 1958). This cannot be said of Sasse. Cf. F. W. Hopf, "Die Abendmahlslehre der evangelisch-lutherischen Kirche," in *Abendmahlsgemeinschaft?* For Vajta on consubstantiation, *Theologie des Gottesdienstes*, 177f. ET 95. Sasse, *TMB*, 44, 81ff. 129f.

[33] Sasse, *TMB*, 81; emphasis mine.

[34] *BS* 984.3; 983.40. *Triglotta*, 985. Tappert, 575.

[35] Sasse, *TMB*, 82, n. 53. "Die Lehrentscheidung der Konkordienformel," *VSA*, 147: "Wenn Christus uns das Brod im Abendmahl gibt, so gibt er uns auch sein Leib, und wenn er den Kelch oder Wein gibt, so gibt er uns auch sein Blut. . . . Wenn auch unsere Kirchen brauchen die uralten Wörtlein, Im Brodt, Mit dem Brodt, Oder unter dem Brodt wird der Leib Christi genommen, so wird dadurch kein Inclusio, oder Consubstantio oder Delidescentia, Einschließung, zusammenverfügtes Wesen, oder ein Untersteckung gedichtet . . . ." Cf. 136. Gollwitzer, *Coena Domini*, 53f.

[36] Hardt, *Venerabilis et adorabilis Eucharistia*, 138, n. 49.

[37] *Examination of the Council of Trent*, trans. F. Kramer (St. Louis: CPH, 1978) II:268.

[38] *Examination*, II:275. *The Lord's Supper*, trans. J. A. O. Preus (St. Louis: CPH, 1979), 37-44. 153: Gelasius again along with Justin, Cyprian, Augustine, Chrysostom, and Theodoret. Christological errors "were refuted by nearly all the ancient fathers on the basis of the dogma of the Lord's Supper." Cf. AC xxii, 7.

[39] Gerhard, 5, 65. Locus 21, Caput 10, 69: "Proinde credimus, docemur et confitemur, in eucharistiae sacramento veram, realem et substantialem corporis et

sanguinis Christi praesentiam, exhibitionem, manducationem et bibitionem, quae praesentia non est essentialis conversio panis in corpus et vini in sanguinem Christi, quam transsubstantiationem vocant, neque est corporis ad panem ac sanguinis ad vinum extra usum coenae localis aut durabilis affixio, neque est panis et corporis Christi personalis unio, qualis est divinae et humanae naturae in Christo unio, neque est localis inclusio corporis in panem, neque est impanatio, neque incorporatio in panem, neque est consubstantiatio, qua panis cum corpore Christi et vinum cum ipsius sanguine in unam massam physicam coalescat; neque est naturalis inexistentia, neque delitescentia corpusculi sub pane, neque quidquam hujusmodi carnale aut physicum: sed est praesentia et unio sacramentalis, quae ita comparata est, ut juxta ipsius Salvatoris nostri, veracis, sapientis et omnipotentis institutionem pani benedicto tanquam medio divinitus ordinato corpus, et vino benedicto tanquam medio, itidem divinitus ordinato sanguis Christi modo nobis incomprehensibili uniatur, ut cum illo pane corpus Christi una manducatione sacramentali et cum illo vino sanguinem Christi una bibitione sacramentali in sublimi mysterio sumamus, manducemus ac bibamus. Breviter, non ἀπουσίν, absentiam, non ἐνουσίαν, inexistentiam, non συνουσίαν, consubstantionem, non μετουσίαν, transsubstantiationem acceptam, sed παρουσίαν corporis et sanguinis Christi in sacra coena statuimus." D. Hollaz, *Examen theologicum acroamaticum* (Rostock & Leipzig: Kiesewetterus, 1750), Part D 3, Section 2, chapter 5, Question 12, Instance 6, p. 1124: "Quicunque nolunt asserere consubstantiationem in S. coena, illos non oportet asserere, corpus Christi esse in, cum, & sub pane. . . . Particulae illae explicativae non praesentiam physicam, sed hyperphysicam; non localem inclusionem, sed singularem unionem; non carnalem impanationem, aut consubstantiationem, sed praesentiam mutuam & sacramentum communionem panis benedicti & corporis Christi, vini benedicti & sanguinis Christi inferunt." In the previous paragraph he met the charge of bread worship. "Aliud est objectum adorationis, aliud locus adorationis. Ubi distribuitur panis eucharisticus, ibi Christus est adorandus; at panis eucharisticus non est objectum adorationis." Part 2, Section 1, Chapter 3, Question 20, p. 665: ἀνυποστασίαν, p. 667: ἐνυπόστατος ... "adeoque non est persona, sed personata." Cf. WA *Br* 9:419: "Adoratio in sumendo per sese accedit, dum genibus flexis verum corpus et verus sanguis sumitur sine disputatione."

[40] B. Lohse, "Dogma und Bekenntnis in der Reformation: von Luther bis zum Konkordienbuch," in *Handbuch der Dogmen-und Theologiegeschichte* (Göttingen: Vandenhoeck & Ruprecht, 1980), II:58, n. 12. Hereafter *HDTG*.

[41] Latin in Hilgenfeld, *Mittelalterlich-traditionelle Elemente*, 468.

[42] *Brotvergötzung*. P. Meinhold, *Phillip Melanchthon* (Berlin: LVH, 1960), 121. Here also Hardenberg. Meinhold regards Melanchthon's *mit, cum,* as expressing the true Lutheran view. Sasse, *TMB*, 256.

[43] Sermon on Second Christmas Day, 1527. WA 23:737.6: "In brot, dico est corpus, sed non nach dem brot. Quis dixit verbum? Non secundum rationem humanam nec secundum panem, sed secundum verbum dei." Sasse, *TMB*, 303.

[44] *Insubsistentia*: Denzinger, *Enchiridion*, 424-26. Tanner, *Decrees of the*

Ecumenical Councils, 114f. M. Chemnitz, *The Two Natures of Christ*, trans. J. A. O. Preus (St. Louis: CPH, 1971), 31, 42, 135. Beyschlag, *Grundriß der Dogmentgeschichte* II, 1:178-85. Cf. n. 329. W. Elert, *Der Ausgang der altkirchlichen Christologie* (Berlin: LVH, 1957), 62, 118, 144. H. Dembowski, *Einführung in die Christologie* (Darmstadt: WBG, 1976), 114f. F. Pieper, *Christian Dogmatics* (St. Louis: CPH, 1951), II:79-85. A. Ritter, "Dogma und Lehre in der Alten Kirche," *HDTG* I:277.

[45] W. Pannenberg, *Systematic Theology*, trans. G. Bromley (Grand Rapids: Eerdmans, 1994) II:389, n. 188. P. Althaus, *Die christliche Wahrheit* (Gütersloh: Mohn, 1969), 448f.

[46] P. Gray, *The Defence of Chalcedon in the East* (451-553) (Leiden: Brill, 1979), 97.

[47] Denzinger, *Enchiridion*, #428; Tanner, *Decrees of the Ecumenical Councils*, 117; *BS* 1037.11; *Triglotta*, 1036; Tappert, 603. Chemnitz against equations, *Two Natures*, 113, 287.

[48] Fifth Ecumenical Council 9, "una adoratione." Denzinger, *Enchiridion*, #431. Tanner, *Decrees of the Ecumenical Councils*, 118. Cf. Luther, n. 39 above.

Hermann Sasse, a Man for Our Times

Edwin Lehman

Unlike some of you, I never had the privilege of knowing Hermann Sasse in the flesh. I never listened to his lectures, I never corresponded with him.

I was introduced to him, however, through one of his contemporaries who, like Sasse himself, was born in Germany and transplanted to Australia. She was Margaret Appelt, a pastor's widow, whom I was privileged to serve as pastor for a number of years. It was she who presented me with a copy of Sasse's work, *This is My Body*, thus introducing me to the mind and heart of the man whose work is the focus of this symposium.

Many men are greater in death than they ever were in life. Time lets us forget a man's failures and concentrate on his strengths. But I have no intention of using these moments to re-write the course of Sasse's life. I have neither the desire nor the inside knowledge to give you the true, unadulterated version of what the oldest son of that local pharmacist was really like! In other words, I have not come to bury Sasse, nor to praise him!

Instead, I would like to use these moments to reflect on what Sasse's contributions mean—or should mean—to the church and the church's ministerium today. I do this from the perspective of a church which has old roots but a rather young identity, and I do it especially because of the large number of parish pastors here today, for whom theology—whether Sasse's or their own—is much more than a mental or academic exercise.

As we read and ponder Sasse's works, it seems to me there are several specific lessons to be learned, especially by those of us who hold or aspire to the *Predigtamt*.

1. Think theologically:

A few years ago, when asked to suggest the characteristics that should be sought in one who graduates from the seminary and is about to serve as a pastor, I put, at the top of the list, "the ability to think theologically." Some misunderstood what I meant. They felt that it was far more important to know how to get along with people, or to have a heart for reaching the lost. Of course, but I would contend that those are attributes for which every Christian should strive. In the midst of mounting pressures and conflicting choices that beset Christendom and every local congregation, somebody needs to be there to ask the theological question, "what is the will of God in this matter?"

To think theologically is not the same as to think traditionally or even dogmatically. It is not the same as hiding behind formulae or explanations that have been given to us by others—although we surely do not despise any of these. It is, rather, to think according to the Word of God, to apply Law and Gospel in our preaching, teaching, and care of souls, to guard the truth faithfully, and, at the same time to give the truth away freely and purely.

There is a story that one day the nine year-old son of the now sainted Martin Franzmann came to him and asked, "Dad, when the kids at school ask what you do, what should I tell them? I mean, Jimmy's dad is a doctor and Billy's dad drives a fire truck? How do I explain what you do?" And Franzmann replied, "Tell them that I teach isagogics, exegesis, and hermeneutics." That, of course, should impress any nine year-old; so Franzmann added (with a customary "harrumph," I'm sure), "Tell them that I teach people how to think."

Sasse was a thinker who challenged others to think, although sometimes to our dismay, for just when you think he's on your side he says something that causes you to think some more. To some, his thoughts were old-fashioned—as if from another era. Albrecht Peters wrote that, "to the chorus of present-day Protestant theology, Sasse's voice sounds foreign and shrill."[1]

But we would agree with another assessment, that "Sasse's remarks seldom conformed with the general trend, also in regard to the church. Should they not precisely for this reason then occupy our interest again?"[2]

Today's parish pastor faces many demands for his attention: church attendance, Tuesday's voters' meeting, the congregational budget, whether or not to take that particular wedding or funeral, how to win back the members who are losing interest. And there is no shortage of those who would help: courses, seminars, workshops, books, programs—most of them, for a price.

It is surely not asking too much, or expecting the unreasonable, that in the midst of these pressures, the pastor would also stop to think what God's Word has to say: about his own sin and the sin of his people, about God's grace and how it is given as the remedy and cure for sin, about the church and what it really is, about his ministry and what he is called to be, not merely what he is expected to do.

2. A sense of history:

Sasse's appreciation for history did not develop without some pain. Studying under Adolf von Harnack at the University of Berlin, he learned that "The great historian of dogma actually did away with the dogma of the church."[3]

And, as we heard yesterday, following his disastrous experience at Paschendale, he concluded: "You can perhaps live on Harnack's theology in happy times, but you cannot die with it." For Sasse, liberal theology and the optimistic view of man died in the catastrophe of the First War.[4]

The church today, like the world, has largely lost its sense of history, and desperately needs to reclaim it. Sasse's comments, translated by Norman Nagel in *We Confess Jesus Christ*[5] about the importance of the Council of Chalcedon in 451 are classic. Faced with the tremendous upheaval brought about by the migration of nations and the threats of the barbarian Huns, all the church did was confess Christ, and that's all it needed to do, for in so doing, it had something to give to the new world that was replacing the old.

In a similar vein, Sasse wrote elsewhere that the church had no option but to sing the *Te Deum* even over the ruins of a collapsing world.[6]

If the saying is true for secular history, it is even more true for the history of the church: "The farther backward you can look, the farther forward you can see." The Lord of the church and the Lord of history are one and the same. The events of history, with their unexplained twists and turns, are not merely the footprints of a drunken deity staggering his way through time, but of a gracious and loving God who condescended to act within the restraints of time and history which He created.

Although history is being made all around us, and often at a dizzying pace, our generation has little appreciation for history. We are the generation that depends on the ten second sound bite. Even pastors often think that the only history that is important in their congregation is the history that bears their name. Again and again we see statistical reports which trace things such as church attendance, membership, giving, etc., but the comparisons only go back to the time the incumbent pastor arrived—as though that marked the "big bang" from which everything else evolved. We are willing to buy into "micro-history," but little beyond that. Yet micro-history is a contradiction in terms.

3. A sense of the whole church:

With his long view of history, it is not surprising that Sasse also had a broad view of the church. Under the influence of Adolf Deissman, he became an ardent supporter of ecumenical work, earnestly harboring the hope of visible unity within Christendom. But following the Lausanne conference of 1927, Sasse was more convinced than ever that the way to the united church of the future was "not the way of compromise. It is to begin with the way of the deepest religious self-examination and change. The mind of Christ must draw into the churches."[7] When the Church of South India was being formed, he wrote, "The praise of the Church of South India which we hear everywhere, and in all ecumenical circles, proves nothing but the sad fact that the decay of doctrine and doctrinal thinking is going on in the whole world of modern Protestantism."[8]

Yet throughout his life he would refer to both Reformed and Roman Catholics as "brothers." And though he wrote extensively for the *Reformed Theological Review* while in Australia, he could not imagine an ecumenical perspective that was confined to the Protestant world and left out Rome. Only a few months before his death, commenting on the inadequacies of the Leuenberg Concord, he wrote:

> In this ecumenical age, it should not be forgotten that there are also catholic churches and that the overwhelming majority of Christians in the world believe, and are firm in that belief, that the consecrated elements in the Holy Supper are really, not just figuratively (*wirklich nicht nur figürlich*) the true body and the true blood of the Redeemer. Whether our Reformed brethren like it or not, whether they understand it or not, it could well be that in the doctrine of the Sacrament, Lutheranism stands closer to Catholicism, than to the churches of Geneva.[9]

Few of us venture into the deep and murky waters of true ecumenism as Sasse was willing to do. Perhaps we fear that our actions would be misunderstood. Perhaps we would be seen as less than Lutheran. One has to be very sure of where he stands and of where others stand. We tend to think of involvement in ecumenical activity as something like performing an exorcism. You don't mess with it if you don't know what you are doing.

But, surely, our narrow parochialism stands in pitiful contrast to Sasse's view of the *oikoumene*—unlimited by either space or time, yet comprised of the "little holy flock or community of pure saints under one head, Christ" (LC II:51). If we shared and operated with such an understanding of the church, we would have a more wholesome view of our responsibility within it.

4. A readiness to confess:

Within this context, Sasse was a bold and tireless confessor of God's truth. In his view, the establishment of the *EKD* in 1948 was a denial of the Lutheran Confessions. He wrote: "The evangelical Lutheran church is a confessional church in the strict sense of the word. It ceases to be a church of the Lutheran reformation as soon as it ceases to be the church of the Lutheran confessions. Of that there can be no doubt."[10]

Today there is much talk about confessional Lutheranism. But there are games being played with that term that would raise Hermann Sasse's blood pressure to the boiling point if he were still with us.

Present LWF documents, which claim to speak for the majority of world Lutherans, state "Lutheran *communio* requires that the churches be in altar and pulpit fellowship." The same document unapologetically admits, "*Communio* ecclesiology assumes there will be theological diversity."[11] Yet, throughout the church's history, it has been accepted that church fellowship requires agreement in doctrine. A bishop of one of the ELCA's predecessor bodies reaffirmed, only a generation ago, "Insistence upon agreement in doctrine as a precondition of church fellowship is the distinguishing mark of Lutherans . . . and should never be relaxed."[12]

So then, *communio* requires church fellowship. Church fellowship requires doctrinal agreement. But *communio* assumes theological diversity. We need to be wary when the call for Confessionalism is voiced, while the term is never defined.

But to be confessional means more than to confess doctrine. In anticipation of the 450th anniversary of the Reformation, Sasse wrote, "A confession is nothing if it is only in books and on paper. Being confessional is about confessing Christ. There is no such thing as a confession of Christ without confessors."[13]

We have had a brief glimpse into the conscience struggles of Sasse and his contemporaries, especially during the Hitler era. We do not know what confronts the church in the 21st century. Other Hitlers? Other ideologies? Of course—they are all out there, just waiting to be named.

The challenge to confess—to confess without counting the cost—will surely be there for us, for our children and for our grandchildren. Are we, as pastors, preparing our sheep for the day when the wolves are again let loose among us?

5. A pastoral heart:

The last point I want to make is to underscore that for all that he did, wrote and was, Sasse maintained the heart and mind of a pastor. After all, for more than a decade he served as pastor in an inner mission in and near Berlin. Though he was never a national or regional bishop or president, he felt a responsibility for communicating with pastors of his church, through his extensive series of "Letters to Lutheran Pastors" beginning in about 1948.

For all his fierce contention for the truth, he also knew that the struggle was not to be waged according to weapons of the flesh. In one of his last articles in the *Reformed Theological Review*, he wrote:

> St. Paul connects truth and love in his great chapter on the unity of the church, Eph. 4, by his admonition "not to be tossed to and fro and carried about with every wind of doctrine, but speaking the truth in love, grow up into him in all things." And in his high priestly prayer for his church our Lord connects the two petitions, "that they may all be one," and "Sanctify them in the truth; Thy word is truth."[14]

It's my sense that many pastors are trying to deal with truth and love as though they were opposites that need to be kept in tension. They are not opposites in God's way of dealing with us. God is truth.

God is love. Sasse would give no sanction to any pastor who thinks he can compromise the truth for the sake of love, nor to the pastor who thinks he can withhold love for the sake of truth.

Like all good pastors, Sasse was concerned about the sheep: those already in the fold as well as those wandering away from the Shepherd. But he reminds us also that while we spare no effort reaching the lost, the ultimate response to that search is in the hands of God:

> The duty to proclaim the gospel is the duty of the church at all time, irrespective of success. There are times when the gospel seems to find open ears. There are times when the hearts seem hardened. This was the experience of the prophets and of the Lord himself. True evangelism will never despair of the power of God and his word. But it will always remember that we cannot open the hearts of men. This is God's privilege. The Holy Spirit alone can cause men to say in the hour of the great temptation, "Lord, to whom shall we go? You have the words of eternal life."[15]

Conclusion:

In the century since Hermann Sasse took his first breath, the world has gone though cataclysmic changes. We need only think of what has happened in the area of communications, transportation and travel, warfare, and medicine for obvious examples of the oft-made, but unprovable claim that the changes witnessed in this century have been more dramatic than those of all the preceding centuries of mankind's pilgrimage on this planet combined.

The church has not been immune to these changes. It has, in fact, both benefited and suffered from them. On this eve of All Saints' Day, it is appropriate for us, as children of the Reformation, to remember how the hammer blows of an Augustinian monk forever changed the face of the church. But as heirs of Luther, as co-heirs with the likes of Chemnitz and Walther and Sasse and—add whatever name you will—we dare never lose sight of the truth that is of God, nor dare we ever re-direct our hope or our love in any direction but God. In our part of the world particularly, it is not merely Christians who are in constant danger of becoming worldly, but the church itself which risks conforming itself to the world.

It seems appropriate, therefore, to close with this word of warning and encouragement from Hermann Sasse:

> ... it must be noted that the strongest influence upon the world is never exerted by a church that has become worldly. That is the end discovery of all epochs of secularized church life. The church in the days of rationalism failed to exert even the slightest influence upon the world. Liberalism and modernism in the church have made no impression whatsoever upon the world. The Reformation, on the other hand, shook and transformed the world. When does the church exert its greatest influence in the world? When it is church, wholly church and nothing else! When it brings its message which is alien to this world, to a world which wants to know nothing of it. This does not imply that the church then will be successful under all circumstances. But the church will never be successful, will never exert any influence upon the world at all if it runs after the world and attempts to ignore the great gulf which separates it from the world. It is only the church that is alien to this world which shall inherit the earth.[16]

> We have not come to bury Sasse
> Nor to praise him.
> The evil things he did—who knows 'em?
> The good we celebrate in this symposium.

Notes

[1] Albrecht Peters, "Review of *In Statu Confessionis* by Hermann Sasse," *Theologische Literaturzeitung* 92 (1967): 700.

[2] Hermann Dietzfelbinger, "Aus der Treue zum Bekenntnis. Hermann Sasses Vermächtnis," *Lutherische Monatshefte* 16 (1977): 7; my trans.

[3] Hermann Sasse, "The Impact of Bultmannism on American Lutheranism with Special Reference to his Demythologization of the New Testament," *Lutheran Synod Quarterly* 5 (June 1965): 3.

[4] Ibid., 5.

[5] "The 1,500th Anniversary of Chalcedon (1951)," *WCJC*, 55-58.

[6] *TMB*, 364.

[7] Sasse, ed., *Die Weltkonferenz für Glauben and Kirchenverfassung* (Berlin: Furche Verlag, 1929), 8; my trans.

[8] Sasse, *Church Union in South India* (Adelaide, n.d.), 13.

[9] Sasse, "Ten Years after the Council; Some Thoughts of Ecumenical Discussion," *RTR* 35 (Jan.-Apr., 1976/May-Aug., 1976): 41.

[10] Sasse, "Concerning the Nature of Confession in the Church, Letters to Lutheran Pastors II," *Theologische Quartalschrift/Theological Quarterly* 46 (1949): 168ff.

[11] Eugene L. Brand, "Toward a Lutheran Communion: Pulpit and Altar Fellowship," *LWF Report* 26 (June 1988): 32.

[12] Richard C. Wolf, *Documents of Lutheran Unity in America* (Philadelphia: Fortress Press, 1966), 547.

[13] "Gedanken am Vorabend des Reformationsjubiläums von 1967," *ISC* II:272; my trans.

[14] *RTR* 35:41.

[15] Sasse, "Why did Churches become Mosques in the East?" *Christianity Today* 10 (21 June 1966): 981.

[16] "Ecclesia Migrans," *ISC* I:331; my trans.

Contributors

Ronald R. Feuerhahn, Ph.D.—after parish pastorates in Wales and England, preceptor of Westfield House, Cambridge (the theological college of the Evangelical Lutheran Church of England); now associate professor of historical theology at Concordia Seminary, St. Louis; co-editor of *Scripture and the Church: Selected Essays of Hermann Sasse*; frequent conference speaker on worship and church and ministry issues.

Lowell C. Green, D.Theol.—began and ended his active ministry with parish pastorates in the American Lutheran Church and The Lutheran Church—Missouri Synod respectively; spent 20 years in parish ministry and 16 years teaching at various colleges and seminaries in the United States and Canada; in retirement adjunct professor at the State University of New York, Buffalo, NY; author of many books, including *How Melanchthon Helped Luther Discover The Gospel*, and of many articles in the area of historical and systematic theology; a keen organist and a frequent speaker at theological conferences.

Tom G. A. Hardt, Th.D.—pastor of the independent Evangelical Lutheran Church of St. Martin in Stockholm, Sweden; author of *Venerabilis et adorabilis Eucharistia* (a magisterial study of early Lutheranism's understanding of the Real Presence) and translator into Swedish (*Kristen Dogmatik*) of J. T. Mueller's condensed version of Franz Pieper's *Christian Dogmatics*; a prolific essayist.

John W. Kleinig, Ph.D.—lecturer in Old Testament at Luther Seminary, Adelaide, Australia, where in his student days he was taught by Dr. Hermann Sasse; author of *The Lord's song: the basis, function and significance of choral music in Chronicles*; writer of articles on worship and spirituality and a frequent speaker on these and other topics.

Edwin Lehman, D.D.—after parish pastorates in Western Canada, President of the Alberta-British Columbia District of The Lutheran Church-Missouri Synod (now LCC), two-term President of Lutheran Church-Canada, and Chairman of the International Lutheran Conference; currently President Emeritus of Lutheran Church-Canada and Director of the Missionary Study Centre at Concordia Lutheran Seminary, Edmonton AB.

Kurt E. Marquart, M.A.—after serving parishes in Texas and in Queensland, Australia, was called to Concordia Theological Seminary, Springfield IL (now at Fort Wayne IN), where he is currently associate professor of systematic theology; author of *The Church and Her Fellowship, Ministry, and Governance* (*Confessional Lutheran Dogmatics* IX), and of many learned articles; a frequent conference speaker.

Gottfried Martens, Th.D.—currently pastor of St. Mary's Evangelical Lutheran Church in Berlin-Zehlendorf, Germany (a parish of the *Selbständige Evangelisch-Lutherische Kirche*); author of *Die Rechtfertigung des Sünders—Rettungshandeln Gottes oder historisches Interpretament?* [an historical-systematic study of justification with analysis of recent Lutheran-Roman Catholic dialogue] and of several learned articles.

Norman E. Nagel, Ph.D.—after parish pastorates in England and ten years as preceptor of Westfield House, Cambridge, was dean of the Chapel of the Resurrection at Valparaiso University, IN, before accepting a call to teach systematic theology at Concordia Seminary, St. Louis, where he is now graduate professor of systematics; translator of Werner Elert's *Eucharist and Church Fellowship in the First Four Centuries* and of the three-volume *We Confess* series; author of many learned articles.

John R. Stephenson, M.A., Ph.D.—after a parish pastorate in Lewiston, NY, assistant (now associate) professor of historical theology at Concordia Lutheran Theological Seminary, St. Catharines, ON; author of *Eschatology* (*Confessional Lutheran Dogmatics* XIII); General

Editor (in succession to Dr. Robert Preus) of *Confessional Lutheran Dogmatics*; frequent conference speaker and writer of many articles on historical and systematic theology.

John R. Wilch, Dr. theol.—born of missionary parents of the American Lutheran Church and himself a keen missiologist; after a parish pastorate in British Columbia and a college professorship in North Carolina, now professor of exegetical theology at Concordia Lutheran Theological Seminary, St. Catharines, ON; author of *Time and event. An exegetical study of the use of 'eth in the Old Testament in comparison to other temporal expressions in clarification of the concept of time* and of many learned articles.

Thomas M. Winger, Th.D.—the only Concordia, St. Catharines, graduate and the youngest among the speakers; now pastor of Grace Lutheran Church, St. Catharines, ON; received his theological doctorate from Concordia, St. Louis, in 1997; author of several learned articles.

www.ingramcontent.com/pod-product-compliance
Lightning Source LLC
Chambersburg PA
CBHW050555170426
43201CB00011B/1702